We Also Served

Dedication

For Ivan, Rosalind and Elizabeth: thank you for never doubting I 'could do it'.

This book is in memory of my Great War grandfathers: Major Arthur Scott-Turner, Surgeon, RAMC; Doughboy Percy Adler; my grandfather-in-law Private Samuel Newman of the Loyal North Lancashire Regiment; and also of my mother-in-law, Captain Edith Newman (née Jacobs) ATS, who volunteered on 4 September 1939. If her brother could serve, so too would she!

Jenny
I do hope that you enjoy reading
about these extraordinary women

Viv

We Also Served

*The Forgotten Women of the
First World War*

Dr Vivien Newman

Vivien Newman

PEN & SWORD
HISTORY

First published in Great Britain in 2014 by
PEN AND SWORD HISTORY
an imprint of
Pen and Sword Books Ltd
47 Church Street
Barnsley
South Yorkshire S70 2AS

ISBN 978 1 78346 225 4

Printed and bound in England
by CPI Group (UK) Ltd, Croydon, CR0 4YY

Typeset in Times New Roman by
CHIC GRAPHICS

Pen & Sword Books Ltd incorporates the imprints of Pen & Sword
Archaeology, Atlas, Aviation, Battleground, Discovery,
Family History, History, Maritime, Military, Naval, Politics, Railways,
Select, Social History, Transport, True Crime, and Claymore Press,
Frontline Books, Leo Cooper, Praetorian Press, Remember When,
Seaforth Publishing and Wharncliffe.

For a complete list of Pen and Sword titles please contact
Pen and Sword Books Limited
47 Church Street, Barnsley, South Yorkshire, S70 2AS, England
E-mail: enquiries@pen-and-sword.co.uk
Website: www.pen-and-sword.co.uk

Contents

Acknowledgements

My first and greatest debt is to the hundreds of women whose writings have enabled me to enter vicariously into their wartime lives. My aim has been to do them justice.

The interest, encouragement, and generous sharing of ideas of many friends and colleagues has sustained me during the writing of this book.

Debbie de Boltz ferried me around York Minster, willingly taking 'just one more photograph' of the Memorial Panels.

Caroline Carr-Whitworth, Curator at Brodsworth Hall, graciously responded to my plea for entry to the Hall and provided so much information about eight-year-old Amy, her knitting and her letters.

Keith Dolan has shared his font of knowledge about the Western, and especially Gallipoli Fronts over many years; his abilities to bring campaigns to life and guide pilgrims round battlefields are second to none.

Colour-Sergeant Christopher Earl ferreted out obscure military information and provided insight into today's Armed Forces. I like to think that his being mentioned in the June 2014 Queen's Birthday Honours is for his 'Meritorious Service' to this book, but I understand it is in recognition of his dedicated military service.

Nelle Rote Fairchild, George Fletcher, Chris Went, and the New Zealand Granthams shared family history about Nurse Helen Fairchild, Lieutenant Arthur and WRAF Alice Armer, munitions worker Martha Alderson, and Alexandra and Hugo Grantham.

Dr Vicky Holmes' ability to spot blogs, tweets and calls for papers started the whole project.

Dickie King kindly lent the WAAC uniform. My daughter who modelled it for a photograph in this book is less grateful!

Clare Russell's endless enthusiasm for 'my' women and their stories extended to going on a day trip to Brussels merely to visit a prison, a firing range, a tram-stop and a statue.

Lucinda Semeraro is always able to find the perfect translation from French into English. Her enthusiasm for her sister's book has been constant.

ACKNOWLEDGEMENTS

David Semeraro went beyond the call of duty in trying to find out information about Regina Diane; we almost found her at the eleventh hour – and one day we will! His nursing knowledge has also been invaluable.

Brita Smith genealogy sleuth *extraordinaire*.

Jen Newby has been the perfect editor – calm, encouraging and quick to respond to panic emails. My gratitude to her is immense; any faults that remain in the text are, of course, my own.

My daughters Rosalind and Elizabeth's belief in their 'Funny Mummy' is more sustaining than they realise. Their willingness to sacrifice their fashion principles to model First World War service women's uniforms is heartening.

Above all my wonderful husband Ivan: his love, technical abilities with websites, scanners and recalcitrant computers, know no bounds. Not only did he expertly play 'devil's advocate' as he read multiple drafts, but without his culinary skills I may have lived on bully beef throughout the writing of this book.

Illustration Acknowledgements

The Black Cat 'Women on War Work' cigarette cards are in my personal possession; there is a family wartime connection to Black Cat and the former Carreras Ltd.

My thanks to: Sally Day for the photograph of her grandmother Mary Lampard who worked at Chilworth Munitions Factory; Frances Olley for the photograph of her family member – sadly her name is now forgotten but she herself is not; Debbie de Boltz for the York Minster panel of women's names which forms the background of the book jacket; Ivan Newman for patiently scanning in hundreds of potential images.

Introduction

'It used to be said that war did not concern women'
(Queen's Nurses' Magazine October 1916)

I have always known about my grandfathers' First World War service. Her father's photograph was on my mother's bedside table, his eyes, haunted by all he had seen, staring into the middle distance. He was a Royal Army Medical Corps surgeon, specialising in abdominal wounds, and he served in France from November 1914. Like so many who returned, he spoke little about his war service, although post-war he worked with those still suffering from shell shock – teaching my mother to drive in the grounds of one of the 'lunatic asylums' he visited weekly.

Less is known about my father's father. He was a Doughboy in the American Armed Forces, dying of Spanish influenza in early 1919. Widowed in her mid-twenties, by the time I knew her my American grandmother could remember nothing of the young husband who had left her with two small boys to bring up alone. My teenage grandfather-in-law served at Gallipoli and in Mesopotamia. He was Mentioned in Despatches and returned with a bayonet wound that never fully healed. It used to terrify his grandsons. His war-related drink problem marred his own and his descendants' lives. These stories are typical; many of my generation are familiar with male ancestors' war service. But they are only one part of a family's history: the part that is easy to trace.

As a child, I accepted that both the First and the Second World War in which my father served, also pictured in uniform on my mother's bedside table, were 'Men's Business'. Then, one day, my nanny decided it was time I learnt to knit. Desperately unskilful, I tried distracting her and asked when she had learnt to do this complicated task: "During the First World War, I was five and I had to knit a scarf for a soldier. Lots of little girls did. We knitted in school and couldn't go out to play until we had done enough rows." I thought about this. Was knitting all that women and girls had done in this distant war? I asked more questions, only to come up against a brick wall.

Although as young mothers my grandmothers would have been

occupied with their families, what about their sisters, my great-aunts? What had they done in the War? My mother did not seem to know, indeed, nobody seemed to know – or even appeared interested. They could tell me about women in the Second World War but not the one that had already gripped my imagination. In many ways, this book is the result of my ongoing attempts to find answers to those questions. While I never have discovered what my own female ancestors did, I know what they might have done and the early battles they would have fought in order to be able to do anything at all.

In August 1914, the population of Great Britain was just over 46 million. With a tiny Regular Army (of some 733,514 officers and men), supported by around 269,000 Territorials and Reservists, Secretary-of-State for War Lord Kitchener made it abundantly plain to men aged between 18 and 45 that their country needed them. But the country had no need of its women. Out of a female population of some 27.6 million, only the 297 regular members of the Queen Alexandra's Imperial Military Nursing Service (QAIMNS), the 70 Queen Alexandra's Royal Naval Nursing Service sisters (QARNNS) and the 273 members of these services' Reserves had a designated wartime role, whilst the approximately 2,117 Territorial Forces Nurses (TFNS) anticipated serving in military hospitals or military wards at home. Where professional military nurses led, other qualified nurses rushed to follow. By the end of the war, nurses from across the world had served in every theatre of war, closer to the guns than anyone would have ever imagined on 4 August 1914 – and significant numbers died or were killed as a result.

Whilst nurses were soon wanted, the vast majority of the female population's labour and skills were still not required, even those with expertise any nation-at-war must surely need. The advice given to one eminent surgeon, 'Good lady, go home and sit still', was replicated the length and breadth of Britain. Other nations were less prejudiced and eagerly accepted the service of female physicians and surgeons who proved that they were just as competent as men. On the Western Front, professional doctors and volunteer nurses established and ran hospitals and drove ambulances ferrying the wounded across war-torn terrain. On more distant Fronts, both professional and volunteer women faced living and nursing conditions hardly less primitive than those of the early nineteenth century, and they earned the perpetual gratitude of the soldiers and civilians they selflessly succoured, sometimes losing their own lives.

One English woman even served with the Serbian Army; an annual service is still held in Serbia to commemorate and recognise British women's sacrifices.

The War's insatiable appetite for men was soon apparent. If the country and the war effort were not to grind to a halt, women were now told their labour was essential. Rather than sitting still, women were encouraged, even coerced, into playing their part. They made munitions and tilled the land, feeding the guns and the nation. Those too young or too old to work outside the home took up their needles and produced literally millions of pairs of much-needed socks, scarves, shirts and simple but essential comforts for soldiers, as well as equipment for hospitals. With much of Belgium and parts of France occupied, eyes and ears behind the lines were essential. Overshadowed by the female spies of a later war, those recruited in the First War proved as adept, brave and vulnerable.

As casualty lists lengthened, few homes were untouched by death. Although the majority of the bereaved mourned a husband, son, sweetheart or brother, others grieved for a beloved daughter, mother, fiancée or wife. Some, but not all, would have the comfort of a headstone or at least the knowledge that colleagues had accompanied her body on its last journey, however far from home she had perished. Many women have no known grave: some sleep in the ocean's deep waters; the bodies of others were blown to smithereens in munitions explosions or mangled in factory accidents.

Some mourners who participated at the memorial ceremonies held for both men and women during and after the War felt they had gained closure. Others grieved for the rest of their lives. The writings of those whose loved one's life, irrespective of gender, had been cut short show the human anguish behind the regimented headstones, the sweeping monuments to the missing and the local memorials which dot our landscape, frequently inscribed with both men's and women's names.

What women succeeded in doing and the roles that they created for themselves between 1914 and 1918 still have the power to astound and amaze. Had Mummy, rather than Daddy, been asked, 'What did you do in the Great War?' she could justifiably have replied, 'Without me the war may well not have been won.' This book shows why.

Dr Vivien Newman,
Chelmsford 2014

CHAPTER 1

Recruiting Women:
Sending the Boys, Knitting for the Boys,
Writing for the Boys

'We answer not the call to Arms, we answer the call to…'
(Mrs Peel)

On a late July evening in 1914, Nursing Sister Violetta Thurstan attended a military tattoo on Salisbury Plain. It was, she wrote at the time, 'one of those breathless evenings in July when the peace of Europe was trembling in the balance, and when most of us had a heartache in case England, at this time of international crisis, did not rise to the supreme sacrifice.'.The evening of military displays, riding demonstrations and massed bands drew to its close, 'The *Last Post* followed,' and, as the notes rose into the sky, this was the moment when, 'I think somehow we all knew'.

Hilda Sebastian wrote home on 26 July 1914 from her boarding-school, Wycombe Abbey, in Buckinghamshire, 'the soldiers all came to church this morning.' Reflecting decades later, she believed that with the pending school holidays, 'The appearance of the soldiers held little significance for me then,' although her 3 August diary entry reads, 'No one talks of anything but the war. What is England going to do?'

Sixteen-year-old Clare Leighton was unaware of 'what was happening in the world' beyond Suffolk; the war only impinged on her consciousness when her 18-year-old brother Roland 'became a Second Lieutenant and disappeared to a camp.' In Buxton, Roland Leighton's contemporary and friend, Vera Brittain, was recording events in her diary. On 3 August she states that if England remains neutral, 'we should be guilty of the grossest treachery'; the following day she concludes, 'this war is a matter of life and death to us.'

Twenty-four hours earlier, near Westroosebeke, Belgium, Martha

Cnockaert's father had, 'burst into the kitchen of our old farmhouse. "The Germans have invaded Belgium," he breathed.' Left to the mercy of the Germans by the retreating Belgian Army, Martha's home was set alight by the invaders, 'We stared fascinated [*at the conflagration*] till my mother gave a moan like an animal in pain, then we slowly walked into Westroosebecke.'

With Belgium invaded, many in Britain wondered, 'When are we going in?' During the evening of 4 August 1914, the answer came. Many of the thousands of citizens who gathered around Buckingham Palace to cheer the King and Queen felt, like 17-year-old subsequent Voluntary Aid Detachment (VAD) nurse Angela Trotter, 'frightfully excited', 'thinking it was splendid that we were going into the war.'

May Cannan, Quartermaster in the Oxfordshire VAD, realised that for women this was 'our war too'. In the north of England, 16-year-old farm worker Olive Taylor remained oblivious to what was happening, 'England had been at war three months before I knew. I was in domestic service on a farm near the River Humber and one day as I was attending to the ducklings a shell whizzed over my head from the direction of the river.' This was the first she knew about a war in which she would be closely involved.

Britain's last European War had ended in 1815, 99 years ago. Popular opinion – if not Lord Kitchener's – was that this one would be 'over by Christmas'. As the 120,000 men of the Regular Army which formed the British Expeditionary Force (BEF) mobilised, swiftly followed by the Territorial Army, one army wife knew she would 'never forget the almost unending roar of troop trains on the way to Southampton. My husband was one of the first to go.' Another woman sat at a station, 'watching trains full of soldiers go past. Suddenly I felt the tears come… all those men… those boys'. A young girl living close to where one Division was camping and who had friends in the regiment 'got a telephone message to say that they were off that night… There was no time for more than the most hurried farewell'. However, most citizens with no obvious connection to the Army knew little about how, or even when, the Army would arrive in the field; heavily censored newspapers were not enlightening.

On 18 August *The Times* finally lifted the veil of secrecy which had surrounded the BEF's movements, announcing, 'BRITISH ARMY IN THE FIELD'. Hints of the desperate situation developing across the

Channel emerged when, on 25 August, news broke of 2,000 casualties already sustained. *The Sunday Times'* 30 August headline was stark, 'MORE MEN NEEDED'. By the end of the first three weeks of war, the Press Bureau announced losses of 5,000 to 6,000 men. On 3 September, Vera Brittain noted a 'call for 500,000 men to arms'. Yet, after the initial rush to the recruiting stations, by mid-September volunteer numbers began to dwindle. Nonetheless, casualties had to be quickly replaced.

'One Word From YOU and He'll Go'

In a nation with no history of conscription and a small Regular Army suffering devastating casualties and rapidly falling enlistment rates, the women of the British Empire would also be conscripted, not into the Army, but into encouraging, coercing, and indeed even humiliating men into enlisting.

As early as 30 August 1914 Admiral Charles Penrose Fitzgerald organised 30 women in Folkestone to distribute white feathers to men not in uniform. As members of the Order of the White Feathers their mission was to shame men into enlisting or fear being branded a coward. The *Daily Mail* enthusiastically reported their activities, hoping, like Fitzgerald, that the gesture would 'shame every young slacker' into enlisting. The generally female white feather distributors achieved much notoriety by frequently misjudging their targets: stories of men on leave, wounded, or in reserved occupations being handed these odious symbols abound.

How many women were actively involved in the Order of the White Feather is impossible to establish, but the numbers are almost certainly lower than popular history leads people to believe. Although in *Three Guineas* Virginia Woolf argues that the numbers were infinitesimal, the Imperial War Museum (IWM) Collections indicate that, whilst not widespread, there were more than Woolf's supposed 'fifty or sixty'. White feathers continued to feature in stories in popular women's magazines long after the introduction of conscription, which should have laid the campaign to rest; the IWM has records of a few being distributed even in 1918. Knowledge of the White Feather Campaign remains alive and well in the collective imagination, even in the twenty-first century. The popular television series *Downton Abbey* featured white feather women in an episode relating to World War One.

On 4 September 1914, Baroness Orczy, author of *The Scarlet Pimpernel*, addressed an appeal 'To the Women of England', telling them that if any of them were wondering, 'What can I do?' the answer was simple, 'Give your sons and sweethearts'. Orczy made it plain:

> I want your men, your sweethearts, your brothers, your sons, your friends. Will you use your influence that they should respond one and all... to my crying need? ... [*Mothers*] your sons cannot stand aside any longer... you his mother will be ashamed to look all the brave English men and women in the face.

Would-be adherents had to complete a form, and, if they included 2d in stamps, they would receive a badge and their name placed on the Active Service League's 'Roll of Honour'. Women had to pledge to 'persuade every man I know to offer his services to his country and never to be seen in public with... any man who has refused to respond to his country's call.' The response was relatively unenthusiastic: only about 20,000 women, as opposed to the 100,000 Orczy wanted, subscribed within the first week.

Newspapers also encouraged women to undertake the recruiting sergeants' work – frequently publishing material by contributors who felt that a man's duty was to don khaki. A 29 August 1914 letter to *The Times* reminded every 'English Girl' that she would 'give good help to her country by shunning a man, be he 'lover, brother, friend' who did not 'take up arms'. In December 1914, the *Contemporary Review* advised girls to 'cut the acquaintance' of any sweetheart not in khaki. On 8 July 1915 'Ethel M' informed 'Jack G', via a letter to *The Times,* that 'if you are not in khaki by the 20th I shall cut you dead.' Although we cannot know if 'Ethel M' really existed, it was sufficient that contemporary readers believed that she did.

The press did not depend solely on letter-writers to swell the ranks. The *Daily Mail* initiated its own campaigns; one which achieved notoriety used music halls, popular long before the War and renowned for the singing of patriotic songs. It commissioned prolific lyricist and composer Paul Ruben to write a women's recruiting song to be sung nightly in 'Music Halls, cinemas and theatres in the West End'. The resulting 'Your King and Country Want You' first appeared in print on 12 September 1914, having been successfully sung in Bournemouth the previous week. Profits from its 1s 1d sale (equivalent to about £2.50 in 2013) were donated to the Queen's Work for Women Fund and by November it had run into a fifth edition. According to the commissioning newspaper, there was hardly a home in the country without a copy and, 'all those who have heard it believe it will act as a powerful aid to recruitment.' The newspaper patriotically waived its performance fee.

From mid-September a list of venues where it would be sung and the relevant artistes appeared in the paper – arguably this alerted the White Feather distributors, as the performance ended with those who did not show themselves ready to enlist being handed a feather, frequently by children. Social commentator Mrs Peel noted in *How We Lived Then*, 'It seems strange that a call to a man perhaps to give his life, in any event to face almost unbelievable horror, did not incite words of more dignity.' Judging by the song's appeal, many disagreed with her.

Although sung by female artistes, other stridently pro-enlistment songs were also written by men. Arthur Wimperis and Herman Finck's 'I'll Make A Man of You' was widely sung in music halls, both to drive up recruitment numbers and raise funds. Vesta Tilley, one of the biggest stars of the day, was closely associated with such songs; she frequently strode on to the stage dressed as a Tommy wishing, 'Jolly good luck to the girl who loves a soldier,' and drumming up recruits.

In this context, the story of mill worker Kitty Morter (sic Eckersley, IWM Sound Recordings 4089) is simply told. A recently married young couple, Kitty and Percy Morter went to their local music hall. Army officers were also on stage. To Kitty's distress, when Vesta Tilley marched up and down the auditorium, encouraging men to enlist, Percy was one of many who fell in behind. She remembered, 'When we got home that night I was terribly upset.' To no avail. Lance Corporal Percy Morter was killed on 7 July 1916, leaving Kitty pregnant with their first child. In Vesta's defence, she became closely involved with morale-boosting concerts, performed for soldiers in military hospitals and raised thousands of pounds through her appearances in charity shows for hospital and rehabilitation funds.

Mothers were also directly targeted in songs: F.V. St Clair's 1914 'Follow the Drum', subtitled 'Every Mother's Son is Ready to Carry the Gun' (with profits mounting apparently to over £1,000 given to various 'Relief Funds'), combines 'Mother England' and England's mothers whose patriotic sons will, in the words of the chorus, 'be ready to carry a gun'. A number of mothers felt that their sons should indeed carry a gun and the question of whether an individual should enlist could divide neighbours and families.

In Buxton on 9 August 1914, Vera Brittain reports how their neighbour Mrs Ellinger was, 'quite rude to Mother… Maurice [*her son*] intended signing on for 3 years.' On 3 September, Vera noted her father's reluctance for his son [*Edward*] to enlist. Mr Brittain was subjected to considerable pressure from Edward, 'Mother and I [*who*] tried to make him see it from the point of view of honour.' Mrs Brittain wrote to one of her husband's business partners 'asking him to use his influence over Daddy'. This conflict was a major preoccupation for the Brittain family: 'we all discussed again Daddy's refusal', and the debate stretched beyond the four walls of the Brittains' home. 'We saw Mrs Ellinger later & she seems very strongly to disapprove of Daddy.' Further pressure is put on Mr Brittain during a discussion of a letter in *The Times* 'of a mother who said to her hesitating son, "My boy I don't want you to go, but if I were you I should".' Eventually, bowing to female pressure, Mr Brittain relented, 'Edward may enlist although he wishes it to be known that this is "in direct opposition to my wishes".'

The subtext of Mrs Ellinger's disdain was undoubtedly the idea that Maurice was protecting the Brittain family – something that posters and pamphlets soon conveyed to women, especially mothers. In wartime, mothers willing to offer their sons to the nation in her time of need can be portrayed as selfless and patriotic; those who 'expect other Mothers' sons' to defend her and hers are condemned as unpatriotic and selfish. One early pamphlet exhorted mothers to 'Give Your Sons', thereby proving that they were the 'right sort of Mother for Old England'.

A 1915 recruiting leaflet blends ideas of civic and maternal responsibilities, 'One word from YOU and he will go.' Others, such as the leaflet asking the 'Women of London', 'Is your "Best Boy" wearing Khaki? If not, don't YOU THINK he should be?' implied that a man who 'neglects his duty to his King and Country,' might well 'NEGLECT YOU'.

Posters directly addressing mothers' psychological power over men soon entered the fray. According to social commentator Caroline Playne in *Society at War*, recruiting messages were 'proclaimed on all available wall spaces' in the 'most soul-convincing way.' One that has achieved a measure of notoriety is the Essex Recruiting Committee poster, 'Go! It's Your Duty, Lad, Join Today.' The mother's pointed arm makes it plain to her seemingly reluctant son where his duty lies. Inevitably, not all mothers were convinced. In Essex, Alexandra Grantham saw war as 'depriving the mother of ownership in what so essentially belongs to her, the children to whom she has given birth.' Although her published writings make her own views clear, she may have concealed these from her sons, one an officer in the Essex Regiment, the other in the Hussars.

Another widely reproduced Parliamentary Recruiting Committee poster, E.V. Kealey's 'Women of Britain "Say Go",' appeared in May 1915 when recruitment numbers were dwindling. Its sentimental image of a mother gazing out of the window as soldiers march by, whilst clutching her two children, is amongst the war's most famous and also ambiguous posters. There is a wistful resignation on the woman's face; she may accept the need for the men to go, yet there is little obvious enthusiasm or jingoism, more an acceptance of the necessity. Women who, embarrassingly, had no sons to give could nevertheless do their duty, as another 1915 poster addressed 'To the Women of Britain' makes plain: 'You can prove your love for your country by persuading them to go.'

During the first two years, just under three million men volunteered to serve in the British Armed Forces. Such numbers joining of their own free will represented a considerable achievement. Whilst the majority enlisted out of a sense of duty and patriotism, some admitted to being 'shamed' into volunteering – and were resentful of those who had coerced them. Nevertheless, the numbers of volunteers remained insufficient. On 28 December 1915, according to Caroline Playne, the 'long drawn-out controversy, round which all the emotionalism that could be spared from actual war measures… drew to its close.' On this historic day, 'statesmen whittl[ed] away [one of England's] three greatest institutions, free military service.' The Cabinet had decided to 'introduce a measure of compulsion for military service.'

This opened the way for the January 1916 Military Service Act and the conscription, initially of single men aged between 18 and 41, and married men soon after. Writing on 9 January 1916, Kate Courtney felt that 'the outlook seemed very black – a bitter contest against conscription added to the fierce war, perhaps a beginning of social strife which we fear will follow this war.'

In the Dominions, the need for more men was also urgent and governments considered their options. After intensive campaigning, in August 1917, the Canadian Government voted in favour of the introduction of conscription – a move that deeply divided the broadly pro-English and anti-French-speaking Canadians. Meanwhile, in Australia, full conscription was attempted twice via plebiscites. The first in October 1916 was narrowly defeated: 51 per cent of Australians voted 'No'. A second plebiscite was scheduled in December 1917.

Inevitably both sides used posters and leaflets to gain support. Constructed to prey on the Australian males' sense of masculinity, one striking leaflet reminded readers how the [*British*] Women's Auxiliary Army Corps were 'doing work in the shell-swept zone,' in order to release soldiers for 'the grim work of the trenches'. The message from the Australian Government to both women and men was clear, they should give 'An Overwhelming Yes' in the forthcoming plebiscite. A slightly increased majority of Australians disagreed; this time just under 54 per cent of the population remained opposed. Australian soldiers would finish the War as they had begun, as proud volunteer members of the Australian Imperial Force. Although it would continue for Australian women, by early 1916, British women's task as recruiters was done.

'It's not a sock she's knitting it's a web of love for him'

Lord Kitchener's pointing finger telling men, 'Your Country Needs You', has become one of the iconic images of the War. Women who wished to contribute their services to the war effort being advised to 'Go home and knit socks' has similarly entered into popular imagination. Less well known is how, requiring 300,000 pairs of socks by November 1914, Lord Kitchener and Queen Mary called upon the women of the British Empire to knit them – and Kitchener gave his name to a stitch which ensured that toes and heels were turned seamlessly to avoid blisters. Before the War, the Army Ordnance Service had annually provided the Regular Army with, *inter alia*, 220,000 shirts and a million pairs of socks. These quantities now had to be found within a week and, with more and more men under arms, demand could only increase.

On 18 August 1914, the Queen Mary Needlework Guild was launched, offering a delicate medal and certificate to its most industrious members. Knitting was class-less: apparently the Queen ensured that knitting materials were strategically placed in many rooms at Buckingham Palace and she herself took up her needles. Following her example, many patrician women organised working parties for the women of the villages dependent upon their estates.

From the earliest days, Lady Horner (whose only son, poet Edward Tennant, died in November 1917), 'had a big Work Party' for the local

18

village women. Sitting 'in the Loggia' of the Manor House, 'we started making shirts and socks and sharing all the [*War*] news' she had acquired from friends in high office, including Prime Minister Asquith. She felt that, 'working for their men and hearing all the latest news I could get for them was a great comfort.' Ettie Grenfell was another of the countless wealthy women to set up working parties. By '11 December 1914, [*her*] working party at Taplow Court had sent 955 garments to hospitals and soldiers abroad.' Ettie lost two of her three sons: war poet Julian in May 1915 and Billy a few weeks later.

In her *Roll Call of Serving Women* (n.d. – c.1915) Mrs Billington commented that 'the great era of knitting [*had*] set in.' London teenager Mary Coules remarked in her diary, 'Everybody developed a craze for knitting socks, all our conversation was punctuated by "purl, plain, purl, plain",' with occasional interruptions to deal with dropped stitches making conversations problematic. According to Mrs Peel, from August 1914 England resounded with the click of knitting needles, as women knitted in private and public spaces, 'in trains and trams, in parks and parlours'.

Volunteers could apply for financial assistance to purchase wool. The 5 October 1914 *Daily Graphic* lists not only the numbers of knitted articles received, but also the names of subscribers to the funds set up for purchasing and distributing yarn and needles. Mrs Peel cynically comments on how purveyors of these items 'must have amassed fortunes'. This is unsurprising if the women of Dundee were in any way typical; they contributed some 6,000 pairs of socks in the War's early months alone.

Although fun has been poked at the Knitting Army and at its truly staggering output, in letters from the Front, serving men and women begged their families to encourage knitters to greater efforts, often through emphasising gratitude for 'comforts' received and showing how desperately socks were needed. As early as November 1914, Territorial Forces Nursing Service (TFNS) Sister Jentie Paterson wrote, 'Please thank the ladies of your committee and tell them how I distributed the last lot [*of socks*].' Some soldiers' socks being 'moulded to their limbs, generally been on 5, 6, 7 weeks,' helps explain her appreciation. Frost-bitten feet could lead to amputation, and as they strove to keep patients' feet warm in the frequently tented hospitals overseas, on inadequately heated hospital trains, hospital barges and ships, most nursing staff would have agreed that it was upon Home Front knitters that 'Soldiers' Feet Depend'.

Canadian Sister Agnes Warner wrote home from a Mobile (*French*) Hospital on 7 November 1915 to express gratitude for the wool that 'Mrs S. sent' and which the women in the village were already knitting into socks for her 'Beloved *Poilus*', whose need for socks is chillingly obvious, 'So many of the men have just straw in their boots and are almost frozen' A subsequent letter afterwards confirms, 'Mrs. S.'s socks and bandages have just come.' These, 'being white… often save the men from being infected by the dye of the stockings.' Socks are dispatched, 'to the dressing station by ambulance, and from there they go to the trenches at once.' Agnes' letters home continue to praise knitters and their dedication. Her own dedication was recognised by the French authorities, from whom she received the *Médaille d'Honneur*, *Médaille des Épidémies* and the *Croix de Guerre* – as well as earning the unfailing gratitude of the *poilus*, whose sufferings she and the citizens of St John, Brunswick had striven to alleviate.

First Aid Nursing Yeomanry (FANY) Pat Beauchamp took knitted comforts to entrenched Belgian troops. She remembered her anguish when she saw that her supply of socks and scarves was insufficient to go round the men who so desperately needed them; some had not had clean ones in three months. Finally she donated her 'own scarf', then, with nothing left to give, turned 'sorrowfully away'. With so small an area of Belgium unoccupied, Belgian soldiers were particularly dependent upon the generosity of Allied knitters. It was generally impossible for letters, let alone socks or comforts, to reach them.

As many nurses' letters and writings make plain, knitted garments provided both physical comfort and psychological links with home, both for the soldiers who received them and for the women who distributed them. According to Pat Beauchamp, both genders remembered the 'kind hands' that had knitted them at home. However, knitting items for soldiers, not for servicewomen, was considered 'war work', and although nurses also needed warm stockings and knitted items, they often had to *buy* these out of their own pockets.

In a letter to her father, VAD Josephine Pennell MM, working with the St Omer Convoy in the bitter winter of 1918, wrote, 'Please ask Mother if she could get me three pairs of winter stockings. This is in the nature of an S.O.S. The great point is they should never need darning, and three in number unless they are very expensive in which case two pairs will have to do.' American Nurse Helen Fairchild, in an October 1917 letter home, told her family how she had bought herself 'four pairs of heavy woollen stockings, a heavy knitted underskirt'. Before their entry into the War, Americans had knitted in response to appeals from the International Red Cross. Once American troops were engaged overseas, knitters concentrated their efforts on their own servicemen. African-American soldiers were less well catered for. They, like servicewomen, seem not to have been the knitters' priority. However, a 'Self-Improvement Club' was set up by African-American women who knitted for 'their boys'. There is no documentary evidence of any group prioritising service women.

American troops needed one and a half million knitted wristlets, mufflers, sweaters, and pairs of socks respectively, although socks, due to the nature of trench warfare, were, always paramount. A Japanese women's group was founded in Seattle. As the 23 December 1917 *Seattle Times* enthused, the 'fair maidens of the Orient have aligned themselves with patriotic movements' – and were busily knitting.

The *New York Sunday Sun* newspaper found an imaginative way both to maintain the supply of socks and the motivational knitting poems it published weekly: prizes (of balls of wool) were offered for the best 'sock songs' submitted. If the subsequent published volume is representative, the competitors were numerous and the pairs of socks they knitted must have equipped many a battalion. For those without sufficient poetic talents to win wool, the American Red Cross provided knitters with patterns, wool too if necessary (75c per allotment), and shipped the finished items overseas.

On one of her 1915 trips to the Belgian trenches, Pat Beauchamp had noticed how some comforts had notes attached to them. This was common practice. In February 1917 Trooper A.B. Beattie of the Australian Light Horse in the 'Egypt Desert Sinai Peninsula' received some socks from Tasmanian Marjorie Lyn. She had included 'a note' with her name and address inside one of the 'well-knitted socks' which he had received. The correspondence (subsequently donated to the Australian War Memorial) between Beattie and Marjorie, whom he considered 'a little dear', flourished.

As his existing socks were almost 'finished', hers, he claimed, arrived in 'the nick of time'. On 7 June, 'Yours dated 6th May very gladly received... You were a sport to write such a nice long letter.' He is delighted to learn that she is 'only a flapper aged 18' and asks for a photograph. He jokes about a friend, Clarence Moore, who also wrote to his benefactor but discovered that she 'was not a bashful young lady at all' but a woman 'of 45 years of age'. Clarence starts writing to Marjorie as well. Both soldiers express their homesickness and Marjorie's socks and letters provided physical comfort and a link with a homeland half a world away.

In December 1916, writing from the mud of the Somme area, an Australian Lance Corporal told his benefactress that, 'Though we endure hardships [*which he enumerates, indicating that the letter may not have been censored*] we can never fully appreciate the wonderful kindness of the women folk which has been a little ray of sunshine from our dear Australia.'

Canadian soldiers' need for socks and letters was equally pronounced and Canadian women responded. Marion Simpson of Hamilton, Ontario, a prolific knitter and correspondent, included a letter with every garment and helpfully included a self-addressed envelope. Fourteen of these replies have been preserved in the McMaster University Archives; they speak to us across the century, showing women's 'webs of love' stretching almost literally across the world.

Younger knitters and correspondents were also hard at work across the combatant nations. Little Lucy Bateson's knitted gifts were warmly welcomed. One 12-year-old was assured in April 1919 that 'it's thinking about nice little girls like you that has helped us to beat the Germans.' Another child remembered she 'started knitting for the Red Cross at the age of nine years, and was knitting up two pounds of wool and cotton per week by the age of eleven.' She donated the Red Cross certificates she received to the IWM. Her knitted facecloths were sent to hospitals, indicating that she may initially have been a novice knitter, as children made these before progressing to scarves and socks.

Children were assured that their knitting was 'war work'. Irene 'Reeny' Turtle, born November 1910, was not allowed to go out to play until the scarf she was knitting reached a certain length; she found an imaginative solution, 'I pulled it as hard as I could in the hopes of making it appear longer.' Her efforts were rewarded, and as an old lady she still remembered the letter from the soldier who had received her scarf. Reeny's knitting skills improved and she continued to knit

22

well into old age, teaching the present author to knit – by way of facecloths.

In Yorkshire, Amy Tyreman was hard at work throughout the War. Along with other children at Brodsworth School near Doncaster, she knitted a truly impressive collection of socks, mittens, mufflers and scarves. Her sisters, 11-year-old Hilda and 3-year-old Constance, were equally dedicated. The local newspaper commends the whole school's efforts – 'about 745 warm comforts' but singles out the Tyreman family, who contributed a total of '194 articles'. Apparently, as much wool as the children could knit into 'warm comforts [*was*] freely provided.' Children's enthusiasm for their 'war work' was even mentioned in their funeral cards: one little boy had been knitting 'almost as he drew his last breath'. The children of Brodsworth and nearby Marr produced a total of 1,145 items.

Amy preserved the letters she received, some just a few lines long, others long enough to give a sense of the soldier's character and homesickness as well as his appreciation of the gift and the care that had gone into the knitting. Amongst the most poignant are from Royal Naval Division Seaman J.H. Norman, written just before the evacuation of the Gallipoli Peninsula. Covering two sides of YMCA notepaper, and dated 26 December 1915, he tells Amy that he has just spent his first Christmas away from home and he hopes that his family will send her a small gift as a token of his appreciation of the socks he was 'lucky to receive'. Norman subsequently told her:

> I was very pleased to hear from you and dear friend I like your little photo, I must thank you for it, and I am so sorry that I have not got one to send to you but may be when I get back to Dear Old England I will send you on one to remind you of the Sailor that received your socks and dear I think it awful good of you children to make such things for they are needed very bad [*sic*].

One wonders if Amy ever learned what had happened to her 'Sailor', who was killed on 26 October 1917. Her letters, her knitting needles, wool, badge and certificate from the Queen Mary Needlework Guild are now in the safe-keeping of Brodsworth Hall. Her efforts, and the undoubted solace they brought to the soldiers and sailors who received the gifts she and her contemporaries created, remind us that whilst the War might have been physically fought in the trenches, on the high seas and in the air, those at home sought ways of sending physical tokens of love to the troops.

In distant Australia, 'Champion knitter' Nora Pennington was hard at work. She won the district record for 'the number of socks, mufflers, mittens and balaclava helmets knitted by anyone under the age of thirteen.' Neither knitting nor the war effort brought out the best in her schoolmates: one, a David Gleason, remembered decades later, 'the rest of us longed to grab her knitting, rip the stitches out and snarl her wool for her'! Perhaps there was rivalry between the children, as David's mother was 'a leading light in the... Red Cross'. Whenever he returned from school, 'the house was full of women clicking needles... making huge quantities of socks, vests, mittens and mufflers.' In a further hint of resentment, he reported that, 'Mum spent more and more of her time on the war effort.' At the other end of the age scale, the elderly were equally busy knitting. On 15 September 1915, the *Ballarat Courier* included an obituary for Mrs Lavinia Rhys who, a month short of her ninetieth birthday, was 'busily engaged knitting socks for the soldiers.' The obituary is such that it almost sounds as though she, like the little Brodsworth boy, had died needles in hand.

A semi-official Australian Comfort Fund (ACF) was established to coordinate civilians' efforts to provide all forms of material comforts for troops. Knitters from across Australia supplied their boys, the famous 'Diggers', with staggering quantities of knitted and other handmade garments. The State of Victoria Division reported that since the ACF's August 1916 foundation, it had provided a total of 512,542 knitted articles for the troops, encouraged perhaps by the Melbourne newspaper *The Age,* which often published knitting poems and also patterns for the new longer trench 'stocking' and directions on how to ensure that these were waterproofed. The Melbourne Lady Mayoress' League published 'Directions for Knitting Two Socks at Once for Our Men On Active Service,' with the perhaps unnecessary caveat that this endeavour was not for 'beginners'!

In 1917, the New South Wales Division of the ACF, anxious that it would not be able to source sufficient wool, turned to its own immediately available resource, sheep, and proudly announced that 'knitting direct from the fleece' contributed materially to the ever-growing pile of socks. Perhaps this inspired one of the War's many poetic parodies for, when Mary took her lamb to school:

RECRUITING WOMEN

The little maids at school that day
Forgot their sums and letters.
They pulled the wool all off its back
And knit it into sweaters.

North American schoolchildren were equally busy with their needles, and in Canada blind as well as sighted children were knitting for their troops. Young American children who could not knit were reminded in school magazines and stories that their patriotic duty lay in enabling adult knitters to participate in this activity. The 1918 *Seattle School Bulletin*, in its long list of 'How Children Can Help Win The War', included several hints regarding knitting: 'Do mother's work so she can knit'; 'hold yarn for mother while she winds it into a ball'; 'be careful of clothes so mother will not have to patch and can knit.' Finally, any child unfortunate enough to have a mother who could not knit, could 'help grandma so she will find time to teach mama to knit.' Although children were not actively encouraged in these leaflets to tell their mothers to do so, knitting was considered acceptable in church, and even when attending trials in court.

Many schools, charities and newspapers across the Allied nations organised competitions offering prizes (not infrequently balls of wool) and knitting societies; names of the most prolific knitters were listed. Perhaps desperate to have their names recorded in a Knitters' Service Record, a number of girls prided themselves on the number of pairs of socks and mufflers they knitted per week, often unravelling their own garments to acquire the necessary yarn. Archived copies of the *University of Washington Daily* show how this university provided knitting lessons free of charge, as well as yarn and knitting needles – although a deposit was required to ensure the finished item was returned. Aspiring knitters were informed that knitting in pink wool was unpatriotic and 'selfish'.

The headmistress of the North London Collegiate (Girls) School reported in *Our Magazine* in 1914 how, 'Every girl who could not knit is learning to knit now', and competitions with prizes for the most prolific knitters were organised. This school's Roll of Honour included not only the names of former pupils who were serving in an official capacity, but also those of current pupils who were doing their bit using their sewing and knitting needles – of which there was soon a growing shortage. Members of the school's Dorcas Society met monthly in order to increase their knitting and sewing output. At the annual prize-giving ceremony, the Chairman of the Governors encouraged the girls not to dwell on the hatred 'engendered by war', but to 'turn their hearts and hands to works of mercy.' Pupils had also voted that, instead of awarding flowers to prize-winners, donations should be made to enable them to purchase knitting wool.

Knitting became an extra-curricular activity at Wycombe Abbey School. On 18 February 1915 Hilda Sebastian noted: 'One of the girls is going to play the violin while we knit tonight and another is going to sing. I think I have just enough wool to make a helmet.' As Gustav Holst was singing master at the school, the songs may have been both uplifting and soothing to the listening knitters. Soon, girls 'awoke at 6.00 am on Saturdays to fit in 30 minutes' knitting.' On 24 June 1915, they were heartened by listening to the gramophone they had bought for convalescent soldiers by depriving themselves of sweets and donating money to a gramophone-purchase fund. They were delighted to 'try it' before it was forwarded on to the chosen hospital in Nottingham.

Following an appeal from Serbia for (very fiddly-sounding) 'muslin milk-jug covers', Hilda reports on 6 June 1915 that the headmistress 'has undertaken for the school to make 900.' Hilda successfully achieved one between Friday and Sunday. Then she writes, 'Another thing, Miss Whitelaw has undertaken is for the school to make 200 sandbags. I believe they are going to let us off lessons one afternoon to do them.' If Hilda struggled with milk-jug covers and sand-bags, some aspiring knitters were more willing than talented. Mrs Peel remembers a small girl asking, 'Mummie, shall I *live* to finish this sock?'

Women's magazines reassured those who favoured their sewing needles that soldiers would also appreciate shirts, pyjamas and even handkerchiefs. One magazine's 'Agony Aunt' provided a useful solution to a correspondent's dilemma. Apparently, the best way of cheering up a soldier was 'by sending him half a dozen of the beautiful hem-stitched Tit Bits khaki hankies.' The implication is that khaki handkerchiefs are a better way of showing affection than sleeping with a soldier home on leave. Sadly, history has not revealed whether the correspondent took this advice.

Soldiers needed socks. Had volunteers not knitted, factories would have had to produce them. Women's knitting therefore made a crucial, now overlooked contribution to the war effort. But it did more than simply replace a production line, it brought precious memories of 'Home' to the

Front for both servicewomen who distributed the gifts and servicemen who received them. It linked civilians of all ages who took up their needles with such dedication on behalf of their own or another woman's loved one, and frequently provided companionship for women and children as they sat and knitted together. One poet intuitively understood her mother's emotional need to knit, 'It's not a sock she's knitting, it's a web of love for him.' As the Empire resounded with the click of knitting needles, Lord Kitchener's August 1914 request was met threefold: as Mrs Billington noted, even by November 1914 'a total of 970,000 pairs of socks,' not to mention, scarves, mufflers, balaclavas and letters, awaited the Empire's 'heroes'.

Neither Private, Major nor Countess:
A Hospital Letter-Writer in France

For many, writing letters as well as knitting was a pleasure, creating a vital link between home and loved ones. By 1917, the British Forces Postal Services were handling an average of two million letters and postcards a day. However, for sisters in hospitals, letter-writing was part of their official duties, needing to be fitted into their nursing shifts which occasionally exceeded 40 hours. Military hospital protocol required that the next-of-kin of patients considered 'Dangerously Ill' be informed of their relative's possible imminent demise; sisters' duties included writing these 'Break-the-News' letters. They frequently could not keep up with them. In just one morning during the Somme offensive, Sister Edie Appleton wrote about 60 such letters from her hospital in France, this in addition to being in charge of wards overflowing with the wounded and dying.

Aware as early as December 1914 of nursing staffs' near unmanageable non-nursing workload, 60-year-old May Bradford, wife of the Consulting Physician and subsequently Surgeon General to the BEF, had arrived in Boulogne, 'with the view of undertaking work of a suitable kind in one of the service hospitals.' She wrote letters for the sick and wounded as well as 'Break-the-News' letters. *A Hospital Letter-Writer in France* (1920) gives an insight into her service in Boulogne and Étaples, which lasted until after the Armistice, 'without any break save a week's illness due to some fever.'

Deeply conscious of how recipients would cherish her letters – frequently the last contact they would have with their loved one – she would write sitting by the man's bedside and, to ensure that each letter sounded personal, she would try to include homely details and allude to his children by name. Armed with 'writing materials, a camp-stool, newspapers, two baskets of comforts, and often a third large basket of oranges for the gassed cases,' she made her way round the 'distant huts', linking wounded men with their homes, reassuring families or gently preparing them to accept that despite every effort being made to save him, he would soon, in soldiers' terminology, be 'going West'.

Friendships were formed, not only with the patients, but also with correspondents. Having written many letters to an Irishman's sister, 'About six weeks after [*his*] death she wrote, "I wish you would go on writing to me; I am so lonesome without your letters".' May complied. Another soldier, Private C.J. Reynolds, had his foot amputated: his mother donated May's letters to the IWM. In one, she wrote:

We are so sorry your son was delayed from going to England. It must have been a great disappointment to you, he was not well enough to travel, it is a terrible anxious time for you in England. All my heart goes out to you in sympathy. The sister-in-charge says your son's wounds are not doing very well, he has so many. He is now asleep on his bed in the sun and that is very good for him. I will keep you informed of his progress. He sends his love.

Yours Faithfully,
(Lady) May Bradford.

She soon prepares Mrs Reynolds for the worst:

Your son I regret to say keeps very ill, his condition is so septic. He is anxious I should say that he cannot write himself but sends his best love.
May Bradford

In a more deferential age than our own, many patients wondered if she would 'know how to write' letters to those whom they considered important recipients. Unsure of her social standing, they would tell her that the requested letter was, 'quite different from writing to my mother'. One 'street sweeper' received Christmas greetings from the Corporation of London. Wishing to acknowledge these, he asked 'Do you know how to write it, Sister?'. He felt reassured when, as instructed, she signed off 'Your obedient Servant'.

At times ingenuity was required, as some soldiers were so badly wounded that they were unable to speak or even remember their address. Linguistic issues could compound the difficulties. As a Welshwoman, Lady Bradford ascertained that one delirious soldier was speaking Welsh; her letter was 'the first intimation his family had had of his whereabouts for considerable time.' Other Welsh soldiers were unsuspectingly grateful for her linguistic fluency. An up-the-line letter to a Welsh wife 'who knew no English' had been languishing in the Censor's Department. These worthy gentlemen, 'not knowing in the least what treason might be in it, would not send it on,' until she assured them it contained no threat to national security. The fact that the letters she wrote were not censored caused considerable joy to a young lad, who decided that, as no male eyes would fall upon his letter, he could send his *inamorata* 'as many kisses as he wished'!

Some recipients were anxious about this letter-writer's identity. One mother demanded that the matron of the hospital, 'tell me who May Bradford is? My son is very susceptible.' Another mother was reassured when her son, finally able to write for himself, provided an explanation. She was 'glad your letters are written by a nice old lady.' To May's amusement, the age was 'trebly underlined!' Younger women at home were equally wary; more than one asked, 'Who is this pretty V.A.D. who wrote for you? Tell me all about her.'

Lack of official status created uncertainty as to how to address May. 'There was no official name for the post or position which I filled,' the confusion was neatly summed up by 'one boy, "I calls you Mother, my mother calls you Nurse, and the Sister of the ward calls you Lady Bradford. I'm fair 'mazed".' Others were similarly ''mazed'. One relative wrote to 'M. Bradford, Commanding-Officer in charge of Private T.' At times she was 'reduced to the ranks and called "Private Bradford",' at others elevated to 'Major'. One mother felt comforted, 'Major Bradford must be a kind-hearted sort of man... I expect he has a mother of his own living, that's why he feels for me so much'. Another soldier told her that 'Mother thinks you're a mon [*sic*].'

The men themselves found a solution, 'Early in 1915 [*they*] took to calling me Mother', some going on to tell her that she was 'the very "spit" of their mother and would show me her photograph. It was sometimes rather startling to see the figure which I was supposed to resemble.' Intriguing insights are given into the treatment some of them meted out to their mothers; 'the calls of "Mother" here and "Mother" there' resounded around the wards as she was asked to '"go under the bed and get my pipe out of my kit",' or other similar tasks.

The emotional comfort Lady Bradford gave as she knelt on the ground to speak to those lying on stretchers knew no bounds; her skirt was often clutched by 'seven or eight men' pleading '"Don't leave me out!" "Don't go away without writing for me!".' To the dying she would sometimes replace a beloved mother at home and many soldiers were eased into the next world convinced that they were holding their own mother's hand, 'He died thinking that she [*not I*] was at his side.'

On hearing in June 1916, that May was 'Mentioned in Despatches', one man summed up the feelings of the many, quite simply, 'We are proud'. Her work amongst the wounded and suffering continued until 7 April 1919. Post-war, she received an OBE, a well-deserved accolade for a woman whom many soldiers felt had 'smiled me well'. She humbly commented that her service was 'an experience on which I could never look back without a deep sense of gratitude that it had been given me to fulfil.' Judging from the comments of those she wrote for and those who received her letters, the gratitude was reciprocal.

This was Our War

The events that were put in train following the declaration of war irrevocably changed countless women's lives. Many accepted the propaganda telling them that it was their patriotic duty to encourage a man, however beloved he might be, to enlist in the Empire's cause. Posters and leaflets often appropriated a woman's, even a mother's voice, and shouted 'Go!' But the combination of women's actions, the official recruiting committees and recruiters failed to supply enough volunteers and, in 1916, the sacred freedom of voluntary military service was sacrificed in Great Britain and in Canada. A different voice now compelled men to 'Go!'

Anxious to find physical ways of showing affection and gratitude to soldiers so far away, those at home took up their needles. Young and old, they endeavoured to knit 'love and luck' into every stitch, earning the gratitude of thousands of serving and auxiliary personnel. Those who distributed and those who received these poignant, yet practical, gifts were eager to make contact with the frequently unknown army of knitters and sewers whose webs of love linked the Home and War Fronts. For children, here was essential war work in which they too could be engaged and even those barely out of babyhood showed remarkable tenacity in producing scarves, socks and face cloths. Knitters of all ages earned the appreciation of Queen Mary, treasuring their medals and certificates.

Letters from the Front provided those at home with immense comfort. May Bradford gently prepared some families for sorrows that would soon be theirs; those anxiously awaiting news were reassured that, irrespective of rank, social status or age, everything possible was being done to save their soldier's life. She comforted the dying and became quite simply, 'Mother to the British Army.'

CHAPTER 2

'Thank God We Have The Sisters': Nursing Personnel at the Front

'Every soldier will be required for fighting and every nurse for the care of the wounded,' (Nursing Times, August 1914)

Unlike the majority of women who were eager to assist the war effort but who found that the nation had little use for them, professional nurses were a case apart. Before 1914, 1,800 trained nurses (including 80 from Canada, Australia and New Zealand) had served overseas with the Army, mainly but not exclusively during the South Africa wars. These women were the forerunners of the approximately 24,000 professional nurses whose active service between 1914 and 1919 involved caring for occupants of the 637,746 hospital beds at home and in all theatres of war.

In addition, about 900 nurses served on hospital ships which evacuated and treated the wounded. (These figures exclude the widely researched and much written about members of the Voluntary Aid Detachments (VADs) and other volunteer organisations.) Whilst a small number were already members of the QAIMNS, QARNNS, QAIMNS(R), QARRNNS(R) or TFNS, the majority were civilian nurses working with the Army and unless their status (or rank) is directly relevant to their story, no distinction is made between them in this chapter. All did their utmost to save the lives, or at least ease the dying, of the men in their care. Their official ages ranging from 17 to 54 years, these women confronted the realities and the horrors of technological warfare on a daily basis.

'The nurses were most adaptable and made the best of everything'

The Army Medical Services exist primarily to expedite a man's rapid return to fighting strength. With the Army constantly facing manpower shortages, nursing personnel were deployed in hitherto unimaginable ways and places, and nurses' memoirs and diaries show that they embraced the challenges they faced. On 18 August 1914, 24 QAIMNS nurses proceeded to Le Havre to join their Matron-in-Chief to the BEF, Maud McCarthy. Her tireless energy soon became a hallmark of QAIMNS leadership; she was the only head of a British Army Department not to be replaced during the war years. Born an Australian and having deducted four years from her age, she was 'officially' 55 years old when war broke out. Her detailed war diaries (held in The National Archives) provide a day-by-day account of the experiences of those 'the stirring bugle' called not to 'War and deeds of lust and hate', but simply to 'Ward and tent'. (Lieutenant-Colonel Brockway, Australian Army Medical Service)

The British Army's 23 August to 5 September 1914 Retreat from Mons is well-documented militarily, yet the involvement of the medical services, including nurses, is often overlooked. One nurse present during the retreat was Sister Millicent Peterkin. Her private papers and diary, held at the IWM, give a sense of the headlong rush to evacuate hospitals in the face of the advancing enemy. The wounded were loaded onto troop trains or cattle trucks accompanied by sisters, 'they were lying eight or nine in each truck, and in beside each lot were two sisters. [...] They had to fly from Amiens, abandoning 700 beds, all their tents and equipment and all personal belongings, having nothing but what they stood up in.' Patients' sufferings in this headlong retreat gave Boer War veteran QAIMNS(R) 42-year-old Kate Luard cause for anxiety. Her *Diary of a Nursing Sister on the Western Front* (1915) describes men being 'picked up without a spot of dressing on any of their wounds, which were septic and full of straw and dirt.'

Once the very early days of mobile warfare ended, a series of medical services were established which, like the soldiers, began to dig in: staffed by male medical orderlies and providing some minimal medical care, Regimental First Aid Posts were established in the trench reserve lines. From these, the wounded were transported, (generally by horse-drawn ambulance) to Advanced Dressing Stations and thence to Casualty Clearing Stations (CCS), where operations could be performed. Initially male-only preserves, CCS (rapidly increasing in size and number) were often sited near railway sidings or waterways to facilitate the movement of the wounded, making them vulnerable to attack.

Patients were processed and moved further back, generally on Ambulance Trains (ATs) or even barges (after September 1914 staffed with nurses), to Stationary, General or Base Hospitals in the rear, some tented, others set up in huts, casinos, hotels and even sports stadia; 500 beds was the minimum capacity and venues had to be capable of expanding indefinitely. Casualties with so-called 'Blighty' wounds were shipped back to the multitude of hospitals at home. Some were permanent military hospitals, others civilian ones with military wards and additional auxiliary hospitals were temporarily established in stately homes up and down the land.

Before October 1914 female nurses were not stationed in Casualty Clearing Stations. However, on 29 October 1914 the Adjutant General asked Matron McCarthy to provide 10 nurses for two CCS. Countless others soon followed. The tasks facing nurses were gargantuan, and their morale exemplary despite 'patients pouring in in dreadful conditions. The stretchers were placed in rows on the floor, with barely room to stand between each' (McCarthy). Often all that could be done was to 'kneel on the ground, feed the patients, dress their wounds and bathe their feet.' Here the most urgent operations were performed. Initially staffed by between seven and nine nurses, rising to 45 during a big 'Push', CCS could handle from 200 to 1,000 patients a week.

Matron McCarthy's diary reveals the vulnerability of these posts. For three successive days in April 1915 'the shelling was continuous and shells fell in and around No.3, Casualty Clearing at Poperinghe [*Belgium*]'. Aware that 'the mental and in some cases, the physical strain was very severe', McCarthy decreed that nurses should only undertake six-month tours of duty in CCS before being relieved. It soon became apparent that a patient's chances of survival on evacuation directly correlated to professional nurses' presence in CCS.

Kate Luard proudly reports how, 'One Sister on a Barge wrote to Sister D. that they always knew which came from here [*Kate's CCS*] as they were so clean, happy and well-clad.' It appears that their being 'well-clad' owes something to the citizens of Witham in Kate's home county of Essex, as she comments on gifts received including 'pretty, gay soft cushions' for the head injury cases. Throughout the war, nurses galvanised well-wishers at home to send over comforts. They not infrequently spent their leave giving 'lantern-shows' and talks to raise awareness of soldiers' needs.

'More ghastly than anything I have ever seen or smelt'

The majority of professional nurses of all nationalities who served overseas worked primarily in Base Hospitals and in CCS. However, by the end of 1914 a significant number were staffing the seven hospital ships, the barge flotillas and the twelve ambulance trains (ATs) which were ferrying casualties to the rear hospitals. According to Maud McCarthy, the first AT to carry a sister aboard left Le Mans 'on about 7th September 1914'. The approximately 42-hour journeys were not without hazards for sisters and patients alike, yet many longed to become AT nurses.

'My luck is in this time. Miss _ has just sent for me to tell me I am for permanent duty on No._ Ambulance Train which goes up to the Front Line… Did you ever know such luck?' wrote Kate Luard on 27 September 1914. She had already experienced AT service, having taken '480 sick and wounded down to St Nazaire' on a train 'miles long'. The pressing need for permanent staff and QAIMNS Kate's status as a veteran of the Boer War undoubtedly fired her enthusiasm for this novel nursing experience for women. She quickly became a well-established train sister, dealing at times with as many as '510 cases. You boarded a cattle-truck, armed with a tray of dressings and a pail; the men were lying on straw; had been in trains for several days; most had only been dressed once, and many were gangrenous… no-one grumbled or made any fuss… More ghastly than anything I have ever seen or smelt.' Louisa Bickmore expressed similar sentiments, 'No tongue can tell what these patients have gone through and none who have not seen them in their battledress can form any conception of it.'

Initially the trains' facilities for patients and staff were non-existent. Kate remembered 'one wash only on a station platform at a tap which a sergeant kindly pressed for me while I washed! One cleaning of teeth in the dark on the line between trucks.' Nurses made 'tea in cans' using the engine's water. The early ATs had no corridors and, despite official prohibitions, nurses 'clamber[ed] from coach to coach while in motion by way of the footboard' – wearing, of course, ankle-length skirts. In addition, they carried:

a load on their backs. The load was a bag, as aseptic as possible under the conditions, which contained dressings, medicaments etc. and in addition, during the night, when going from one coach to another, the Sisters had to carry hurricane lamps suspended from their arms. It is needless to say to what dangers they were exposed in the fulfilling of their duties. (Matron McCarthy)

Kate Luard was proud of her expertise 'at clawing along the footboards'. McCarthy accepts, even condones her staff contravening the interdiction on changing coaches. After all, 'it was not possible for them to do otherwise, knowing as they did that men on each coach might perhaps be dying for want of attention.' By the end of November 1914, the quiet courage and dignity of these sisters was brought to the attention of the Commander-in-Chief and, in due course, to Queen Alexandra who, 'in the first week of December, most graciously sent to all of them a gift of tea and sweets, which they truly appreciated.'.

With the passing of time, such acrobatics became a memory, as purpose-built trains had corridors and stretcher-racking, although Kate regretted that despite her train becoming 'very smart' it still lacked a bathroom, which 'I should like added!' Life on board was certainly hazardous as 'German airmen usually regarded a British hospital train, Red Cross and all, as a legitimate and even desirable target. Frequently the windows of a train were shattered. When one was targeted at Amiens on the night of 10 November 1916, three of the sisters were awarded the Military Medal for their gallantry.

ATs were not without difficulties and even some scandal, as Matron McCarthy's diaries reveal. On 4 July 1916 a letter informed her that a Staff Nurse on one AT 'was getting herself talked about with one of the MOs, a married man.' The outraged writer requested that the Matron-in-Chief deal with the situation – which she appears to have done. Then, in January 1917 McCarthy notes the receipt of a 'confidential letter [*from another sister*] who was anxious to see me at an early date'. Apparently 'certain things [*were*] occurring on 27 Ambulance Train which she knew I would not approve of and which did not bear writing about.' Sadly for the curious, no information is provided about what these 'certain things' were.

As McCarthy well knew, every story has at least two sides and she investigated further, discovering that one of the AT nurses was engaged to a Lance Corporal orderly working on the train – in itself potentially shocking as nurses held officer rank and fraternisation between Officers and Other Ranks was frowned upon. Despite her best attempts, McCarthy was unable to get to the bottom of the 'other irregularities'. One is left wondering if the romance petered out following the sister's removal from the train, as there is no obvious record of a wedding having taken place. Understandably, much of the historiography relating to nursing personnel praises these women's professionalism and dedication. Snippets such as these reveal their human side and, for a few seconds, we get closer to the flesh and blood women behind the starched aprons, impeccable collars and cuffs of their uniform.

'Crawling on all fours': Hospital Barges

Although ATs transported many of the wounded from CCS to Base Hospitals or ports, from September 1914 hospital barges travelled across Northern France's extended waterways carrying the most severely wounded patients, whose lives depended on being jolted as little as possible. It is almost miraculous that many survived the embarkation process, which involved being lowered by ropes and pulleys through the open top of the barge to the wards below. Despite these apparent shortcomings, the nursing and popular press extolled the virtues of barges as an ideal mode of transport for the wounded, if not necessarily for staff. Depending on the weather, journeys could be delayed by as much as 42 hours, putting additional pressure on the two sisters, nine RAMC orderlies and the one Medical Officer shared between barges, which were towed in pairs. Nurses preferred not to be on the same barge as MOs; relationships between the two were not always harmonious.

Barges were attractive to some nurses as well as patients. One anonymous contributor to the November 1915 *British Journal of Nursing (BJN)* 'Letters from the Front' is 'getting used to life on a barge, quite a nice change really.' The tone is eminently cheerful despite frustration that wartime censorship prevents her from revealing much factual information about her whereabouts, her barge, or even the life and death battles in which she was engaged.

Yet, hints of what conditions were like occur in nurses' personal writings and letters. Millicent Peterkin excused the brevity of one letter, as she had worked a 15-hour shift. By April 1918 when this letter was written, physical tiredness was not the only enemy. Although barges were painted grey, with the Red Cross prominently displayed on each side, as the enemy increasingly ignored the international symbol of neutrality barges, like all other medical facilities, became a target for fighter pilots. With lights turned off at night, nurses made their rounds in the pitch dark, a small torch their only means of light.

Nurses were constantly begging for comforts for the men as well as for surprising necessities; one even pleaded for the abrasive cleaner VIM, whilst Millicent Peterkin longed for a simple pudding recipe book as, on her barge at least, the cook was either unimaginative or unskilled: when it came to 'puddings' his repertoire was 'sago' or 'stewed fruit'. Her family obliged.

Difficulties of life on board extended beyond needing VIM, recipes or even onerous nursing duties. Although barges were believed to be 'warmer and drier' than tented hospitals (*BJN*, 21 November 1914), some were barely fit for purpose. One sister reported, 'Our barge became more and more leaky, until we simply paddled from bed to bed, and then had to lie up for repairs.' In winter, slippery decks resulted in nurses taking an unexpected dip in the freezing canal and many resorted to crawling along the decks on all fours. In addition to their nursing duties, when patients were offloaded, cleaning (with or without VIM) was undertaken – a demanding and essential task, as often filthy and lice-ridden soldiers could be evacuated straight to the barge from the battlefield (as opposed to via a dressing station). When they had been gassed, poor barge ventilation meant that other patients and staff could suffer a mild gas attack, leading to breathing problems; being bitten by lice could cause nurses to develop typhus and trench fever. Nevertheless, the *BJN* cheerfully asserted in spring 1916, 'Our Sisters enjoyed working on [*barges*] last year [*even if*] the noise of gunfire is at times tremendous, and as there are guns quite close, the shells go whistling overhead.'

Soon the noise of gunfire increased. When the Battle of the Somme opened, one barge sister wrote how the canal is 'about 10 miles from the firing line and the guns are going all the time – just one continuous thundering noise,' ominously reminding both patients and nurses of the action continuing close by. Barges were in constant service. In the first 20 days of the Battle of the Somme Mildred Rees' barge, 4 Ambulance Flotilla Barge 192, carried '300 patients in this one barge alone – all of them serious cases.' Her matter-of-fact tone barely conceals her compassion for the 'poor things out on the ground 12 to 40 hours before even being brought to the first Field Dressing Station. They are splattered with blood and mud.' She finds it miraculous that many of them survive – doubtless thanks in part to her and her colleagues' ministrations. In November 1917, Mildred was Mentioned in Despatches 'for gallant and distinguished services in the field'.

After the War, Matron McCarthy concluded that Hospital Barges were 'perhaps our most difficult units', largely, she felt, because 'the Medical Officers are temporarily employed, and in many instances do not give the nurses the support they require.' Dangerously wounded patients almost certainly knew little and cared less about VIM, puddings, or even inharmonious professional relationships. Many who experienced an evacuation by barge quite simply felt that after the horrors of the Front, they had 'died and literally wakened in heaven'.

'My heart is aching terribly': Nursing on Hospital Ships

If relatively few nurses served on ambulance barges, a far more significant number worked on hospital ships (HMHS). It is easy nowadays to forget that every wounded man who was evacuated to England, irrespective of theatre of war, was transported by ship. Those wounded on the Western Front had a relatively short crossing home, fortunately, as according to one nurse, 'the patients made very bad sailors'. Others underwent long, arduous and at times perilous voyages.

Many HMHS nurses were often, in the more distant theatres of war, close to the guns. Serving on HMHS *Delta*, 36-year-old QAIMNS(R) Anna Cameron's letters were written between May and December 1915 within sight, sound and range of the Gallipoli guns. Her 8 May 1915 letter makes clear that she is uncomfortably aware of the irony of the ship's personnel watching, 'through our field glasses', the fighting taking place on the land whilst awaiting the nightly harvest of wounded. Nevertheless, there is an element of excitement: 'Shells from the Turks were actually dropping round our ship. We were actually in the firing line. We saw only one ship hit. Her aft torn away. We weren't a bit nervous. It all seemed so matter of fact somehow, but the awful noise of the guns was trying.'

By 10 pm everything has changed:

We had taken in 400 horribly wounded men straight from the field. Some were shot further in the boats which took them to us. The gangway ran with blood. Some of the poor fellows hadn't had one dressing on. One needed all one's common sense and courage. We 3 sisters had 200 of the wounded and only 6 orderlies at that time, so many were needed for stretcher bearers... They came pouring in. The orderlies were good but untrained for emergencies. [*The wounded*] were so dead beat that we wrapped them in their filthy clothes poor fellows and let them rest. Faces shot away, arms, legs, lungs, shots everywhere. One said 'Thank God we have the sisters.'

Having sailed to England with her cargo of horrifically wounded men, by 26 August *Delta* had returned to the Dardanelles where, 'We saw the long line of stretcher-bearers dashing along to the shore and the boats put off thick and fast. Our turn soon came.' With 1,240 men on board a ship staffed for 536, *Delta* started once more for home. In her diary Anna confesses, 'the hopelessness of struggling against heavy odds and unable to relieve suffering adequately tries me so dreadfully. The other Sisters keep calmer inside – I can't. If only I could.' Three months later, her need to abandon the dying to attempt to minister to the still-just-living is almost torturing her, 'the memory of some things which have often had to be left undone in the stress of War nursing stabs and stabs in the quiet days.'

Several nurses comment on the experience of being bystanders, awaiting a military action knowing that its aftermath will stretch them to the limits of their professional and emotional resources. In early 1916, Kathleen Mann felt guilty that she and her colleagues were what she called 'Kitchener's Tourists just lounging in deck chairs on a very comfortable steamer... But what we are in for we do not know.' In home waters, on board Grand Fleet HMHS *Plassy* before and during the June 1916 Battle of Jutland, Mary Clarke noted, 'It has been a weird sort of day, waiting about for news the whole time & afraid to settle for anything for fear of any sudden news.' Not for long – 'Soon they begin to arrive, drifters by the dozen, six and seven deep on the starboard sides waiting to unload their sad burdens... and they said the worst were still to come. Then the bad cases began to come in, poor things, it was pitiful to see some of them.' With 46 'acute cases' in her ward, Mary worked a 17-hour day, welcoming the '5 minutes blow on deck after lunch [*as*] the smell of burns is awful one gets almost nauseated sometimes.' First-hand knowledge of the extent of the casualties leaves her unconvinced by the newspapers' claim that it 'was a Victory for us'.

Hospital ship staff could be posted from one vessel to another seemingly at random. Mary Clarke's much-anticipated leave was suddenly and unexpectedly cancelled. Posted to Malta, she had two hours in which to bid colleagues farewell and pack for a three-year commission in what she dubbed 'the tropics' after a similar amount of time in the North Sea. She had merely 'five minutes' with her family as her train passed through Exeter. Her reaction to her posting at Royal Navy Hospital Bighi is bleak:

My heart is aching terribly, and I feel like going away by myself and having a good cry but the only thing is to fight against the feeling of homesickness and loneliness, I think the more one gives way to it, the worse it becomes... The men aren't a bit friendly like our men were, they sit on one part of the deck and the sisters on the other. I felt very lonely without anyone to talk to and tho' it is Sunday, I hadn't the heart to put my silk stockings on.

In October 1918 Matron Helena Hartigan RRC led a party of 14 sisters to Archangel, on the White Sea, close to the Arctic Circle, on board HMHS *Kalyan*. Few Army nurses served there, although volunteer units did. Before her departure, attempts had been made to transform *Kalyan* from a previously near-tropic to Arctic carrier. 'Inner wooden walls were set up about three inches from the ship's side, and the intervening space was packed with sawdust, converting *Kalyan* into a species of floating thermos flask. Glass skylights were covered with asbestos matting.' Those serving aboard this carcinogenic thermos flask were issued with 'a special kit of truly formidable warmth, consisting of leather jerkins, windproof linen coats lined with sheepskin, cloth caps with fur peaks and earpieces and serge gloves... Not ornamental but proof against frostbite.'

Winter closed in and the realities of Arctic Circle nursing soon became apparent, 'Sick and wounded were brought to the *Kalyan* by barge... The small cots on board were not ideal for surgical cases, there was not sufficient room for the splints, etc.' Other patients arrived by sleigh in what they themselves called 'coffins'.

As the sick and wounded had received only minimal care before being transported hundreds of kilometres to reach *Kalyan*, their condition on arrival defies imagination. *Kalyan*'s staff and patients were marooned in their own world, although one crucial event reached them, 'the wireless gave us... the news of the Armistice'. However, with Archangel 'icebound until May or June', so too were the ships, and the Armistice meant relatively little to those so far away. Eventually, spring came with an unpleasant result: it 'liberated the odours which the snow had mercifully corked!' Assisted by a passage cut by ice-breakers, patients, crew and nurses were homeward bound. Their odiferous vessel arrived in Leith in June 1919, in time for the Peace Day celebrations – and for Hartigan, a Bar to her previously awarded Royal Red Cross. For her exceptional devotion to duty she was twice Mentioned in Despatches and decorated with the Belgian *Médaille de la Reine Elizabeth*. We will never know if her death in 1932 at the age of 54 was related to the asbestos present in the matting covering *Kalyan*'s skylights.

'How we had longed to go':
Nurses From Across the British Empire

Whilst Maud McCarthy and the first QAIMNS were arriving in France in August 1914, patriotic nurses from all over the Empire were also eager to serve their 'Mother Country'. Amongst the very first were the Australian Army Nursing Service (AANS); proportionately, Australian nurses outnumbered those from all other Dominions. On Friday 14 August 1914, the *Sydney Morning Herald* reported that in the ten days since War had been declared, 150 nurses from the Australian Trained Nurses' Association had volunteered their services and 'more names are constantly being given in. [*They*] had expressed their readiness to leave for any part of the world at the shortest notice.'

Three months later, the ship carrying the First Australian Clearing Hospital, including 11 Army sisters, set sail, the vanguard of the 2,562 Australian nurses who served overseas between 1914 and 1919. The oldest was 'Mother Anzac' – 57-year-old Staff Nurse and masseuse Esther Barnett, who had reduced her age by 10 years when enlisting for overseas service in August 1915.

Irrespective of nationality, many professional nurses had never left their native shores and, notwithstanding their sense of excitement and duty, those detailed for overseas service had to confront the likelihood of not seeing loved ones for many months, maybe even years. Ardent admiration for their patients, heartfelt belief in 'the Cause', as well as homesickness and a sense of isolation became these women's familiar companions. Their diaries, letters, and memorabilia preserved in the Australian War Memorial in Canberra bear witness to an extraordinary journey undertaken with enthusiasm, courage and dedication. These sources also give personal insight into the agony and the camaraderie of nursing service so far from home.

Prolific correspondent 31-year-old AANS Evelyn Davies looked beyond the sense of euphoria that the prospect of active service overseas engendered in so many participants. In her first letter (May 1915), she confided that she, 'would just hate leaving everyone when the time comes … still it seems a duty to go.' Her widowed mother proudly preserved her daughter's correspondence from Lemnos, Egypt, India, England and France; having typed out nearly every letter, she circulated these amongst family and friends. They provide a fascinating insight into the wartime life of this woman who struggled to overcome loneliness, self-doubt and perhaps a slightly abrasive personality.

Once at sea, Evelyn, like many nurses of all nationalities, discovered that the voyage's first obstacle was sea-sickness, 'Oh I have been so sick. The cabins are fearfully stuffy.' Seasickness is a common theme on the seemingly endless journey. Some women tried to make light of their misery, 'supper on board and then over board', writes one; sea-sickness was the 'main preoccupation for the first week.'

On embarkation, many Australian nurses were unaware of their ultimate destination: a common experience. British nurses embarking in August 1914 noted being, 'bound they knew not wither ... Sealed Orders'. According to Kate Luard 'nobody knows anything for certain'. Even in June 1917, after a week at sea, Australian Christina Strom writes, 'They say we are *not* going to Salonika but no-one appears to know where we are going.' Ironically, Christina did in fact serve in Salonika.

When their transports stopped to refuel, nurses had a welcome opportunity for sightseeing; including the Egyptian pyramids, Sphinx and Museum. Women 'with their veiled faces' fascinated one nurse. As they neared European waters, the risk of being torpedoed increased. Evelyn Davies' mother may not have been reassured to learn, 'We have to wear our life belts all day now and have them and our coats and boots all ready to slip on beside us at night. The ship is rocking and creaking horribly.' When nurses travelled with troops on transport ships they were vulnerable to attack as, unlike Hospital Ships which were, in theory at least, protected by the neutral status of the Red Cross blazoned upon them, troop ships were legitimate targets.

As a grim reminder of the realities of war, soon after her arrival in France, another Australian and equally prolific correspondent, 28-year-old Elsie Tranter, 'had to attend the funeral of Sister [*sic*] Dawson. Her body was washed up near our camp. She was on a hospital ship that was torpedoed in the Channel.' Dawson, a much-loved missionary nurse, was Matron of HMHS *Salta*.

Elsie Tranter had left Australia in December 1916; her lively record details her service, predominantly on the Western Front, whilst her account of her outward voyage aboard *Orsova* draws attention to the endless restrictions placed on nurses irrespective of nationality. Negative feelings towards authority quickly emerge in her writing, perhaps because the Australian Matron-in-Chief's attention to uniform transgressions almost prevented nurses from hanging over the deck, spotting those who had come to bid them a final emotional farewell as their transport prepared for departure.

> Miss Richardson inspected us and criticised the hat-pins we wore, the angle of our hats and various other trifles. When all the wrong-coloured hat pins were removed and all the ration hats (as we call our ugly little grey felts) were placed at an angle of 45 degrees we were ever so eager to rush on deck... the last bell sounded – up came the gangway. Goodbyes were called out and we pulled away from the pier. When the last streamer broke such a funny lump came in my throat and I began to think that I was not a very brave soldier after all. But tears had to be brushed aside so that we could watch and wave till it was impossible any longer to distinguish anyone on the pier.

Perhaps this matron did not know that once in the field many nurses would, according to Kate Luard, be wearing 'skirts and aprons very short'. If skirts and aprons were no longer regulation length, undergarments were often lacking, particularly if, like Kate's, nurses' possessions did not keep up with their multiple moves: 'I have to wash my vest overnight when I want a clean one... We have slung a clothes-line across our room. The view is absolutely glorious.' One Australian nurse even had her clothes-line stolen – her colleagues teased her endlessly about this.

Elsie Tranter's Matron Richardson was determined to enforce her iron will, treating her Australian nurses as wayward schoolgirls. She forbade them from speaking to the 950 soldiers and 18 officers on board *Orsova*. Elsie records how, having been seen ashore in the company of males:

> All the naughty little sisters in grey have been on parade and have been absolutely forbidden to talk to the NCOs or Naval Officers while if we dare go out with them while in port our shore leave [*in Egypt*] will be stopped and we will be 'shot at dawn' or something or other horrible like that – I think – My mind was wandering at the time. I never can remember these toe-to-carpet lectures.

Human emotions, always heightened in time of war, find ways to bypass regulations; nurses and soldiers proved resourceful. Elsie recalled how, 'The immediate result of this lecture was the establishment of a travelling post office between the promenade and the troop decks.' Tensions between the younger nurses and military personnel on the one hand and the Matron and Senior Medical Officer on the other spilled over; officers devised a witty list of 'Ten Commandments' – giving wonderful insight into the interdictions placed on the women. Commandment Six warns, 'Thou shalt not adulterate thy miseries with joy as it is not good for thy health.' Fiercely independent, once in France Elsie successfully hitched lifts on lorries, caught midnight trains and even dried her hair in an oven.

It was not only on board Australian ships that relationships between nurses and senior personnel were tense. On HMHS *Plassy* Mary Clarke and colleagues tried to snatch some rare relaxation. However, 'the Fleet Surgeon has stopped us playing ping-pong in the music saloon. He was very apologetic about it but said that some of the officers had been complaining of the noise. It is rotten, every sort of recreation we have seems to be stopped. I suppose he will soon stop us walking on the deck.'

Australian nurses' anger about such infantilisation is understandable. These highly-trained professional women in their twenties, thirties and even forties, had volunteered to travel thousands of miles to nurse servicemen, placing themselves at considerable personal risk. The rules and regulations imposed upon them seem inappropriate, particularly as overseas service often left them out of pocket: 'Look at how much it cost in Australia, then since coming to London we have had to buy Primus Stove, Mackintoshes, Gum Boots, Mess Kit and several odds and ends', writes Evelyn Davies – items naturally supplied free-of-charge to males.

For several weeks at sea, irrespective of nationality, nurses received no mail. Once ashore, letters become a recurrent theme – joy when they arrive, despair when 'Home Folk' appear to have failed to write or anguish when the longed for 'budget of letters' is known to have been on a torpedoed transport. Letters were nurses' only link with distant families and friends. Even a century later, readers share Evelyn Davies' joy when, three months after embarkation, she finally reads precious words from home, 'Your first letter has just come and my word I was thankful to have it. I used to nearly howl when I saw others reading theirs and me not getting any.'

British nurses in France were equally desperate for letters. In August 1914 Kate Luard is delighted to have, 'had my first letter from England'; she provides details of how mail is handled between home and the front. The British Army being renowned for improvisation, 'two Tommies sit by a packing-case with a slit in the lid for the letter-box.' On board HMHS *Kalyan*, Matron Hartigan noted how 'the arrival of a mail was a great event – we were sometimes six weeks without one – the mail came by dog sleigh across the White Sea.' From her barge Millicent Peterkin is continually writing letters, curtailing some in order to post them when she stops off to buy provisions.

Not all home correspondents were conscientious, however. VAD Aileen Woodroffe frequently chides her family for not replying to her countless letters, 'Letters flow from here in great quantities but I don't seem to notice any incoming tide. This must be rectified.' It is impossible to know what proportion of mail going in both directions was lost. Each missing letter was a moment of personal sadness – the sorrows of war include the minutiae of small losses as well as devastating loss of life.

Once at their destination, the tone of nurses' letters changes. Daily irritations fade when placed alongside the job that they travelled so far to do. One of Elsie Tranter's letters makes it clear that Anzacs were closest to Australians' hearts, 'Needless to say, we are all tremendously proud of our own Aussie boys. They always seem to be the nicest, the bravest, and the most humorous of all. But then perhaps it is just because they belong in a special way to us that we like them best.' Relationships with English nurses could be problematic for Australians, who often got on better with other 'Colonial' nurses. Evelyn Davies explains, 'There are two Canadian girls here, Mum, who are great sports, funny how overseas people have so much in common. They are far more friendly than the English folk.'

The importance of comradeship is well-documented amongst serving men; it is less well-researched among serving women. Australian nurses such as Christina Strom talk frequently about 'the joys of fellowship; the teamwork that was there.' Women shared in colleagues' joys and griefs and told families at home about outings with friends – simple pleasures the more precious for being rare. Sadly, Evelyn Davies appears to have had few friends. She writes, 'One needs a special pal here in a place like this.' Although she did briefly find a companion, Elsie Deakin, she was soon posted elsewhere, 'I miss her dreadfully'. Evelyn admits to feeling 'too old' ('my poor hair, Mum, is almost grey') to continually make new friends. Mary Clarke faced similar problems, confiding, 'I wish I had a few congenial spirits to talk to. I so dread starting life again amongst new people, I wish I didn't take such a long time to make friends.' Such intimate revelations are rare and poignant; nurses more usually write of the 'poor, poor boys, all smashed up' (Evelyn Davies).

Serving personnel came to replace women's distant families. In 1917, after three years with the AANS, Elsie Eglinton married Scotsman 3rd Engineer George Mackay, whom she met on service. Two Australian nurses were her bridesmaids; all wore nurses' uniform for the ceremony (reminiscent of the servicemen who got married in khaki); wounded soldiers formed a Guard of Honour comprised of walking sticks, and, rather unusually, the Matron gave the bride away. Elsie, who resigned on marriage, was subsequently very isolated; she remained in England whilst her husband served overseas. The forced retirement of this highly professional woman, who had served both in France and on hospital ships off Gallipoli, must have been a significant loss to the AANS. Resignation was not expected of QAIMNS personnel, although one staff nurse was reprimanded for only informing her superiors of her marriage to Australian Private Bryant after the event (he appears to have survived the war). Many of McCarthy's diary entries reference nurses' marriages and their requests (granted) to be 'retained in the service after marriage'. Married nurses were not allowed to serve in the same theatre as their husbands.

Nursing personnel were constantly on the move. According to Elsie Tranter, 'that is the beginning and the end of an army sister's life: Packing, unpacking, awaiting orders.' Sometimes the orders were to report to a base hospital relatively far behind the lines, on other occasions tented ones close to the guns. Serving at CCS 62 in Belgium in July 1917 during the Battle of Passchendaele, one nurse reported, 'A heavy barrage started about 2 am here, we are about 8 miles back.' Being within striking distance of the enemy's fire-power was a part of overseas service: 'Bombed by Boches at lunch time and at 8 p.m. heavy firing started.'

In a heavily censored 23 August 1917 letter Elsie Grant explains to a friend, 'We have been up in Belgium at the 3rd Australian Casualty Clearing Station. We have been shelled out three times but this last time was too dreadful. The English hospital next to us [*had*] one sister killed and one wounded... Our hospital is a total wreck now.' In March 1918, Elsie was again within sound of the guns, 'We can hear the guns quite plainly here [*Doullens*].' On another occasion, 'Such a noisy night.

Barrage commenced at 1.15 a.m. Shells were whistling and screaming. … there was a horrific explosion and everything was lighted up. The dump at Bapaume was struck... the wounded [*began*] pouring in'; another day on the wards was underway. This constant exposure to shells and guns, as well as the death of her beloved brother, took its toll on Elsie Grant. According to a friend, by 1918 she was suffering from a nervous condition (painful swellings in her face) and was considered physically unfit to carry on. She was detailed for transport duty with the AIF. Tragically, despite marrying after the war and having four young children, she took her own life, aged 37, in September 1927.

Although the press eulogised nurses' steadfastness, Elsie Tranter is more cynical, or perhaps realistic, about women's need for companionship to bolster fragile nerves. 'Being with others made us feel safer, you can't face these things alone but with a pal beside you, you feel strong to face danger. If alone in your hut you live every moment in dread until the bombing is over.'

Proximity to the guns was part of life in all CCSs. As early as 1 April 1916 *BJN* reports how nurses from CCSs who were convalescing at Hardelot, 'have generally the sound of the guns still in their ears, and are worn out for the time being.' The convalescent home's gentle regime eased their condition, at least for the majority, although, 'for the first few days [*they are*] too tired in body and mind to care to do anything, and so many are unable to sleep from the strain they have been going through.'

Aware of the strain nurses faced, McCarthy restricted the length of time those under her command could serve in the most traumatic facilities (jaw and face wound wards, CCSs, barges and ATs) to six months before a spell of duty in the rear – occasionally to the nurses' annoyance. Her diary details daily the numbers of 'Sick Sisters', a part of nurses' service generally overlooked by historians. McCarthy strove to improve the well-being of those who reported sick and several aristocratic ladies provided convalescent facilities. The menus at Hardelot (and the cook's qualifications) suggest the nurses may well have eaten their way back to good health.

If for some women mental traumas proved insurmountable, for those fit at least in body, ordinary life inevitably continued even against the backdrop of war. Elsie Eglinton, anchored off Lemnos in the Aegean Sea and dealing with Gallipoli casualties, reported, 'We have one sister on board with a beautiful head of hair, she washes it and comes on deck to brush and dry it. It's bold of her but really it's such lovely hair I don't wonder she likes showing it off.' (August 1915) Others developed a 'craze to see who can wear the most swanky boudoir cap and dressing gowns'. It is reassuring to find these nurses enjoying brief moments of relaxation; soon they took on board, '770 sick and wounded... we've had a hard night and lost several patients.'

Inevitably service life had some precious humorous moments. In April 1917, desperate to get her long, (apparently filthy) hair washed, and with a few hours off-duty, Elsie Tranter walked into what remained of Camiers in Northern France. To her dismay, 'All the hairdressers seemed to have left town. However I saw a little shop with all manner of toilet requisites in the window and Mme [*sic*] who looked as if she couldn't say no standing at the door.' Putting the French lessons she had taken on board ship to good, if unexpected, use, 'I made my request in the best French I could command.' Soon there is another problem: drying the hair:

Madame became greatly distressed... then she was struck with a brilliant idea. Opening the oven door and placing a cushion on the floor in front of it, she bade me sit down and put my head in the oven. A novel way no doubt but it answered the purpose. Then she got a large book, it seemed to me like a register for the important events in the family history, and in the centre of a clear page she wrote, *'Aujourd'hui j'ai lavé la tête de l'australienne'* (To-day I washed an Australian woman's head). Underneath, she had to write my name and home address.

Elsie was soon back at work amidst horror and frightfulness. In May 1917 she:

had to assist at 10 amputations one after another. It is frightfully nerve-racking work and I seem to hear that wretched saw at work whenever I try to sleep. We see most ghastly wounds and are all day long inhaling the odour of gas gangrene. How these boys suffer. This war is absolute hell we see and hear every day the results of its frightfulness.

Gas was perhaps the greatest 'frightfulness', physically affecting nurses too, 'those of us who are working amongst the gassed men have lost our voices and can just about manage to whisper. This is unfortunate for the men seem to like us to talk to them.' Ever since the first deployment of gas in April 1915, the medical profession had struggled to deal with its effects. In November 1915, *BJN* includes a piece by an unidentified sister, 'We have had the biggest rush we have had yet. On the 23rd October, 277 men, suffering from poisoned gas were admitted after a few hours' notice. It was quite the worst experience we have had during the months we have been here. Nothing can describe the scene, one must be there to realise the horror of seeing men in the pitiable condition they were in.'

Two years later, Evelyn Davies writes, 'We are getting gas cases now, Mum, such cruel stuff it is, burns their skin, causing blisters, causes inflammation of the eyes and all mucous membranes, chokes up the lungs... Fritz is fiendish alright. Not warfare at all it is slaughter absolutely.' Nurses were issued with gas masks; at times these served unexpected purposes. In March 1918, whilst awaiting orders to evacuate her mobile hospital, Elsie Tranter explains how some exhausted nurses simply lay 'on the floor with a gas mask for a pillow, trying to snatch a few minutes sleep'; others waited outside with their tin hats 'at unbecoming angles'. They gazed up the road to see which would arrive first, their transport or the Germans now engaged on their desperate 1918 Spring Offensive 'Operations Michael and Georgette'.

By 27 August nurses came on duty 'in short dresses to knees – high military boots – gas masks and tin hats handy.' What would Matron Richardson have made of her Australian nurses wearing tin hats at an angle other than 45 degrees, with skirts only reaching to their knees? Some nurses slept with tin hats protecting their stomachs. Experienced in abdominal wounds, this seemed to have been the area that they wanted above all to protect.

When the guns fell silent, few nurses, irrespective of their nationality or theatre of war, embraced the joy of the Armistice. On 11 November 1918, Elsie Tranter recorded, 'Our day in the hut was altogether rather a heart-breaking one and when duty for the day was finished we did not feel able to enter fully into the joy of Armistice.' Australian nurses were soon on their way home. Evelyn Davies was the only woman from her town to have volunteered for overseas service, and she finally returned in July 1919 to a hero's welcome.

For many, the homeward journey was hard. Some were unimpressed by what was now expected of them. Returning on *Orsova*, one of the vessels carrying Australian soldiers' English wives and their families, Jessie Tomlins complained, 'we have to act as nursery maids on those family Boats, mind the babies while the mothers dine etc – that's hardly the job we came for.' Others returned on 'regular' troop transport ships, packed this time with men who were not the 'Conquering Heroes' of their dreams but the flotsam and jetsam of battle. What understated horrors must be contained in one nurse's undated letter, 'We came home on a hospital ship almost full of legless and limbless men.'

As they neared their own shores, these nurses could not have known that their hitherto grateful nation would soon overlook them. Although Australia is alone amongst the combatant nations to inscribe the names of all serving personnel, including nurses, on war memorials as opposed to just those of the dead, post-war Australia did little else to honour women's contributions to her war effort. Yet Australian nurses' war record is a proud one: 25 made the 'Ultimate Sacrifice', dying 'On Active Service'; some returned physically to the land of their birth but, like Elsie Grant, were forever scarred by the traumas they had lived through and witnessed.

Three hundred and eighty-eight, or 15 per cent of those who served, were summoned to Buckingham Palace – which involved them in the slightly resented expense of purchasing new uniforms – where they received decorations including the Military Medal for courage under fire, for being Mentioned in Despatches for 'gallant devotion to duty in the Field' and 154 received the Royal Red Cross. But, eclipsed by the ANZAC 'Diggers', the devotion, courage and personal sacrifices of these nurses on the Western and all other Fronts faded from memory, and their story is but a footnote to rather than an integral part of the ANZAC legend.

Sublime Heights of Valour and Daring: Female Medal Recipients

Before 1914, decorations for women were exceedingly rare. Despite Queen Victoria decreeing on 23 April 1883 that 'ladies [*brought*] to 'Our notice by Our Secretary of State' would be eligible to be honoured with a Royal Red Cross, by 1914 only 246 women had been decorated.

From 1915 to the end of the war, awards of the RRC increased dramatically. Sue Light believes that this:

was now expected by many wealthy, philanthropic women as an accolade for services rendered in spending their own money and opening their own homes to care for the sick and wounded of war. The names in the Royal Red Cross Registers held at The National Archives show that the Commandants of many voluntary hospitals, with little or no nursing training or experience, received recognition, while their staff went empty-handed. They were the figureheads and as such accepted the bouquets.

Perhaps because so many professional staff 'went empty-handed', the *BJN* reports nurses' awards with palpable pride, often with accompanying pictures of recipients attending investitures at Buckingham Palace, sometimes taking tea afterwards with Queen Alexandra. Judging by the citations, they had undoubtedly earned their awards through their 'exertions'. Nurses who served with the French, Belgian and Serbian forces received decorations from their hosts and a number were decorated by more than one nation.

Whilst nurses were decorated for their professional services and patrician women for philanthropy, some of the most senior (such as Maud McCarthy, who was elevated to Dame) received various orders of the British Empire. There was, however, one decoration reserved for those who demonstrated unusual courage: the Military Medal (MM). Women's eligibility for this had only been confirmed by Royal Warrant in June 1916. The 1 September 1916 *London Gazette* carried the names of the first six women to be gazetted 'for bravery in the field'. Perhaps to feminise the medal, the King also approved 'of the following emblem being worn on the riband of the Military Medal: a small silver rose, which does not form part of the decoration.'

Justly proud of her nurses (in total, of the 135 female MM recipients of all nationalities, 55 were either members of the QAIMNS or TFNS), Matron McCarthy's diaries mention when nurses were decorated; occasionally this happened in the field. At one investiture held on 19 August 1917, representative sisters from nearby CCSs, as well as those who were being decorated, were invited to, in Kate Luard's words, 'gad over' to what was expected to be an impressive ceremony.

In late January 1917 sisters Evans, Mahoney and Thompson were gazetted. Their Commanding Officer had reported that when the facility on which they were serving was subjected to enemy attack, each of these modern Florence Nightingales 'carrying a hand lamp, went about her work coolly and collectedly and cheerfully and by her magnificent conduct she not only allayed alarm among the helpless patients and those suffering from shell shock but caused both patients and personnel to play up to the standards which she set.' Such courage is unsurprising if impressive. What is surprising is that these were the very sisters serving on 27 AT, over whose conduct McCarthy spent many anxious hours. Whatever disputes were taking place on this train, exceptional bravery was rightly recognised and rewarded.

Nurses showing exemplary bravery 'in the field' seems to have astounded the male military hierarchy. It was as though they had not anticipated women prioritising the safety of their wounded patients over their own and demonstrating outward sang-froid. Yet almost every citation, however brief, hints at nurses' exceptional courage when hospital facilities were bombed, shelled, and generally fired upon. TFNS Dorothy Laughton's gallantry citation gives a glimpse of a night that must have been a vision of hell:

On the night of the 19th August 1917, the Asylum at St. Venant, which is in part used as a Casualty Clearing Station [57], was hit by five bombs dropped by an enemy aeroplane; 5 female lunatics were killed or died of wounds, and fifteen injured. Miss Laughton, in spite of being knocked over by the blast of a bursting bomb, behaved with the utmost coolness, and it was mainly by her example and presence of mind, amidst a maniacal chaos, that order was restored, and that the wounded were speedily attended when extracted from the ruins.

Five months earlier the Acting Matron-in-Chief had visited this rather strange CCS and its seven nurses and felt that despite it being 'established in one wing of an asylum building, the wards seem to be suitable for the purpose for which they are required.' Perhaps this would have been so, had it not been targeted by the enemy.

Nurses from across the British Empire were eligible for the Military Medal. For their actions on the night of 22 July 1917, when 2 Australian CCS was subject to a German raid, Alice Ross-King, Clare Deacon, Dorothy Cawood and Mary Derrer became the first of the seven Australian recipients. Alice wrote, 'I could hear nothing for the roar of planes and Archies [*artillery*]. I seemed to be the only living thing about ... I kept calling for [*Orderly*] Wilson to help me and thought he was

53

funking, but the poor boy had been blown to bits.' Information in the AWM reveals that she was attending a patient 'when the first bomb hit. Despite calls to get down, Alice kept going, and the bomb landed in front of her. She was thrown to the ground but got up and tried to continue. With all the lights out, she failed to see the bomb crater in front of her and fell headfirst into it.' She felt, 'I shall never forget the awful climb on hands and feet out of that hole about five feet deep, greasy clay and blood (although I did not then know that it was blood).' She remembered little of the rest of the night, simply that she and her colleagues just 'kept going', risking their lives to rescue patients trapped in the burning buildings.

On Christmas Day 1917, Alice was Mentioned in Despatches and on 31 May 1918 she received the Associate Royal Red Cross – a proud war record for any individual, irrespective of gender. Eight members of the Canadian Nursing Service were also awarded MMs, two for their exceptional courage and composure when the Base Hospitals at Étaples were bombed on 19/20 May 1918 with considerable loss of life. The Canadian women were singled out for their 'courage, coolness' and disregard for 'personal safety'.

The award was not without snobbish controversy, as all nursing personnel were considered officers; Canadian Wilhemina Waugh stresses how 'we were given the rank of lieutenant and wore the two stars on the shoulders of all uniforms.' But the MM was reserved for 'Other Ranks', with the Military Cross being awarded to Officers (of the rank of Captain or below). The *British Nursing Times* editor was the first to voice concern. Her open letter to the Secretary at the War Office on 26 January 1917 makes the point that although military nurses should, by virtue of their officer status, be awarded the Military Cross, they are in fact being awarded the Military Medal, a non-officer decoration. She hopes that what she considers an 'anomaly' will be rapidly addressed.

She received a convoluted reply from B.B. Cubitt at the War Office. Cubitt's explanation was that the Military Medal was being awarded to women who 'have shewn bravery and devotion under fire'. The sub-text appears to be that they, or the editor who had raised the point, should be grateful. Matron McCarthy certainly appears so: 'it [*is*] a great honour to be given a medal which is awarded solely for bravery in the field.'

From the war's earliest days, the achievements and accomplishments of the professional nurses were, and have continued to be, largely overshadowed by those of the volunteer nursing organisations such as the VADs, whose generally superior social status led to considerable press interest in their activities. The post-war publication of memoirs, culminating in Vera Brittain's well-known and televised *Testament of Youth*, and, indeed, the recent BBC programme *The Crimson Field*, has kept their memory and service alive. Yet, testimony by and about professional nurses, supplemented by Maud McCarthy's meticulous diaries, illuminates professional nurses' service.

Whether working on state-of-the-art hospital ships and trains, crawling on all fours along hospital barge decks, or calmly nursing in CCS or Base Hospitals whilst being targeted by the enemy's firepower, these women just got on with the job. Irrespective of patients' nationality, creed or rank, wherever there were wounded there were professional nurses. These women, so admirably led by Dame Maude McCarthy, demonstrated courage, resilience and humanity as well, as at times, understandable human frailties. In her autobiography, Sister Catherine Black summed up the war's long-term effect on serving nurses, 'You could not go through the things we went through, see the things we saw, and remain the same. You went into it young and light-hearted. You came out older than any span of years could make you.'

CHAPTER 3

Making the Munitions of War:
Guns, Shells and Food

'Strong, sensible and fit, they're out to show their grit,'
(*'War Girls'* Jessie Pope)

The majority of British women had neither the training, expertise nor the financial independence to serve overseas. In the early months of the war, there were few jobs that would enable them to both earn their living and participate in the war effort. However, as the armed services sucked in more and more men, female labour became essential. National Service posters proliferated, reminding female citizens that England was engaged in a fight for her life. By becoming 'The Girl Behind The Man Behind The Gun' or eventually, for those reluctant to manufacture the weapons of war, by 'Speeding The Plough', women could play their part in the national struggle.

'Mad on Munitions':
Miss Tommy Atkins in Lloyd George's Army
On 31 January 1916, widowed mother Susan Davey's reunion with her only child, missing for three weeks, and whose age had been successfully concealed in order to serve the nation, was reported by the Woolwich *Pioneer and Labour Journal*. In itself the story was not unusual. Since the war's opening days, under-age boys (and indeed over-age women in the Nursing Services) had rushed to enlist; less common, albeit not unique, was Mrs Davey's case: her missing child had enlisted not in the Army but, being 'mad on munitions', in Lloyd George's Munitions Army.

Sixteen-year old Elsie Davey was working in one of Woolwich's numerous munitions factories, where workers' official minimum age was 18. Elsie was just one of thousands of girls who saw munition-making as a way of, in volunteer Munitions Worker 6676 Monica Cosens' words, 'toil[*ing*] for their country'. Whilst women's factory jobs ranged from lowly, unskilled tasks, like 'hand-picking bones in Fat Extraction Plants,' to those whose skills earned them the position of First-Class Mechanic, all were essential to the war effort.

Although women had long worked in the factories of industrialised Britain, often in appalling conditions, the story of women's munitions work begins in 1915, when the so-called 'Shell Scandal' started a process which brought droves of women into the factories. It was further accelerated by the May 1916 General Compulsion Bill, which conscripted males between the ages of 18 and 41 into the Armed Services. With so many men under arms, recruitment posters made it abundantly clear that soldiers' lives now depended upon women's labour. Before August 1914 only three national factories produced war munitions; by 1918, 150 factories and over 5,000 controlled establishments no longer manufactured peacetime products but instead the munitions of war. It was through the gates of these multiple and varied factories that the 'khaki-girls' soon streamed. Countless women (precisely how many has proved impossible to calculate) would sacrifice their lives in the factories, and thousands more their health.

The mid-nineteenth century's various Factory Acts had protected women, at least partially, from the heaviest labour. Contemporaries expressed surprise at their apparent readiness to 'sacrifice comfort and personal convenience to the demands of a great cause' (L.K. Yates, *The Woman's Part: A Record of Munitions Work*). Almost immediately, women's munitions work evoked considerable interest, with responses published in newspapers, prose texts and in poems. Some writers expressed angst about women's active participation in the business of killing, hitherto a 'male' occupation. Others appear unconcerned. Some, such as popular travel writer Mrs Alec Tweedie, in *Women and Soldiers* (1918), enthused over the commitment of these 'military khaki-girls [*who*] appear business-like and smart'; their dedication was such that, 'I *will* stand it... even when it means working for fourteen hours at a spell'.

Others are more ambiguous. The 8 May 1915 *War Illustrated* is grimly aware of the reality of the female workers of combatant nations 'making thousands upon thousands of cartridges that are destined to take death to tens of thousands of men'. Social commentator Caroline Playne was less affronted by these women's occupation than by their appearance. Were these women, 'clothed anyhow', these 'Amazonian beings bereft of reason or feeling... really women?' Poet Nina Macdonald simply felt, 'All the world is topsy-turvy/Since the war began.'

Idolised or condemned, for the women themselves it was not just the physical conditions that made life hard. Many male factory workers found women entering the munitions workforce in such numbers threatening and intolerable and acted accordingly. Mrs Felstead was frequently harassed, 'My drawer was nailed up by the men, and oil was poured over everything through a crack another night.' Although 'at the end of three weeks my spirit was quite broken', she persevered, eventually working in an aeroplane works where, to her relief, 'there was no antagonism on the part of the men' but also little communication. Girls' benches were on one side of the fitting shop, men's on the other and they hardly spoke to each other.' Promoted to instructor, one (unofficial) task was to keep the girls in her charge 'contented in spite of the men'. In another factory, one woman was sacked for hitting a 'man who chewed tobacco and kept spitting in my pocket'. Being sacked rendered a woman virtually unemployable for a period of six weeks, as she needed a 'Certificate' of good conduct to move from one factory to another.

For most khaki-girls, for whom every penny earned was essential, ignoring such behaviour was the only option. Skilled lathe worker Joan Williams believed that 'the men were always very jealous of the women doing skilled work.' Never encountering real prejudice herself, she believed that, underlying 'this great grievance… was [*the fact that*] so many women came on to skilled work in a short time owing to the exigencies of war when [*men*] themselves had to serve seven years apprentice.' Discharged in 1919 Joan had reached the 'elevated position' of tool-room hand, the only female employee at her factory, Gwynne's in Chiswick, at this level. She was a slightly unusual employee, having also recently achieved a BA with First Class Honours, a rare achievement for a woman in that era. Even so, she, like all women, earned less than a man, even when doing an identical job.

Although, in theory, women doing men's jobs were to be paid at the same rate this was not the case in practice, as ways were found to circumvent this directive. If a man set up the machine on which the woman did all the operating, her work was considered less skilled than his and her pay downgraded. Discrimination went further than pay: when meat was rationed, women were entitled to smaller quantities due to their apparently less skilled work.

Joan Williams' friend Peggy Hamilton in *Three Years or the Duration* was outraged by pay differentials: 'I must admit that whatever our output or whatever skills we learned and performed, we always received only just over half what the men did for doing exactly the same job.' However, she, like Joan, shows understanding of men's attitudes towards and fear of women in the factories. She expressed concern over the even longer shifts most men worked, particularly by wounded, discharged soldiers, wondering if they were 'even fit enough'. She was outraged that some former Tommies were 'discharged [*from the Army*] with no pension, no job' and, in the case of one soldier who had lost an eye to a bayonet slice, 'not even a glass eye which he [*would have*] had to buy for himself'.

The contentious issue of social class could also disrupt factory harmony. In *The Woman's Part* Yates writes obsequiously about how, 'a lady of delicate upbringing could... have been seen arriving at the Arsenal in the early hours of each morning accompanied by her former maid, both being the while "hands" in the employ of the State.' The text does not explore how the servant would have been paid whilst the mistress, almost certainly one of the Lady Volunteers (known as 'Miaows'), may have been drafted in to provide what was seen as a refining influence on more lowly-born workers. 'Miaows' (some 9 per cent of the total workforce) seemingly received the same treatment as paid workers in terms of conditions and hours of work, although they probably received fewer reprimands.

Yates' belief that all munitions workers, including those who had come from the 'four corners of the Empire', worked together in 'perfect harmony' seems idealised. Monica Cosens, who initially saw her fellow workers as 'vulgar little hussies', comments on how, despite working together, 'the first edge of [*mutual*] suspicion is never worn away... They accuse each other of things neither would dream of doing.' Elizabeth Gore, biographer of her aunt, Dame Lilian Barker, head Lady Superintendent at Woolwich and whose own mother (Lilian's sister-in-law) worked at Woolwich, remembers hearing about initial tensions between women of totally different backgrounds and classes. As acquaintance and understanding between the 'swank pot' and factory girl increased, discord decreased but never disappeared.

Harsh economic necessity brought countless women into the factories; once recruited, the official notices posted in all factories and offices underlined patriotism: '*Motive for Work*. Patriotism. A munition worker is as important as the soldier in the trenches, and on her his life depends.' In 1915 *Domestic News* disagreed, arguing that domestic workers who had flocked to the factories had been simply driven by a desire to leave menial jobs as servants, 'it was not all patriotism that prompted them.' This seems to overlook the harshness of many women's financial circumstances and how gainful employment was imperative for most.

Army separation allowances for urban families were often inadequate and mothers' munitions work supplemented meagre incomes – although there was generally a gap between what their factory-hand husbands had previously earned and current household income. The issue of female munitions workers' pay was vexed: many factory owners did their utmost to interpret the government's recommended 'minimum' weekly-rate of £1 as the standard. Nevertheless, by the end of the war, women's wages were on average around 30 to 35 shillings a week, while for some they were substantially more.

Whilst employers bewailed domestic servants' desertion to the factories, who can blame those such as Elsie Bell, who in 1914 had earned half a crown for a gruelling 12-hour, seven-day week and, by the end of the war, working at Pirelli's wire-cable factory in Southampton, was taking home about £3. Even allowing for inflation and that she would have had to fund her own board and lodgings, it is unsurprising that in an interview she commented, 'you was better off in a factory'. Her account of her working conditions as a servant is surely more accurate than one middle-class writer's idealised description of a 'well-fed, well paid, warmly housed and generously considered' parlour-maid, who has resigned from this supposedly idyllic post to 'do her bit' for her nation. A more realistic diarist, middle-class Hornchurch housewife Mrs Purbrook, acknowledged that the chance of 'earning larger wages, contributed to the so-called patriotism but who shall criticise it?' Higher wages were essential as, workers 'have travelling and food to pay for and no doubt other expenses'.

Much ink was spilled over munitions workers' salaries, the flames fanned by middle-class writers and newspaper columnists. Volunteer Monica Cosens was aware of how her co-workers eked out their hard-earned pay. Rose 'has a mother to keep and is no shirker. She wants every penny she has the strength to earn.' Having detailed the pay, the deductions and the unforeseen circumstances that could reduce pay packets, Monica felt it was 'difficult to believe that the preposterously high wages sometimes quoted as being earned by "munitions hands" exist.' Generously many workers would try to buy 'a small gift for a brother or friend at the Front', often only having a very few pence left for simple treats, such as a visit to the cinema or a bag of sweets.

In her 1919 account for the Women's War Work Committee, Mrs Felstead remembered how in Messrs G's aero-engineer works near London, 'we fared badly', as there was no piece work available. She 'could not possibly live' on her £1 for 53½ hours per week, eventually wheedling an extra 8d out of her employer who, when she left, admitted '[I] was worth more than I had been getting all along.' Perhaps reflecting a lower cost of living, some Birmingham workers felt that £1 a week was a good wage; for one ex-glove-factory worker it was 'more than I ever had before'. As this woman had 'an invalid mother to keep' the extra hard-earned money was welcome.

Few workers seem to have been able to afford the fur coats and other luxuries which certain sections of the press accused them of purchasing with such profligacy. Writing in 1963, social commentator Stella Davies criticised workers for 'the high jinks they got up to in their free time. Many wore expensive seal-skin coats, and their morals were said to be "no better than they ought to be", [profiting from] the "wages of sin".' There is barbed criticism in Juliet Nicholson's 2009 comment that 'girls from munitions factories spent their money on gramophones and tickets to dance-halls.' Middle-class women were not criticised for how they spent their money, even if it was earned in factories.

Still frequently overlooked is how many 'khaki-girls' contributed their hard-earned money to the war effort. Posters urged citizens to invest in War Bonds and supervisors encouraged 'thrift through War Savings Associations or by other means'. Khaki-girls complied, conveniently returning the Government's money to its coffers; they 'crowded the post offices to buy war savings certificates', they also contributed to wartime charities and benevolent funds. Such generosity is particularly remarkable when many workers simply could not afford to eat in the subsidised factory canteens, but brought their own food in a paper bag, which they re-heated in the ovens made available to them, at the cost of 1/2d. Journalist Mrs Usborne, visiting an Airship Factory for *Cornhill* magazine, remarked on how the 'excellent' meal, which cost 6d, was beyond the pocket of 'the majority' of workers.

For those who could afford the canteens' prices, and even for those who merely ate their own food there, some canteens were oases of calm where the half-hour meal break could be spent in comfort. However

61

altruistic the idea of a factory canteen may sound, there was a more practical reason for their introduction. Previously workers had often spent their lunch-break in overcrowded local pubs, where service was slow but alcohol flowed freely. The need to increase productivity rendered it essential that workers (of both genders) were fed quickly and remained sober for the afternoon shift. The *Health of Munition Worker Handbook (HMW)* lists this as one of the key benefits derived from factory canteens.

Despite the Munitions Committee being eager to establish canteens, they were less keen to run them. A plethora of voluntary organisations such as the YMCA/YWCA and Women's Legion (already experienced at cooking for soldiers) stepped in, and volunteers wore medals to show they too were doing their 'bit'. By 1918, the 31 dining halls and 14 coffee-halls at Woolwich Arsenal were supplying 80–90,000 daily meals, taking £1,000 a day and employing 1,000 workers. As one worker pointed out, the canteens being so heavily used did not necessarily mean workers were satisfied with them, it was just 'there was nowhere else to go'. Nevertheless, for women workers who could afford it, having a meal cooked for them and even somewhere to sit, made a welcome change. In many poorer homes of the period, there would only be one or at most two chairs, with seating priority going to 'Father' and any working sons, in age hierarchy. 'Mother', who had invariably been on her feet all day, ate standing up.

Standards in canteens inevitably varied. Diarist Gabrielle West was in (salaried) charge of the canteen at the Royal Aircraft Factory, Farnborough, Hants. Her January 1916 entry states, 'Voluntary workers are the limit. About 8/10 are married women but yet there is only one of the whole 37 who knows the very barest elements of cookery and housekeeping.' She was amazed at 'two dashing young ladies', whose skills did not match their enthusiasm for their domestic work. They were the Duchess of Wellington's nieces, who before the war may never have realised that potatoes needed peeling, let alone that they would one day be required to peel them for factory-hands to eat.

Politics also intermittently entered the factories; Gabrielle West, now a Woman's Police Service Sergeant (WPS), remembered one occasion at Pembrey in Wales where a fight broke out between striking munitions workers and one 'Well reared... little creature' who, unaware that a strike had been called, was 'seen as a blackleg'. Chased from one end of the factory to the other, 'the strikers threw water at her'. At Woolwich

Arsenal, Superintendent Barker confronted would-be strikers head-on. Hiding her extreme nerves by sticking her hands in her pockets, she told her hostile audience that 'to strike in wartime was like giving arms to the enemy'. She added that she empathised with their grievances and successfully defused a situation on the point of igniting.

Strikes, which so outraged those at the Front, were not infrequent in munitions factories. However, it appears that women were less apt to strike than men, although in Wales at least Gabrielle found women 'relatives of the miners from the Rhondda and other coal pits nearby' often threatening strike action. One of the disputes instigated by the women left 600 men idle. Relatively few munitions records dwell on such events, preferring to demonstrate the extent to which khaki-girls were doing their bit to ensure that the boys at the Front were armed with sufficient ammunition to lob at 'the Hun'. Writer Mrs Tweedie, ever quick to take women's part, draws readers' attention to how, in February 1918, 4,000 'girls in Renfrewshire passed a resolution stating that they had heard with horror of the Glasgow ship-building strike threat and vowed never to do the same. The Minister of Munitions telegraphed his acknowledgement of their patriotic resolution' and undertook to 'ensure that the frontline troops were told of women's loyalty'.

Before 1914, factory conditions and the health of many factory workers were appalling. If it was indeed 'On Her Their Lives Depend', munitions workers' health needed to be looked after and, as far as possible, healthy workers engaged. Peggy Hamilton remembers that before being taken on, 'we stood naked, like saints in a row, while two women doctors gave us a very thorough examination, not forgetting to look for lice in our hair.' Despite being desperate to squeeze the maximum amount of work out of factory-hands, after lengthy deliberations the Health of Munitions Workers Committee decreed that a seven-day week was deleterious to the health of workers who were already toiling a twelve-hour day, excluding frequently lengthy travelling time. Several commentators noticed how 'once rosy-cheeked, bright eyed girls soon looked drawn and haggard.'

Fifty years before the war, night shifts in factories had become illegal for women, but the Government now waived the various Factories Acts. Longer hours, shorter breaks and night shifts were introduced, often under what proved to be the erroneous impression that these would increase output. After an experiment revealed that output on a weekly $74\frac{1}{2}$ hour shift was lower than on a 55^1/$_2$ hour one, some factory owners subsequently reduced shifts, but others did not, and even the most sympathetic increased hours when a big 'push', such as the Battle of the Somme, was looming.

Monica Cosens gives an intimate glimpse of the additional burdens night working placed on women, not only due to the lengthy shifts and the inevitable fatigue, but the difficulties faced by the majority of workers, who lived cheek-by-jowl in the teeming courts and tenement housing of the early twentieth century. Recognising how privileged she was to be able to sleep in the daytime for as long as she liked, and be waited on by her parents' staff, Monica realises that 'Mrs Barrett who has the top part of the house… [*overlooks*] how Daisy underneath who has to work by night, is trying to sleep; so she bangs the zinc lid on the dustbin.' Monica knew many of her co-workers had to look after male kin. 'When they go home in the morning, before they can rest, [*they*] have to clean the house, cook the breakfast, and can only snatch a few hours' sleep between then and midday when the menkind come home and expect a hot dinner.' She is amazed by these women's 'wonderful power of endurance.'

To prevent machines falling silent, should the seven day week be reduced, 'educated women' of the 'leisured class' would, according to a July 1915 pamphlet, be recruited for weekend work. A pilot scheme was run at Erith – as an added bonus for the Government, these leisured women would be volunteers. The successful scheme spread to other factories. Sylvia Warner felt that it was 'rather a good scheme' and detailed her experiences in the February 1916 *Blackwoods* magazine. Intriguingly, when she was handed a list of the requirements for her weekend work, it was pointed out that 'evening dress would not be necessary'!

Trained by one of the workers whom she would ultimately relieve, she recognised the skills as well as the tedium, the interminable hours, and the discomfort factory workers endured. 'Thirst' became the great enemy, 'The air of the shop is feverishly dry, so dry that it feels harsh in the nostrils. It cannot well be anything else, seeing that it is full of microscopic steel-dust and the smoke from hard shells.' Having shared their hardships and understood the reality of their work, Sylvia felt 'a vast and saturnine pity' for the day workers when she saw them rushing to the factories to face another backbreaking day.

Many munitions workers faced gruelling journeys in overcrowded trams, buses and trains to get to work. Peggy Hamilton took 90 minutes to reach No. 4 Gate Woolwich, via Woolwich Square, 'The buses were always full and when we arrived in the Square it would be teeming with people fighting for a place on a bus. No-one ever paid because the conductor had no chance of collecting the fares. Each bus was crowded to suffocation point... We had to fight and push to get on board and were often ejected from several buses.' Desperate workers would 'start climbing in between and over the top of the wagons' that were being used to transport goods and material in and out of the Arsenal, making Peggy's 'hair stand on end'.

Lateness led to severe financial penalties in most factories. One Nottingham tannery worker remembered the 'clanging bell' which rang 'every morning to signal us both in and out. If you were two minutes late... you were fined... three pennies. This we could ill afford.'

Some workers were 'exported' (official terminology) away from their homes to other factories. Both the government and charitable organisations were involved in providing 'temporary hutments, with in some instances [accommodation] for several thousand workers.' Those seeking their own lodgings could turn to the Lodging Committees which regularly inspected accommodation. If an insufficient number of landlords voluntarily offered rooms, compulsory billeting was introduced. The Ministry of Munitions could invoke the Defence of the Realm Regulations to force reluctant owners to rent out non-essential properties or billet workers in their homes, creating a similarity between His Majesty's Armed Forces and Lloyd George's Army of Munitions Workers.

Unsurprisingly, the quality of the accommodation varied enormously. Pre-war some 22 hostels or boarding houses for working men and women existed; by January 1918 there were 524. According to Monica Cosens all available properties were 'commandeered'; weekly charges ranged from 14s to 18s. She felt workers being prepared to pay this for accommodation when, had they undertaken different work, they could have lived at home, is proof that women realised 'munitions are vital to the conclusion of the War and they want to help by making them'. One senses that Monica's was a high-end hostel, where volunteers enjoyed 'large, airy class-rooms turned into cubicle bedrooms' and 'seven downstairs bathrooms'. Some hostels were exclusively for lady workers. *The Englishwoman*, in October 1917, was scandalised by the cost of hostel accommodation at Woolwich, calculating that, with this costing 16s 6d and lunch needing to be paid for, workers were left with almost no spare cash. As some hostels were subsidised, employers felt that this was adequate reason to keep all wages low.

In *The Woman's Part*, Yates stresses how 'Perfect harmony' reigned in the hostels; apparently these were having a 'gentling influence on the poorer classes'. With staggering lack of awareness of the realities of working-class living accommodation, where a bed, let alone a room of one's own was an unheard of luxury, she believes in the future no girl 'will ever again tolerate slum conditions'. In the same vein, she bewails how 'some girls arrive with uncleanly [*sic*] habits', and some remain 'unclean in person'. *HMW* also noted how some workers arrived at hostels in 'such a condition of person and clothing that the help of the sanitary authority had to be invoked for cleaning or disinfection.' Neither author seems to deduce that workers may be arriving in 'insanitary' clothes, with no luggage, simply because they did not own a change of garments, let alone a suitcase.

'Public Order' soon became a cause for concern. The *HMW* provides useful background: 'Just as in military centres there are military police, so, where large numbers of girls are assembled for munitions work, Women Police (WPS) and patrols are required.' Yates constructs this as being for the 'protection of women in factories' and even 'patrolling the neighbourhood of the factory' is done 'with a view to the protection of the women employed'. *HMW* detailed how 'Close supervision of women and girls, especially at night is greatly needed, owing to the strain of the night shift and on moral grounds.' This so-called 'protection' undoubtedly stemmed from fears about women's sexual mores and, by extension, the need to protect soldiers from apparently predatory women, always close to the official breast whenever large groups of women were seen to be employed together, particularly in the vicinity of army camps.

According to Gabrielle West, dislike of the WPS, 'leads to girls taking the law into their own hands'. She noted how in Hereford at least, the 'rough and unruly' girls who seem far from dedicated to their work were not averse to 'attacking policewomen'. Herself generally popular, she acknowledges that the WPS themselves could be 'frightfully undisciplined'. In late January 1916, Gabrielle moved to the 'back of beyond' to Pembrey, in Wales. Formerly run down, the site had rapidly expanded to cover 760 acres and it produced explosives, primarily TNT. A lesser woman may have felt intimidated by the largely antagonistic 3,900 employees, but she slowly began to inspire their sympathy, pitting herself on their behalf against the ineffectual Lady Welfare Superintendent, who ignored their legitimate complaints.

In many factories women put up uncomplainingly with increased working hours, but were prepared to object to poor sanitation and safety. Gabrielle's 10 April 1917 diary entry details how Pembrey is 'badly equipped as regards the welfare of the girls'. She notes, 'There were until recently no lights in the lavatories and as these same lavatories are generally full of rats and very dirty, the girls are afraid to go in.' Explosives factories needed a guaranteed year-round supply of water, but Pembrey's proximity to water brought its own disadvantages as there were 'no drains owing to the ground being below sea level... The result is horrible and smelly swamps.'

Pembrey was in breach of regulations concerning sanitation facilities. *HMW* devotes eight pages to 'Washing Facilities and Baths'; female facilities should include 'shower baths' with shoulder-height horizontal sprays in order to help keep 'the hair dry'. Diagrams demonstrate the ideal lay-out for a woman's cubicle with, ideally, 'a seat and pegs'. Not all owners complied, ignoring Public Health Order (9b) (c) which stated that ablution 'facilities must be so arranged and maintained as to be accessible at all times to all persons employed'. Lord Chetwynd, owner of Chilwell in Nottinghamshire, calculated that giving women enhanced facilities decreased output, and he developed a novel system for preventing the (by his own admission small) percentage of women whom he felt were spending too long 'gossiping' in the latrines as opposed to filling his shells. They had to have what became known as 'a ticket to P'!

A Nottingham tannery was, in one worker's words, a 'grim establishment' whose 'outside is matched by the inside'; toilets 'were only flushed once a day by some unseen method'. Workers' hands could be washed in 'a huge tank filled from the River Leen... no towel or even rag to dry them on' – this was the only washing facility.

Armies wear uniforms and it was decreed that fighters in 'Lloyd George's Army' should also wear clothing that enhanced the appearance of the factory, improved discipline, and promoted *esprit de corps*. *HMW* devotes more space to women's work clothing than to men's. All the photographs are of women modelling the various types and styles of protective clothing, including 'knicker suits [*supposedly trousers*] with tunics and boiler suits for dangerous work'. One has to ask whether the factory fashion so praised by Yates of 'wool lasting-cloth... in cream colour, faced with scarlet' was either practical or favoured by the impoverished workers as opposed to the lady volunteers. With her usual lack of understanding of working-class life, Yates concludes that factory uniforms are 'a model of suitable clothing'. She is sure that, 'once accustomed to the comfort and cleanliness of such garments' women will no longer wish to 'return to the discredited habit of tarnished finery worn at work'.

Many workers wore khaki overalls, hence the name 'khaki-girl'. Peggy Hamilton was unimpressed by her 'thick voluminous cotton overalls with caps to match… tied round the waist with anything we could find. We looked like bundles of old rags.' She may have been surprised to learn that, in Mabel Daggett's view in *Women Wanted* (1918), uniforms reflected 'credit on the fatherly care which the Parliamentary Secretary for the Ministry of Munitions has exercised over the many thousands of the daughters of Eve who look to him as their protector.' Although one London department store stocked 'Coat Overalls for Lady Workers' available from 5s 6d in 'eight charming shades,' most workers would have had to settle for the khaki or blue the factories provided, 'the blue ones being in great demand though when both had faded a bit there was apparently not much to choose between them,' at least according to Elizabeth Gore.

If uniforms and surroundings were drab, at Woolwich 'someone got the idea of substituting brightly coloured ribbon for the government shoe laces' and these seem to have unofficially designated a worker's shop. These splashes of colour must have provided a welcome contrast to the workers' daily surroundings. It would, however, have needed more than coloured shoe laces to cheer up the uniforms at Pembrey. To Gabrielle West's annoyance, 'The girls' danger clothes are often horribly dirty [*laundering uniforms was a factory responsibility*] and in rags, many of the outdoor workers who should have top boots, oilskins and s.westers haven't them.'

Uniforms had workers' numbers stencilled on the back. Some factories referred to workers by their number and Peggy Hamilton recalls clocking in and out through a disk with her number. It was impressed upon Monica Cosens that, like soldiers, she could forget her surname but never her number. Working-class women soon realised that wearing official uniform, even one with a number on the back and unflattering in appearance, conferred status on the wearer, providing a visible sign of involvement in the war effort, and many wore theirs with understandable pride. Just as many bridegrooms and some nurses got married in uniform, there are documented cases of at least two weddings where the bridesmaids wore their tunics and trousers and the bride her overalls. 'The bride was attired in "overalls" and a group of friends... also wore their working dress', reported the *Banbury Guardian* in December 1916.

Women working on machines with moving parts were issued with compulsory caps, as their (almost universally) long hair posed a real danger. Munitions worker Edith Rowley donated hers, with its 'Civil Defence Corps' badge sewn on the front, to the IWM. This militarisation shows that she constructed herself as a member of a force fighting her country's foes. The caps, despite Yates' cheerful assertion that they 'match the overalls in colour and texture; they are all designed so that there is no pressure round the head', were widely unpopular and the wearing of them was supposed to be strictly enforced.

Nevertheless, more than one woman took her cap off with calamitous results; accidents involving a worker being scalped, or narrowly escaping this, did occur although, like other munitions disasters, they were hushed up. Peggy Hamilton was fortunate to escape without even a reprimand when caught without her cap. Defying the Welfare Officer, 'a chit of a girl and her manner annoyed me', she refused to put it on. Summoned to the boss's office she demurely explained she had a headache and he turned a blind eye to her misdemeanour. One cannot help wondering whether her middle-class status let her off where a working-class girl would have been chastised.

If, for many women, the hated cap served to protect their hair and ultimately their person from mishap, some women's caps helped cover hair that had turned ginger from working with TNT. Bright yellow skin could not be similarly hidden. The moniker 'Canaries' tamed the horror of what was happening to these women. Public reactions towards Canaries were mixed, as Woolwich worker Caroline Rennles remembered, 'Some people were quite nice and others used to treat us as though we were the scum of the earth.'

Whatever the provision of basins, baths and showers, no water could cleanse Canaries' hands, hair and bodies, 'it just wore off' – eventually. In a ghastly parody of the Midas myth, Canaries had their own separate canteen, as 'everything they touched went yellow including the furniture they sat on.' Yellow was not the only colour, as one gas shell factory worker remembered, 'your hair didn't go yellow but when you took your head off the pillow, the pillowslips were pink'. Caroline Rennles laughed off dire prophecies from a train conductor who warned her, 'You'll die in two years'. Although she defied his prophecy, she replied 'We don't mind dying for our country.' Caroline's more mature self reflects how 'We were so young we didn't realise. I was very patriotic in the First War, everybody was.'

Seventeen-year-old 12129 Mabel Lethbridge's place of work (7 National Filling Factory, Hayes Common), rather than direct contact with chemicals, had calamitous effects. Keen to serve her country, Mabel concealed from her mother the fact that she was working in a munitions factory, and hid her age from the authorities. Her work in Hut 22 was highly dangerous: new, safer machinery had been delivered but not installed. In late 1917, an explosion killed or burned alive a number of workers. Her autobiography, *Fortune Grass*, gives graphic details of the explosion: A 'deafening roar, and I felt myself being hurled through the air'; of her injuries, 'my leg had been blown off and I held in my tortured hands the dripping thigh and knee.' The 60-strong female fire brigade valiantly strove to rescue the trapped workers, 'up came the fire-girls, flinging themselves bravely into the furnace', but very few were rescued alive. Although Mabel's friend Louie was rescued, she was mentally scarred for life. Mabel's battle for compensation was long and fruitless, the authorities arguing that, having lied about her age, she was illegally employed in the 'Danger Sheds' and not entitled to government support. She was one of 10 Hayes women to be awarded the OBE for 'courage and devotion to duty'. Medals carry no financial cost to the recipient's 'grateful nation'.

Although TNT is the chemical most strongly associated with explosives, cordite was also widely used and it produced noxious fumes. Bizarrely, it was tempting to suck. Lily Truphet, a former housemaid previously earning 5s a week, remembered that 'we used to suck it a bit, it was very sweet' although workers knew it 'would affect your heart'. Working with dangerous materials attracted additional pay and cosmetic manufacturers began to promote restorative creams. 'Ven-Yusa', widely advertised in factory magazines, combined patriotic duty to help the war effort and the need to 'preserve the natural beauty of the skin and complexion.' More than Ven-Yusa was required, however, to prevent the rashes, swelling, temporary blindness and death from the noxious substances Canaries and other 'Danger Shed' women were working with.

These dangers became better understood with time. In August 1916, *The Lancet* carried an article by two female doctors who had studied women munitions workers over a period of five months. They recommended minimum and maximum ages (21–40), that workers be moved elsewhere after 12 weeks and that separate washing facilities and a medical examination be mandatory. Full-time doctors were soon appointed to all larger factories and some attempts were made to balance workers' health with the need to manufacture ever more weapons of war.

Fresh milk was considered an antidote to some substances; Mabel Lethbridge remembered being given a twice-daily pint 'to neutralise the effects of the poisonous explosives'. A crane driver also remembered coming down from her crane at two-hourly intervals for milk. In some cases *HMW* considered respirators or veils 'needful accessories', although subsequent medical reports indicated these were useless. It may have been wishful thinking on the part of the Committee to state that 'in the case of TNT, exposure prolonged over months appears to establish a degree of immunity.'

Regulations in the 'Danger Sheds' were even more strictly enforced than in other areas. Nothing metal, not even linen buttons (which covered metal), nor any jewellery (including wedding rings) could enter the work area. Even regulation footwear was designed without iron or metal fasteners. Whilst steps were taken to protect workers from the dangers, responsibility was also placed on them and infringing the rules, however unintentionally, led to instant dismissal, as one young woman found out to her cost. Returning at night from her factory, someone had given her two matches to light a candle to guide her to her room. The following morning in the 'Shed', the unlit match, which she had unthinkingly placed in her pocket, fell out. Instant suspension followed, despite the circumstances being explained. Her friend remembered her being taken to court and sentenced to: 'twenty-eight days without the option of a fine. They took her away to prison, to Winson Green. And she never got over it. Within a few months, she died.'

Gabrielle West was forced to prosecute one 'poor wretch' for leaving cigarettes in her coat pocket, despite knowing that this was a total oversight on the worker's part. During her spell at Woolwich, 'a very slummy part of London,' Gabrielle noted 'a sort of crèche for pipes and baccy' along the North End Road, where 'for a few pence a week [*owners*] can leave them just outside the gate'. Whilst precautions relating to material banned from the Danger Sheds could be enforced, damage to workers' health was less easy to regulate. One worker's symptoms were initially dismissed as being caused by alcohol. When she was identified as suffering from throat cancer, nothing could be done for her. Her sister remembered, 'She died in terrible agony. They said the black powder had burnt the back of her throat away. She was only nineteen.'

Some ambulance and first aid provision had existed in factories pre-war. From 1 December 1917, these became obligatory in all blast furnaces, foundries, copper mills, iron mills and metal works. Where TNT was handled, one medical officer was obligatory per 2,000 employees. Workers filling gas shells in one factory at least had their own medical provision. Apparently one doctor could tell by the colour of workers' eyes whether the gas was affecting them. Most factories also had nurses and even some VADs; Yates is quick to praise one such nurse 'who worked shifts of twenty-four hours at a stretch during the absence of her colleagues.'

Monica Cosens appreciates having 'a Red Cross nurse of our own and a corner of the Canteen is given up to her for a miniature hospital. Some days she attends as many as forty-three cases.' These ranged from 'a steel splinter into the fleshy part of the hand,' to the extremely painful sounding 'hot swarf into the eye which blisters it', or truly horrific cases such as the one Caroline Rennles remembered, 'one girl had her eyes blown out when some TNT exploded in her face.' There is a fearful symmetry between what could happen to those who manufactured these diabolical weapons of war, and those against whom they were fired. Inevitably, some medical facilities were woefully inadequate. Writing in April 1917, Gabrielle West noted that: 'Although the fumes often mean 16 or 18 casualties a night, there are only 4 beds in the surgery for men and women and they are all in the same room.' Desirability and reality were, once again, poles apart.

HMW complacently calculated that the number of notifiable (serious) accidents in the factories ran to about 150,000 per annum, adding that: 'A somewhat formidable return of accidents is therefore to be anticipated in munitions factories which... include dangerous trades and the manufacture of explosives.' Women by their higher numerical presence in factories bore the brunt of the casualties, and untold numbers of munitions workers died or were fatally injured as a result of explosions. Yet, they remained philosophical, seeing themselves as soldiers prepared to die in their nation's cause.

Russia's withdrawal from the war in late 1917 began the process of demobilisation for factory women, leaving them to face 'the unemployment with which they and the armed forces were to be rewarded for all their sacrifices and hard work of the previous four years,' (Peggy Hamilton). Anxious about what might face the 30,000 women who had worked at the Arsenal – anticipating there would be no place for them in peace-time industry and concerned they would be exploited in domestic service – and faithful to her duties beyond the end of her employment, newly created OBE and subsequently Dame Lilian Barker told women to get in touch with her if they were 'poorly paid or under bad conditions'.

Once hostilities ceased, some women were laid off without even the week's pay to which they were entitled. An 'out-of-work' dole was promised to women about to be dismissed – no time-scale for this was given and deputations of workers descended on Parliament demanding 'guarantees for the future'. Such guarantees were in short supply and those who did not accept a job, however inappropriate or poor the wage (generally in domestic service), soon found their meagre dole withdrawn. *The Daily Mail* of 29 November 1918 felt this was appropriate, 'Women who from simple caprice refuse suitable employment judged by their pre-war abilities will not be entitled to the donation unemployment insurance.'

When the bells rang for the Armistice, they also clanged 'Time' for most munitions women; it was abundantly plain that they had only temporarily entered a man's world. Women workers, whom *The Times* had praised on 15 November 1918 for 'the invaluable services which they have so freely given to the national cause', discovered that they would be cut loose in the new post-war world. Work, if they found any, was all too often the drudgery of the domestic service which, as Barker anticipated, they had merely escaped, 'For the Duration'.

'With bill-hook and stick they cleared out the ditches': Women on the Land

Mary King's 5 August 1914 *War Diary* entry recorded how René Viviani, French Minister of Foreign Affairs, had issued a proclamation to the 'women of France calling upon all those who were young and strong to replace the men in the fields to ensure this year's harvest and prepare the fields for next year's.' French women responded throughout the war; writing in July 1915 while serving in France, Canadian Nursing Sister

Agnes Warner noted, 'There are only two old horses left in the whole village so the women harness themselves into the rakes and wagons and pull them in the place of the horses – and they so seldom complain.'

Also in July 1915, Maurice Hankey, Secretary to the War Cabinet, reminded colleagues of his three recent visits to France. He had been deeply impressed by 'the amount of work [*done*] on the land by old men, women and children'. Whilst not suggesting that Englishwomen replace horses, Hankey concluded, 'it would be a splendid thing if we could get the women on the land in this country too.' Although Cabinet members were unconvinced of England's need of women, Hankey was undoubtedly aware that female agricultural workers in the whole of England and Wales only numbered 190,000. For decades, English women had been increasingly reluctant to enter agricultural work, which, according to Viscountess Wolseley in *Women and the Land* (1916), was thought 'dull, uninteresting and unremunerative'.

The relentless industrialisation of the nineteenth century, Britain's imperial position, and technological advances in shipping, had increased her dependency on imported food; in 1913, British farmers had only produced enough food for 125 days of the year. Demographics had altered in the previous 50 years, and three-quarters of England and Wales' population of 36 million now dwelt in towns. To guarantee the nation's food security, Britannia must continue to rule the waves. Pre-war, the German Government had realised that preventing food reaching the British Isles would seriously undermine her ability to wage war. U-Boats targeting convoys of ships bringing in foodstuffs and starving the population into submission would prove an 'effective strategy'.

Yet, the President of the Board of Agriculture, Lord Selborne's 1914 pleas for early state intervention in food production fell largely on deaf ears, and continued to do so. Once war had been declared, Government departments remained woefully slow to respond to the dangers continuous enemy attacks posed for food convoys. Writing to Selborne in July 1915, Prime Minister Asquith confidently stated there was not 'the least fear that any probable or conceivable development of German submarine activity can be a serious menace to our food supply'. Begging to differ, Selborne took the step of establishing War Agricultural Committees (WAC) to report on the realities of food scarcity and explore ways of increasing production. His measures only became fully effective once the premiership passed in December 1916 from Asquith to Lloyd George.

MAKING THE MUNITIONS OF WAR

In 1915, following a 'Women's Right to Serve' parade organised by Emmeline Pankhurst, thousands of women of all backgrounds had registered their willingness to undertake war service, but they, like Viscountess Wolseley, head of the Sussex (East) WAC, felt thwarted: 'In vain each day we scan the papers, hoping... to [*be*] more vigorously utilised', but there remained a 'large number of still-expectant unemployed'. Of these would-be war workers, those willing to do agricultural work remained in the minority. Few women had real experience of such work and even fewer found it, or the very low wages, appealing. In 1916, landworker Olive Hockin only earned 2s 6d per day for a 10–14 hour day; even this was higher than the 1s 6d women earned at Lyons Hall, Great Leighs, Essex.

As well as poor wages, living conditions were frequently inadequate, and to compound recruitment difficulties, agricultural work was frequently seen as less obviously contributing to the war effort. Furthermore, under intense pressure to increase food production, few farmers were ready to risk employing women and misogyny was rife. Already angry that skilled male agricultural workers had been enlisted by over-zealous Army recruiting sergeants, and indeed by landowners themselves, the received wisdom amongst farmers was, as Olive discovered, 'a woman about the place would be more trouble than she is worth.' Farmers had to be persuaded that a Land Army could feed the nation just as the Munitions Army was feeding the guns.

In *Rural Life in England*, Pamela Horn argues that initially rural women's recruitment to agricultural work was low as, owing to Army separation allowances, a man's absence was not initially a financial loss in the poorest agricultural (as opposed to urban) families, where the obvious pool of such workers lay. However, prices rose substantially throughout the War, and by October 1916 they were 68 per cent above those of 1914. Domestic poverty was rising. Horn states that, in January 1917, one of the reasons for not increasing the separation allowances was Government's fear that providing women with 'generous treatment might reduce their incentive to work'. As this allowance for childless wives and widows never altered throughout the War, and allowances for children did not keep pace with inflation, this argument has merit.

Endeavouring to reduce farmers' antagonism and women's lack of enthusiasm, a series of demonstrations of women's agricultural abilities were staged. Women soon proved their aptitude. The increasingly precarious food situation, women's efforts to prove that they could 'take a useful part in the work of the farms and, by their patriotism and self-sacrifice save the situation', ultimately eased the way for a Women's Land Army, but it was an uphill struggle and land work remained fragmented throughout the war.

The Great War is generally thought of as the first mechanised war, but the Army used horses and mules for logistical support, and from the outset these animals were requisitioned, sometimes being physically removed from carriages and carts, or even from hunts. Farmers faced both a shortage of skilled agricultural workers (of the million men who in 1914 had been engaged in agriculture, it was estimated by 1916 that about 500,000 of them were bearing arms) and they only had old or inferior animals with which to plough – and female labourers to replace the men. Farmers doubted whether women would even be able to ready the horses for ploughing, let alone follow them. Women were 'surely incapable of lifting a harness'.

Drawn to land work through her love of horses, Olive Hockin soon proved doubters wrong, 'I discovered in this, as in many things that are supposed to be beyond the powers of woman, that it is knowledge that is needed more than physical strength.' She mastered both the handling of the 'confusion of chains and leather', so that it 'became on the horse an orderly array of harness', and the art of ploughing, 'an accomplishment I was always told, beyond the wildest dreams of woman's abilities.' Although ploughing 'needs judgment and some experience, given the opportunity [*it is*] as much within the reach of a woman's powers as of a man's', she wrote.

There was, however, one area in which women impressed their skeptical employers from the beginning: tractor driving. Tractors were increasingly used from March 1917; many older farmers refused to have anything to do with them, and it was left to the hastily trained female volunteers to demonstrate their own and the mechanised contrivances' worth, not to mention women's abilities to maintain tractors themselves.

Increasing agricultural production rapidly became a matter of national survival. Irrespective of the Asquith Government's complacency about the U-boat threat, by 1917 supplies were so short that Food Riots occurred in major cities. Food was an overwhelming concern, for the poor who could afford ever less of it, for landowners whose gardens and greenhouses were now committed to growing it, as well as the more lowly back gardens of the middle-classes.

Hornchurch middle-class housewife, Mrs Purbrook's vegetable garden provided a profusion of marrows: 'I expected the family to expostulate at the continuous appearance of marrow on the table for breakfast, lunch and dinner; day after day it appeared in some form, we had it boiled, fried, baked, mashed, cooked with tomatoes and stuffed.'

Pre-war well over two million hundredweight of potatoes alone had been imported annually from Germany. One Norfolk farmer reported that 'between May and harvest' his 18 women workers had 'put up for market about five hundred tons of potatoes'. North London Collegiate School pupils dug up part of their playing-fields for potatoes and Girl Guides in Leigh-on-Sea in Essex used waste ground for potato-growing: they were photographed in the *War Illustrated* patriotically wielding their forks. In the bleak winter of 1917–18, despite potatoes being the size of marbles and the parsnips little bigger, even these were welcome and indeed fought over in starving cities.

But still the WLA's contribution to food production remained complicated by underlying tensions. Agricultural workers foresaw their loss of exemption from military service, their wives feared the erosion of their own part-time jobs, whilst farmers' wives claimed the female workforce billeted on them were simply more mouths to feed. The 1917 National Service poster campaign, 'Speed the Plough', understandably concealed from potential recruits these antagonisms and also how muddy and windswept the land they would till really was. Other forms of propaganda depicted agricultural work against a background of blue skies and green fields, in contrast to Olive Hockin's memories of winter turnip-lifting, 'Our fingers wet with closing round the frosted leaves stung in the wind, as if the living skin was being torn away.'

When advertising campaigns failed to supply sufficient volunteers, two rather formidable members of the WLA High Command toured the country, organising open-air recruiting rallies. Dressed in Land Army uniform, either Lady Denman or Meriel Talbot would, according to Denman's biographer Gervas Huxley, 'attract the startled public's attention by rotating a policeman's very heavy wooden alarm rattle which made an ear-splitting noise. After this, the other would make a rousing speech standing on the top of the car.'

Occasionally they joined forces with processions recruiting for the WAAC or the WRNS but, to the annoyance of these militarised corps, when faced with a seven-mile march, Talbot and Denman processed on horseback, horses being 'indubitably agricultural'!

In 1916, the Board of Agriculture had stated its conviction that women could prove as magnificent an army in the home fields as the New Armies on the battlefields. Optimistically, women's 'patriotism and zeal' would, like those of the soldiers, 'make up for any shortcomings in their professional skills.'

For those who came forward, enrolment was complicated. 'Women's Land Army Conditions and Terms (WLA)' set out the two-way contract between worker and Government. According to Section 5 volunteers had 'TO BE WILLING TO GO TO WHATEVER PART OF THE COUNTRY YOU ARE SENT'; a free railway warrant would facilitate this. Terms of service included uniform and an initial wage of 20s a week, potentially rising to 22s on passing an efficiency test. Inevitably, the uniform caused angst in official male quarters. Hoping this might increase recruitment, uniforms in military 'khaki' were designed.

According to the WLA *Handbook*, 'an English girl who is working for her Country on the land is the best sort of girl.' WLA Edith Storey 'was so proud of my uniform'; she too was on National Service, fighting the Food War. Although some male members of the Board of Agriculture deemed the uniform 'becoming', sufficiently 'feminine' or at least (bizarrely) 'very Greek', to Andrew Clark, Vicar of Great Leighs, it was not Grecian but 'something out of a comic opera'. To others, it was fraught with potential snares (related to sexuality) and workers were told always to cover their breeches with an overall when in public, being reminded, 'You are doing a man's work and so you're dressed rather like a man, but remember just because you wear a smock and breeches you should take care to behave like a British girl who expects chivalry and respect from every man she meets.'

Not all villagers considered the WLA respectable. Hearing that 'horrified tales were circulating about a woman running around the town in a skirt – 'so short you could see her *britches*!' the explanation of the miscreant, Beatrice Oaks, as to why she was wearing such practical clothes fell on deaf ears amongst the 'gossiping Chapel-going folk'. Having seen a trousered worker, one Great Leighs housewife asserted, 'it isn't decent to come out dressed like that... I'm sorry I saw her.' In Hornchurch Mrs Purbook was more sanguine; for her, khaki-girls and farmhands 'dress suitably for all these vocations'. Eventually the Board of Agriculture, despite wishing women to conduct themselves in a 'ladylike manner', recommended a skirt length of 14 inches above the ground, and that a coat reaching to the knees should be worn. Short-skirted Beatrice must have felt vindicated, particularly when, on moving to another farm to become an instructor, she found a woman milking a cow wearing a 'long skirt which trailed in the mud and muck'. She was aware that women's traditional clothes prevented the hygiene necessary to good dairy husbandry.

For women working independently of the WLA, who nevertheless sought appropriate clothing, the London-based Cleveland Manufacturing Company offered a 'well and smartly made Agricola Outfit' for 18/11'. Thirty-five shillings purchased a complete 'Standard Outfit', and the large rather than small-brimmed hat cost an extra shilling. Harrods' 73s top of the range ensemble promised, 'Service boots made on precisely the same principles as men's Army boots.' These were perhaps more comfortable than the official ones supplied to WLA workers: one worker remembered 'Blooming great boots mak[ing] blisters on your feet.' The poorest village women economised by wearing their soldier husbands' boots. With wages still only a weekly maximum 25s, the cost of farming wear, even for those who shopped at the lowlier Co-operative Wholesale Society, was prohibitive. Employers were encouraged to offer uniform loans through the relevant Women's County Committees.

Women were naturally expected to 'conduct themselves in a 'ladylike manner'. Whether this was to protect their own virtue or avoid throwing temptation in the way of male farm workers is unclear. In an acerbic letter to Meriel Talbot, Lady Mather Jackson, Chairman of the Monmouthsire WAC, voices outrage at some workers' behaviour, which included, 'staying out late; they often do not return to their farms until 12 and one in the morning'. In one area at least, Gang Hostels were introduced, where Jackson suggested that recalcitrant workers should be accommodated for a fortnight, working from there, and 'confined after hours to Barracks'.

Jackson's list of 14 'Rules for Training Centres' reads like a boarding-school's rules; the women are referred to as 'Pupils'. The final rule pertaining to 'Bedtime-Winter 9.00 pm' may explain why some defiantly 'stayed out late'. Jackson chose to believe that the issues facing the Monmouthshire Committee stemmed from class, 'No doubt we have here an absolutely different Class of Girls to deal with than they have in most County Districts.' To her credit, Meriel replied that Jackson's rules were over-zealous, that the WLA were not subject to military discipline, as they were working for private employers, and draconian punishments did not, in her opinion, 'lead to desirable results' – indeed quite the opposite, as the 'best results are achieved when the fewest rules are in force.'

WLA accommodation varied enormously; one volunteer was stationed on several farms during her service. Her accommodation on a Duke's estate was her worst, 'only the bare necessities of life and about ten yards from some abandoned pigsties which housed a few hundred rats!' Hilda Rountree volunteered with 14 other Newham College Cambridge students to help with fruit picking, and accommodation was provided: 'The front of the Hall contained our ticking mattresses (which we filled with straw on arrival) on the floor. I remember that by the second night there was not a shoe among the company which did not bear witness to the mortality of the usual inhabitants, the beetles.'

The local doctor offered the use of his bath on a rota basis, but after his boiler burst, bathing involved a trip to the nearby town, often by rented bicycle. Normal washing was courtesy of rain water which was used 'very sparingly' for fear it would run out. Their 15s pay also ran out and by the end of the week the women were down to a 1/2d each. Supper was 'soup, potatoes and rice and bed was officially at 8.00 pm'. Interested by their status as students, the local press reported on their wearing trousers, not on their work.

Efforts were made to construct land work itself as military and enhance its patriotic appeal: green armlets bearing a red crown were issued to WLA members who had worked on the land for at least 30 days, 'implying that the women ranked with Lord Derby's battalions.' Medals were awarded for distinguished service; processions were devised to encourage recruitment and to retain existing volunteers. Notwithstanding official efforts to construct the WLA as Front Line soldiers in the War against Famine, many women still saw themselves as secondary.

Nevertheless, Olive Hockin felt her commitment to land work paralleled that of soldiers: 'Nothing, I am sure but the feeling of urgent public necessity would have kept us going as we did all through that summer – that and the thought of the soldiers in the trenches.' There is more than a hint in her writing that she is as tied to the land as a soldier to his patch of Flanders mud; thoughts of loved ones in foreign fields kept many women tilling the home ones, just as thoughts of those at home kept soldiers fighting. One young worker's teenage husband was in the trenches, in as alien an environment as she was in the fields, he 'never having held a rifle in his hand, not even to shoot a rabbit.' One assumes she had never held a pitchfork.

Irrespective of social background, many WLAs demonstrated real enthusiasm and pride in their work. One wrote to the Committee saying she was 'able to do practically everything that comes round': her 12-hour day began with 'milking ten cows, feeding the young calves, and washing the milk utensils.' Spreading manure, digging mangolds, and dealing with 'wet brewer's grain' kept her busy until her backbreaking day concluded with a stint in the milking parlour and moving the beasts out to pasture.

Dairy work was considered to be 'women's special sphere' and many became dairy maids. Olive Hockin's friend took a while to master the milking art: she 'stood up, wiping her face with her handkerchief. She had not yet learnt to escape the impatient flick of Priscilla's tail…When the tail was dirty… the experience is best imagined than described.'

Like soldiers, many WLA cheered themselves up through songs, recasting soldiers' favourites; these often hint at workers' loneliness, and how women felt starved of desirable male company. Farmers, Conscientious Objectors, and Prisoners-of-War, who also worked on farms, were not a patch on a soldier. In a parody of 'Tipperary', WLA workers felt, 'It's a long way to see a Tommy/It's a long way to go'. Such harmless songs may have helped trigger the inevitable angst about young women let loose far from home. The various WACs tried to occupy the moral high ground; they controlled behaviour through fines levied on those conducting themselves 'in an unruly manner'. Most workers had little scope for 'unruly' behaviour and the majority must have been exhausted at the end of their long days. Meriel Talbot recognised workers' concerns and their loneliness. Anxious to avoid even a hint of scandal that might prove detrimental to the WLA's success, salaried welfare workers were recruited to ensure that conduct becoming to a lady was practised everywhere. These welfare workers organised concerts, amateur theatricals and evening classes, reminiscent of the entertainments provided for the troops.

For women on remote farms, ostracised by the local community for 'taking a man's place and driving him to the Army,' life was particularly harsh. In January 1918, Meriel Talbot launched *The Landswoman*, aiming to give workers 'news of one another', and 'a paper of their own through which to make known their ideas and their needs'. Meriel wrote, 'Dear Girls, The object of this magazine is to bind you all together into one big happy family and I want you to take me on as a friend.'

81

Tilling the soil remained poorly paid, monotonous, unglamorous, essential – and safe. If, as poet Dora Shorter acknowledged, there is in wartime a strange 'joy where dangers be,' then land work needed further militaristic cachet. In March 1918 Lord Ernle, President of the Board of Agriculture, stressed that whilst others had provided 'the silver bullet and lead bullet', agricultural workers' responsibility was 'the food bullet'; their holding the 'food line' was essential to national survival. A Roll of Honour named those who had given Distinguished Service or their lives as a result of their work.

On 27 November 1919, at an elaborate 'Farewell Rally of the Land Army', royalty showed its gratitude to women who had answered the agricultural call. Princess Mary presented the Distinguished Service Bar to 55 members. She praised attendees for their 'devoted service' and wished them 'every happiness in the future'. Three days later, with the potato harvest having ended, the Women's Land Army was disbanded. A few workers who wished to continue with agricultural work were offered free passage to the Dominions; most returned to their pre-war world, moving from raising crops to raising the next generation of workers and soldiers. Many of their sons and daughters would take part in the next war.

Like the munitions workers, most of the approximately 23,000 WLA workers (available figures vary enormously) whose National Service had involved speeding the plough across England's green and frequently unpleasant land, and who had been royally applauded for their efforts, found that both their labour and the plaudits were strictly, 'For the Duration'.

CHAPTER 4

Defiant to the End:
Aristocrats, Doctors and Spies

'Good Lady, go home and sit still,'
(spoken to Dr Elsie Inglis August 1914)

In the early years of the twentieth century, few women had the necessary training, time or economic freedom to pit themselves against the established societal order. Most accepted, however reluctantly, a male-dominated world. When war was declared, they filled positions endorsed by the male hierarchy in which, over the course of the war, they gained justified admiration, plaudits, even military honours. Other women, albeit a small minority, were in a different position. Social privilege or professional training enabled them to carve roles of their own design, which were occasionally derided and frequently overlooked, but nevertheless pivotal to the British and Allied war effort.

Sometimes bored by the luxurious world they inhabited, aristocratic women were convinced that they, like their male relatives, were ideally placed to serve their nation. Without the benefit of formal education or indeed any professional skills, they could still, so they thought, succour the wounded. Denis Stuart, the Duchess of Sutherland's biographer (*Dear Duchess*, 1982), wryly comments how, in a bizarre role reversal, these women 'clamour[ed] to be admitted as nursing probationers even if the job included emptying chamber pots'.

Some, however, aspired to more than bedpan duties. As soon as hostilities were declared, putting their organisational expertise, honed by running huge households and armies of staff, to good use they founded and frequently funded their own ambulance and hospital units. Accompanied by small bands of trained nurses, doctors and ancillary workers, they defiantly bypassed the British authorities and headed for the war's many fronts. As many Allied armies had woefully inadequate medical services, their units were gratefully received, earning the gratitude of thousands of patients and, in some cases, memories of a service still revered today. If the enemy thought they were rather high-class spies, that was all in the day's work.

Since the Crimean War of the mid-nineteenth century, female military nurses had become the norm. Almost unknown, both then and now, is that serving alongside Florence Nightingale was an army surgeon who was not quite what he appeared to be. James Miranda Barry or, more accurately Margaret Bulkley, was not only (unbeknownst to Edinburgh University Medical School, from where she graduated) the first British woman to qualify as a doctor, but so complete was her disguise that she rose undetected through the ranks of the army, serving as a military surgeon, albeit rather a small one with a high-pitched voice. Her gender only became apparent when she died and was laid out, and the news broke following her military funeral in 1865.

However, far from Barry blazing a military trail that other women would follow, her considerable medical achievements in (*inter alia*) stopping the spread of cholera through rigorous attention to hygiene, were either hushed up or forgotten. Still, in 1914, as far as the War Office was concerned, 'It had been ordained that women could not fight, and therefore they were of no use in war time' – not even as doctors (*BJN,* 11 January 1919).

In August 1914, the now legitimately qualified female physicians were convinced that the contribution they could make to the Army Medical Services was self-evident. They assumed that the misogyny they had experienced throughout their training, and which had side-lined them into treating women and children, would disappear. Finally, their hard-won skills and expertise would be recognised. Within days they realised their optimism had been misplaced. Undeterred, they too decided that if their nation had no use for them, they would find Allied Armies who accepted that wounded men and diseases are gender blind. What they would achieve would, in the *BJN*'s post-war words, 'shock the War Office till it rocked to its foundations'.

In all wars, eyes and ears are needed in enemy territory. Desperate to infiltrate, belligerent sides are equally fearful of infiltration and spy mania becomes rife. Ever anxious about the role of women in wartime, authorities were quick to assume that some women were engaged in espionage. 'Spy', along with 'nurse' and 'whore', was then the third accepted female wartime role. Some women were assumed to be spies because their looks, actions, morals or even occupations made this seem probable. Arrest, retribution and condemnation on flimsy evidence could swiftly follow. Other women were less likely candidates: of irreproachable morals and from lowly backgrounds, they could pass undetected and it was betrayal or momentary inattention which sealed their fate. Such was many spies' behaviour in their final hours that even those who condemned them admitted feeling admiration for their bravery and their defiance.

'My God, Duchess they have fired the town': The Millicent Sutherland Ambulance Unit

Following the flurry of titled women rushing to the South African wars, where they had attempted to nurse the wounded, the Army Medical authorities decreed that only professionals would be employed in the future. Millicent, Duchess of Sutherland, was one of several aristocratic ladies who used influential friends to circumvent this prohibition and form private units. Her Unit's story, which she documented in *Six Weeks at the War*, gives a sense of the way these women conducted affairs. One of her nurses, Florence Ford, who trained at Guy's Hospital, kept and preserved her diary of her service with the Unit, providing further details and insight into Millicent's *modus operandi*.

Having reached France ahead of the British Expeditionary Force, Millicent bypassed the British authorities and instead offered her fully staffed and equipped Ambulance Unit to the Belgians, who were woefully short of '*Services de Santé*' (medical facilities). On 16 August, a military doctor came to inspect her hospital, which had arrived in Namur ahead of the German Army's victorious progress westwards through Belgium and northern France. He criticised their carbolic, smiled at the glycerine for the hands and pronounced himself impressed by the surgical instruments – all funded by wealthy contacts at home. Funds did not run to paying nurses a salary, unlike male orderlies who were paid. This common feature of volunteer units in the early years led to significant controversy.

Many units found themselves establishing hospitals wherever they could, in Millicent's case within a local convent, and desperately wounded men soon poured in. Millicent was far from the only volunteer to discover that despite having no nursing experience, 'What I thought would be an impossible task became absolutely natural. To wash wounds, to drag off

85

rags and clothing soaked in blood, to hold basins, to soothe a soldier's groans.' Nurse Florence Ford (who did not feel that the nuns' religion gave them 'much courage'), noted with satisfaction that 'the patients so far have done very well.'

With Namur under continuous bombardment, Florence wondered which was worse, 'being shelled or knowing that you are hemmed in by fires.' Once Namur fell, and with over 100 patients in her care, Millicent set about harrying the German Commander, whom she visited daily in order 'to bother [*him*] and quote the Convention of Geneva and do all I could to lighten the lot of our wounded. I disliked very much trying to get favours out of the Germans but it had to be done.' However she failed to get concrete news out of the high-ranking officers, the dearth of which was getting on everyone's nerves. Other Units, irrespective of the Front they were serving on, also found the lack of news hard to cope with.

Eventually, hearing of the unfolding catastrophe in Mons and having pleaded (for once unsuccessfully) with the garrison's head doctor not to evacuate the Unit's wounded to Germany, Millicent resolved to head for the fighting. In order to achieve this aim, she interviewed the German Commander of Namur – Florence considered this 'most brave'. According to Millicent, this gentleman seemed to be 'getting sick of me and my ambulance'; so sick of her that he even offered transport aboard a German military train. They arrived in Maubeuge two days after the town's surrender to the Germans.

Despite Millicent hoping to get to Ostend and from there to England, they were sent to Brussels. Subsequently interviewed by her local newspaper, the *Northwich Chronicle*, Florence Ford conjectured that this was probably because 'we had crossed the battlefield, seen the trenches, the transport, the guns and the ambulance trains' – the latter she found of professional interest.

In Brussels they were imprisoned in the Hotel Asturias, but Florence considered this makeshift jail 'a very good hotel'; Millicent meanwhile welcomed the 'poached eggs and buttered toast'. To Florence's amazement, a 'Guard with fixed bayonet [*stood*] outside the D's room', inside which Millicent was busy 'interviewing every person of distinction. She really is quite splendid & it is quite the usual thing to do to receive visitors in one's bedroom.' The German Military Governor of Brussels duly sent Millicent compliments and promised to call. Social niceties being essential even in time of war, Millicent 'rose and dressed and, surrounded by my nurses, received him in the salon.' Nurses had to 'put their best bibs and tuckers on to see the German commander which we rather dreaded,' recalled Florence. He granted permission for the Unit to return to England.

After a series of further mishaps, the 'little band' arrived home, six weeks after their departure, having had, according to Florence's *Northwich Chronicle* account, 'a trying experience' – although this did not deter her from further duty with Millicent until ill health forced her to resign in October 1916. Following recuperation, she joined the QAIMNS, giving Millicent as one of her referees. Another referee, the RAMC surgeon employed at the hospital, referred to Florence's 'tremendous energy and unfailing skill. In losing her we have lost someone who was quite irreplaceable.' Others concurred; her QAIMNS record rated her 'an excellent nurse'.

Muriel St Clair Stobart also believed that in wartime women were eminently suited to running hospitals. Like Millicent, she and her Unit arrived in Belgium in August 1914 and subsequently lived through the siege of Antwerp; her improvised hospital, which was in the direct line of fire of the ammunition depot, became a favoured target. Stobart seemed unsurprised when none of her staff 'took the slightest notice' of the shells falling around them, and behaved instead, 'as though they had been accustomed to working under shell-fire all their lives'. As conditions deteriorated she reluctantly realised that the only course of action open to the Unit was to evacuate. To her amazement, she found three London buses hurtling out of the city. She begged the British Tommy drivers to help her and her nurses reach the Belgian frontier. The gallant Tommies seated the women atop boxes of ammunition. The renowned British phlegm enabled the fleeing nurses to, 'laugh merrily at the thought of what fine fireworks we should be in the middle of, if a shell dropped our way.' No shell landed and they reached England safely, where Muriel set about raising funds for another unit, this time to go to the Eastern Front.

Intensive fundraising was part and parcel of life for voluntary units. Like Muriel Stobart, Millicent intended to return 'to the Front, in connexion with the Red Cross; this time I sincerely trust among our own troops. I shall take a fully-equipped motor ambulance, surgeons, and nurses, and all the experiences I have gained in these strange days.' Perhaps she was naive in her belief that the Army Medical authorities would now willingly accept her services. Despite all the horrors and sufferings of the wounded during the retreat from Mons, they remained unconvinced of any need for the specialist unit she was offering. Influential friends pulled more strings and eventually No. 9 British Red Cross Hospital (Duchess of Sutherland's) was established at Malo-les-Bains, as well as a Millicent Sutherland Ambulance Unit hospital barge. A tiny glimpse into the hospital's efficiency occurs in Red Cross ambulance driver Josephine Pennell MM's letter to her GP father in February 1918, 'the wards are wonderfully fitted up. They specialise in fractures and over nearly all the beds are wonderful overhead railways to which the limbs are slung in all sorts of positions. It looks awfully complicated and it must take hours to arrange.' Initially far from enthusiastic about Millicent, Maud McCarthy, Matron-in-Chief to the BEF in France was eventually won over. Visiting the hospital in June 1918 she conceded, 'Her arrangements are first rate, and her little Unit is quite beautiful in every respect, the colours in the different huts being very attractive and quite different from anything else I have ever seen in France.'

In June 1916 Millicent was Mentioned in Despatches; she was also awarded the British and Belgian Royal Red Cross, and the French *Croix de Guerre*. A financial report on 31 January 1919 reveals that during the war 5,914 (predominantly British) officers and men were treated as in-patients by her unit; unknown numbers were temporary patients. Millicent was, and remains, a controversial figure, but whatever the controversies surrounding such units her patients were grateful for the care they received. In his undated letter, former patient Stanley Woollett unfavourably compared his current accommodation in Lewisham Military Hospital to Millicent's. Hers was a 'place of home-like happiness, of light and flowers'.

Many patients felt that she gave them 'hope... something [*they*] longed for'. Millicent also attempted to provide practical help for the future. The first post-war edition of *The Spectator* (16 November 1918) recorded how £600 of the Unit's remaining funds were being invested to create a Benevolent Fund for former patients and staff. With hard times looming, they would have continued reason to be grateful to her.

'Good lady go home and sit still'

Another woman who was also endeavouring to get to the Front was the 50-year-old widely respected Scottish suffragist, doctor and surgeon Elsie

Inglis. She offered the Army her professional services. The response from the War Office representative in Edinburgh was unequivocal, 'Dear lady, go home and sit still.'

Undaunted, if unsurprised, Elsie simply suggested to a Scottish suffragist meeting that they should propose a medical unit to Britain's Allies, equipped and staffed exclusively by women, to be known as the Scottish Women's Hospital Units (SWH). This proposal shaped the rest of her life: as public speaker, fundraiser, surgeon on Active Service overseas, as well as Commandant of several hundred women whose professional backgrounds and skills varied enormously, but who were united in their belief in women's abilities to get things done. Of these female doctors, nurses, administrators and drivers from across the English-speaking world, some were fearless, others showed their fear; some became shell-shocked, and a number died as a result of their service. They got on each other's nerves and developed personal antagonisms and vendettas but also life-long friendships and, occasionally, lesbian relationships. Like their Commandant, some adhered to class hierarchy, others were more egalitarian; some were flirtatious, others, like Elsie herself, were prudes. As an added bonus, many were copious letter-writers, diarists, and autobiographers. In these documents they reveal their hopes, fears and frustrations, as well as the day-to-day humour and horror of their lives, leaving a magnificent picture of a unique movement in women's history.

Although SWH Units served on both the Western and Eastern Fronts, greatest physical and emotional demands were placed on those on the frequently forgotten Eastern Fronts, where female ambulance drivers set off across shell-cratered terrain in Serbia to bring in the wounded; the rank and file women, whatever their supposed role, nursed horrific casualties. The doctors performed intricate surgery and the upper-class young ladies made soup with untreated water from the Danube; apparently this made a lovely-looking rich brown broth, although no mention is made about its taste. They cleaned out cess-pits and dealt with decaying amputated limbs found 'amongst the rubbish' where they had been lying for months. Fulsomely and undoubtedly justifiably praised by the *BJN*, Inglis also reported how 'untrained British orderlies cleaned, and cleaned, and cleaned. That is a Briton's job all over the world.' Fortunately the young women had taken to it 'like ducks to water'.

Over the years, many SWH commented, at times wryly, on Inglis' ability to get her volunteers to rise to hitherto unimaginable heights. The very few stragglers were simply goaded into action by being reminded, 'it is war-time'. Those who achieved the unachievable received her highest accolade, 'Dear girl, I knew you could do it.' Engineer-cum-orderly Jan Gordon and his wife Cora, already in Serbia when the SWH Units began arriving, simply remembered that they 'disinfected typhus-riddled Serbia till it reeked of formaldehyde'. When not disinfecting or caring for the wounded, the sick and the dying, the SWH contrived ways both to get to the trenches and to dances with Serb or Russian officers who Cook Ishobel Ross considered, 'Such splendid men, quite the finest that have passed yet! They are so huge and handsome.'

Moments of relaxation were few and when duty required, the women travelled across hundreds of miles of war-torn country in trains crowded with troops and desperate peasantry; they faced the continuous possibility of enemy fire and, when caught on the wrong side of the line, were, contrary to the Geneva Convention which grants neutral status to medical personnel, imprisoned. The *BJN* was not alone in expressing outrage that 32 women of one of the SWH Units were held in Kevavara, Hungary, as 'common military prisoners of war'. However, fluent German-speaker Dr Alice Hutchison (a Scottish 40-year-old medical missionary doctor's daughter and veteran of medical service in the Balkan Wars, affectionately nicknamed 'the little General'), gleefully outmanoeuvred their gaolers.

With most of their luggage and military supplies confiscated, one precious possession was smuggled into captivity with them – the Union flag. This became their talisman. They dreamed of waving it 'tauntingly in our former captors' faces' when released; the word 'if' did not figure in their vocabulary. In the meantime, it was worn, 'flauntingly'. Considered 'diminutive and pretty with flaming red-gold hair and always gaily and fashionably dressed', Alice used her fashion sense in an unusual way. In order to protect the flag, she 'did a little superficial undressing, wrapped [*it*] proudly round her body and re-dressed'. On multiple occasions she was summoned to the Polizei's office for long and frequently acrimonious interviews, ever bewailing the fact that although she herself knew it inside out, 'The Austrians do not seem ever to have heard of the Geneva Convention.' She endeavoured to remedy this lacuna whilst taking 'great joy in the knowledge that the broad blue and red stripes... stood out beautifully under the thin muslin blouse I wore at the time.' The *BJN* reminded readers that this was 'a lesson in patriotism and resourcefulness of which her compatriots may well be proud.'

Resourcefulness as well as patriotism was required. With an innate understanding of both physical and mental well-being, Alice preferred those under her command to actively fill their long hours of captivity rather than dwell upon their fate and its possible outcome. Her compulsory morning German lesson was followed by honing 'forgotten prowess at rounders and other games in the back [*exercise*] yard.' The scanty lunch of 'soup from a bucket' was followed by a daily walk, with two Austrian guards. These soldiers proved inept. Despite the women only walking 'about six or eight miles', the guards threatened to mutiny. They claimed that far from walking, the women 'flew like geese over the mud'. This daily hike over, personal hygiene followed: 'An "arras" (we believe in keeping up a certain glamour) is erected near the stove and from five o'clock onwards we wash in rotation. The washing-down process is complicated by the fact that one must at the same time feed the fire and see to it that a saucepan full of water is at boiling-point for the next member.' Apparently the local townsmen were so impressed by the women's cleanliness they 'expressed a desire for English wives. Needless to say the unit regards the latter point otherwise.' Charades, followed by singing the National Anthem *sotto voce,* which 'cheered us up wonderfully', ended the day. Finally the women retired for the night on, in *BJN*'s words, 'straw… no beds or bedding… The cubic space of their sleeping room for twenty-two [*sic*] women was equivalent to that of a workroom for nine people under the British factory laws.' Doubtless they slept the sleep of the exhausted.

Eventually, with freedom promised, Alice determined to smuggle out not only the precious flag, but also her diary, which she knew would, if detected, compromise their chances of repatriation. She sewed the loose pages 'into a dilapidated-looking feather cushion.' Using her small stature to her advantage, the 'little General' stood on the cushion, which she subsequently stuffed into her kit-bag. Back in England, Alice hoped that the information she was able to pass on to the military authorities about Kevavara might one day lead to its successful bombing by the Allies. This she felt would be a suitable revenge for their captors' disrespect of the Geneva Convention which, as she frequently reminded them, 'forbids the making prisoners of hospital *personnel*'.

This was but one of the many SWH Units which served on multiple fronts; their leaders were invariably resourceful and inspiring. None more so than Dr Inglis herself; her boundless belief in the ability of British womanhood to perform the impossible was contagious, as new recruit Elsie Butler discovered in 1917. Despite the interviewing committee's initial scepticism about the value of her Cambridge education, Russian-speaking Elsie was engaged as an orderly. Her task was to escort four recruits from Britain to Odessa in the south of Russia. Writing in 1951 she remembered the Committee's implication that to 'fail [*Dr Inglis*] in the slightest particular was tantamount to treason'. The quintet set off into revolutionary Russia. Apparently three of Elsie's four charges were 'no-hopers'; the first was 'lanky, sandy-haired and limp, the second was almost a nymphomaniac and asked nothing better than to be raped; and the third was incompetent, raddled and rouged.'

On arrival in Petrograd, the Russian Red Cross Commissioner tried to prevent them leaving for Odessa on the one (troop) train a week, convinced they, 'should certainly be raped, and probably murdered, [*so they must*] go straight back home.' However, once reminded of the renowned Inglis wrath should he prevent the women's arrival, the official 'crumpled up, being obviously far more frightened of what Dr Inglis would say to him than of anything the Russians could do to us.' Despite, 'Rape and murder being far from their [*soldiers'*] thoughts' the journey proved gruelling, 'practically in a coma and crawling with lice... we were an integral part of the Russian army when days later the train steamed into Odessa.'

Elsie relished her service and the nurses' camaraderie. But as the turmoil of the Russian Revolution closed in, the War Office officials attempted to recall the Unit. Remembering that they had no jurisdiction over Inglis, they decided to ask her 'nicely' to return. Inglis, so patronisingly dismissed in 1914, now fired her final shot at the British War Office, this time to influence the fate of her beloved Serbian Army, which by late 1917 was being massacred on the Russian Front. She opened negotiations with the War Office: the Russia Unit would return, but only if the Serbs were also evacuated and moved from the Russian to the Serb Front.

The War Office pulled every available diplomatic and military string. In late October 1917, the Unit began a race of well over a thousand miles against time, the weather, and a now imploding Russia, arriving at Archangel on 9 November 1917, days before ice closed the port. In the wake of the Revolution, Trotsky and the Bolsheviks had declared a national general strike and all work of any kind was prohibited; Elsie

Butler had been detailed to ensure that their 40 tons of donated equipment were safely loaded aboard their ship. She reported the strike to Inglis, who riposted, 'You must either get the equipment on board before we sail, or stay behind to guard it. Your duty is to the equipment.'

Caught, as she herself expressed it, 'between the irresistible force of Inglis' will and the immovable obstacle of a grand national strike,' Butler decided that it would be easier to break the strike than change her Chief's mind. She succeeded ('Dear girl, I knew you could do it') and remarked laconically that she had also held up the Russian Revolution for a day in the process.

Now in the last stages of terminal cancer which she had suspected in 1914, Inglis had the rigours of a journey over the Arctic Ocean to face. Four days after leaving Archangel, the women's transport became separated from their convoy, their Captain unable to pinpoint their whereabouts to within 100 miles. One woman recorded in her diary, 'I nearly went mad in the night. I am not a coward really, but this continual strain is terrible.' Another, however, felt more confident, secure in the knowledge that amongst their number was a *Titanic* survivor; she had surely proven she was not marked out for a watery grave.

The women had been away on the Eastern Front for nearly two years. They had been close to or in the firing line, and withstood the horrors of retreat and advance. They had covered hundreds of miles in troop trains, ox carts, rickety ambulances, and on foot. They had tended mutilated bodies, nursed the dying and buried the dead – including their own, and had just travelled through a country torn apart by revolution. Many believed it was only Inglis' extraordinary will power which brought them safely through the fury of Arctic storms and the ever-present danger of submarines. The ship's captain earned a British decoration for his achievement in bringing them home – the women went undecorated.

On 25 November 1917, the Scottish Women of the Russia Unit sailed up the Tyne, only a handful of them aware that Inglis was dying. Dressed and wearing her many Russian and Serb decorations, including the Order of the White Eagle of Serbia, Serbia's highest military honour, never previously awarded to a woman, Dr Elsie Inglis stood on deck to bid farewell to the 13,000 Serb soldiers who would be drafted into the remnants of the First Serb Army. They would fight their way back to their homeland, their breakthrough hastening the collapse of Bulgaria, one of the key factors in persuading the German High Command to sue for peace. Barely 24 hours later, she was dead.

Queen Mary sent her condolences to Inglis' sister, dignitaries wrote to *The Times*, journalists rushed to pen obituaries, leading articles, and assessments of her life, SWH staff dedicated their published memoirs to 'our beloved leader'. *The Lancet* devoted nearly a page to her obituary; the Russians and Serbs posthumously bestowed still more awards, the *Daily Sketch* thundered, 'Why not VCs for women?' A service at St Margaret's, Westminster, conducted by the Bishop of Oxford and attended by distinguished representatives of the Allied governments, the Red Cross Societies, and women's societies preceded her lying in state in St Giles' Cathedral, Edinburgh. Royalty was represented at her military funeral, as well as arguably the mourner who would have given her the most satisfaction: the representative from a War Office which, even as late as 1916, had continued to reject her and other British women's offers of service. The women lining the streets jostled for a last view of the doctor who had treated so many of them. Newspaper photographers fought to gain the best shots as the small coffin, placed on a gun carriage and covered by the Union flag, began its final journey to the Deane Cemetery, burial ground of Scotland's heroes.

Millicent Sutherland, Muriel Stobart, Drs Alice Hutchison and Elsie Inglis, and the leaders of the many wartime volunteer units, demonstrated courage and endurance and unflagging beliefs in women's capabilities. Their charismatic leadership qualities most comprehensively defied the stricture that in wartime women should 'go home and sit still'.

'There were spies everywhere':
Spying Women

Women attached to itinerant hospital units and who were temporarily behind enemy lines were, like Alice Hutchison, eager to share information with the British authorities. Their loyalty to the cause was self-evident, and the intelligence they provided welcomed. There were other women, some high-born, others less socially privileged, who lived behind the lines and who spied for the Allies. They epitomised 'good' womanhood; if caught by the enemy they were constructed as heroic martyrs. But there were also women whose loyalty was deemed questionable. With hard news about the war in short supply and heavily censored, spy stories were sensationalised. Those spying against the Allies epitomised all that was evil – and feared – about women. Whilst many 'good' and 'bad' spies have disappeared from the record, the stories of a few can be pieced together, telling us something about authorities' attitudes towards such women and their own, frequently defiant, attitudes towards authority.

In 1914, a significant number of foreign-born nationals resided in Britain; similarly, many Britons lived in European countries. Before the outbreak of hostilities, a secret register carrying the names of some 28,380 aliens (of whom under half were German or Austrian) had been compiled. As war clouds gathered, many hastened to return to their native lands. On 1 August 1914 middle-aged Princess Marie de Croy, daughter and sister of diplomats at the Belgian Embassy in London, rushed home (near Mons, on the Franco-Belgian border) to rejoin her husband. She noticed that, 'the trains were full of Germans leaving for home.' Others, such as the countless German governesses and domestic servants working in England, remained, either through choice or because that was where their livelihood lay. Many would be trapped within a narrow area, the Alien Restrictions Act severely restricting the freedom of movement of non-British citizens.

A 1914 issue of *Punch* captures the public fears directed towards these predominantly middle-aged women; a worried child who is deeply attached to her German governess, asks in an audible whisper 'Mother MUST we kill Fraulein?' Hatred of all things German rapidly became part of the fabric of wartime life, further fuelled by the pre-war popularity of novels such as *The Riddle of the Sands*, which fictionalised a dastardly German plan to invade Britain across the North Sea. Even children's toys were not exempt. One seven-year old remembered how, the day War was declared, her grandmother confiscated 'all our toys that were made in Germany, amongst them a camel of which I was very fond'.

Xenophobic flames were fanned by constructing foreigners as spies. According to Reverend Andrew Clark's 31 August 1914 diary entry, attendees at a meeting at Little Waltham Hall in Essex learned that: 'a most incumbent duty on citizens and police is that of watching for spies.' Locals were quick to comply; three weeks later, an elderly lace seller from nearby Great Waltham spent the night in custody, her crime: to speak with a 'strong German accent'.

Citizens beyond the boundaries of Essex were also on spy-duty. MI5's wartime offices received 300 reports a day of alleged spying. Although few were deemed worthy of investigation, they demonstrate the hatred directed towards those whose allegiance could be doubted. Women were particularly vulnerable in this poisoned atmosphere. The fact that a number of the reported spies were female reinforced the public's belief that espionage is an occupation which suits women.

Many spy stories are anecdotal and largely unconfirmed, but one name has entered the historiography of the First World War: that of Dutch national Margaretha Zelle Macleod, better known to the world as Mata Hari. She epitomises the spy-harlot, allegedly using her *horizontale* role to endanger France. Many who followed the sensational trial would have agreed with Prosecuting Attorney Lieutenant Mornet's summing up: 'This is perhaps the greatest woman spy of the century.' Little matter that the charges of espionage against her appeared flimsy, the possibility that she may have been guilty was sufficient in the eyes of the world to prove that she was guilty and brave were her few friends who tried to track down the truth about her execution and discredit the rumours. Long after her October 1917 death, Mata Hari's case continued to arouse strong feelings and controversy still surrounds it.

There appeared to be some evidence against her. She had indeed been recruited by the Germans, given a codename, H21, and paid 21,000 francs but, having pocketed the German bounty, there is no conclusive proof of her ever doing any spying. In a complicated game of claim and counter-claim, a case was built against her. That she had a 21-year-old Russian lover, a captain in the Russian Imperial Army serving in the Champagne area, appeared to place France at increased risk from her activities.

Defended by a former lover, a septuagenarian lawyer, Mata Hari's case was handled in a way that made a mockery of French justice. In July 1917, the six-man jury found her guilty and the death sentence was a relief to the British and the French authorities. Believing until the end that, as a Dutch citizen, she would be reprieved, the former exotic dancer whose hallmark costume had been multi-coloured veils, glittering bracelets and a brass breast plate, donned a sober dress, a dark tricorne hat and, with a coat slung casually over her shoulders, and looked her 12 executioners in the eye at the Chateau de Vincennes. Refusing the proffered blindfold, she stared defiantly at the firing-party. As the commanding Sergeant-Major put it, 'this lady knew how to die'.

The story spread. A Canadian newspaper accused her of divulging secrets about tanks, and *The Times* that she passed on 'important

Author's daughters wearing 1918 munitions worker and WAAC uniforms, photographed at Woolwich Arsenal, February 2014. (*Munitions uniform, author's collection. WAAC uniform lent by Richard Knight. Photo: Ivan Newman*)

WOMEN'S CALL to WOMEN

WOMEN'S DAY, 1917

Events such as these encouraged women to 'Do Their Bit' for the war effort. (*Author's private collection.*)

Munitions workers rightly saw themselves as contributing to the war effort. 'On War Service badges', equating to the regimental cap badge worn by soldiers, made their contribution visible. Postcards such as this, with the badge prominently displayed, were widely sent. (*Author's private collection.*)

DOING HER BIT

THE 'SHELL' GIRL.

Autograph books were widely owned across the social classes. This drawing of a 'Shell Girl' was sketched by a fellow munitions worker in this autograph book. (*Author's private collection.*)

Postcards from across the combatant nations had similar themes. Ones linking the male sphere of war with the feminine Home Front were very common. (*Author's private collection.*)

Children as well as adults knitted extensively. A ball of Amy Tyreman's wool and her knitting needles have been preserved at Brodsworth Hall and were on display to visitors in June 2013. (*Photograph Brodsworth Hall.*)

Women's Land Army workers were issued with certificates, signed by Lord Selbourne; these were an attempt to make those serving in the Land Army proud of their National Service. (*Author's private collection.*)

This water colour of a Women's Land Army worker shows her daringly wearing the breeches which caused such a furore. (*Author's private collection.*)

Statue of Gabrielle Petit in Place St Jean, Brussels. (*Photograph Clare Russell.*)

WAACs performed numerous roles both at home and overseas; caring for cemeteries and baking were just two of them. (*Author's private collection.*)

Like the boys, members of the WAAC were keen to have a photographic souvenir of their service. (*Author's private collection.*)

Very unusually, two sisters share a CWGC grave in Willingham, Cambridgeshire. Dorothy Willis is probably the only British munitions worker to have a CWGC headstone. (*Photograph Ivan Newman.*)

Known as the 'Dead Man (or Woman's) Penny' due to its size, these were issued to families of the bereaved confirming that 'He [or she] died for Freedom and Honour'. The winning design of the widely subscribed competition (closing date December 1917) was submitted by Mr E Carter Preston (1894-1965) from Liverpool. (*Author's private collection.*)

A Red Cross nurse's military funeral. Nurses' (and all servicewomen's) deaths often caused considerable distress, even outrage, at home and at the front. Funerals were conducted with military honours. (*Author's private collection, almost certainly published by the* Daily Mail.)

Graves of three WAACs killed in bombing raids on 30 May 1918. They were the first servicewomen (as opposed to nurses) to be killed as a direct result of enemy action. They, and their comrades, are buried in Abbeville Extension Cemetery. (*Photograph Ivan Newman.*)

Many organisations donated ambulances to the Red Cross and the voluntary organisations. Some bore the name of the donor on their side. The SWH were adept fundraisers and expert at ambulance maintenance. (*From The War Illustrated.*)

As food shortages increased, the Government issued 'Hard Times' recipe booklets suggesting ways of using every last crumb of food. (*Author's private collection.*)

Tommy Atkins was renowned for improvising, particularly German-found equipment. WAACs were equally adept. Here they are using German helmets as baskets. (*Author's private collection.*)

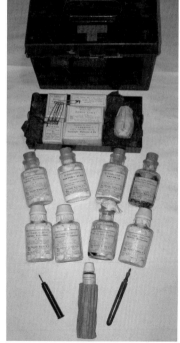

Box of drugs used by a volunteer nurse in a private hospital. This was found in a skip following a house clearance in the 1990s. There was no information about the original owner. (*Author's private collection.*)

WAAC postcard Sent for Christmas 1918 The War was over but many WAACS and nurses were still in France. (*Author's private collection.*)

Face of postcard sent in 1927 by Flora Sandes, the only British woman to have borne arms, to a friend who nursed with her in Serbia before Flora joined the Serbian Army. (*Author's private collection.*)

Reverse of postcard. Flora never really found her way back to Civvy Street. "Best of luck from Yurie [*Flora's husband*] & myself for the New Year. These beasts are hastening to a vodka party, hope you will do likewise & also ourselves. When are you coming to Paris? Love from Sandy & Yurie"

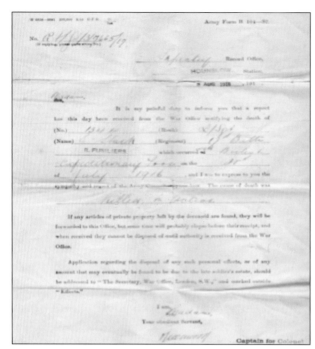

News dreaded across the land often arrived in an impersonal form. (*Author's private collection.*)

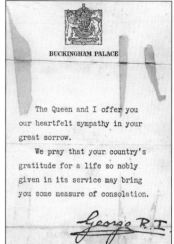

BUCKINGHAM PALACE

The Queen and I offer you our heartfelt sympathy in your great sorrow.

We pray that your country's gratitude for a life so nobly given in its service may bring you some measure of consolation.

George R.I

Many of the bereaved received an official condolence letter sent on behalf of their Majesties. For some it provided comfort that the monarch empathised with them in their grief. Others saw this (and the Dead Man's Penny) as poor compensation for a lost loved one. (*Author's private collection.*)

Memorial at Place Ceres, Reims, France to all nurses who served in France. The inscription pays tribute to the nurses who came from the 'four corners of the world' to succour the French wounded. (*Photograph Ivan Newman.*)

Statues at Roggevelde German Military Cemetery, Belgium, sculpted by the renowned German artist, Kathe Kollwitz for her son Peter, killed in action in October 1914. The huddled figures represent the totality of parental grief and guilt. (*Photograph Ivan Newman.*)

information', but it provides no further details other than saying she was on the German Army's 'spy-roll'. The day after her execution, *War Illustrated* asserted that she had 'proved to be one of Germany's most skilful spies'; it breathes a sigh of relief that 'on going to France her true character was discovered.' Thirty years later, one of the prosecutors admitted that Mata Hari's execution was a miscarriage of justice, 'there wasn't enough evidence to flog a cat'. Meanwhile, according to the movie site IMDB.com, 'her espionage activities caused the deaths of 50,000 Allied soldiers'. Her biographer Julie Wheelwright believes Mata Hari's real crime was to have 'mimed Salome, the powerful but deadly female, an enduring nightmare of female betrayal'.

Whilst Mata Hari's October 1917 execution continues to arouse passions, that of Regina Diane, the stage-name of a 'Swiss singer' (again, a citizen of a neutral state), who was executed in Marseilles in January 1918, is a forgotten footnote to history. One can only wonder if the evidence against her was as flimsy as that against Mata Hari. Perhaps it was Regina Diane's supposed activities that lay behind the comment in Nursing Sister Burgess's diary entry from Marseilles, 'the town is full of spies'; sisters were only allowed out in 'twos or threes during the day or in fours or sixes at night'. Today, both the French and the Swiss authorities seem unable to shed any light on the story. Even a visit to the French National Archives drew a blank. It is acknowledged that she existed and was executed, but the relevant documents are tantalisingly elusive.

Eighteen months before Mata Hari's execution, in the late evening hours of 31 March 1916, Gabrielle Petit, a young Belgian shop assistant, completed the embroidery she had been working on, laid aside the letters she had written and lay down to sleep in her prison cell. Indicted on a charge of espionage, she was neither a socialite nor a promiscuous *horizontale* but had simply been caught up in the war and taken the conscious decision to spy for the British, a role she initially found repugnant.

Contemporary diaries, testimonies and newspapers rarely associated espionage with respectable womanhood, and reports of female spies' activities stressed their *demi-monde* occupations. In *Médécins de la Grande Guerre,* P. Loodts argues that it was the brutality of the German Occupation and the sufferings of her 'violated' homeland which swayed Gabrielle, who became one of the most valuable agents behind enemy lines. Yet, even in her final hours, she felt the need to justify her actions.

Her farewell letter to her sister Hélène stressed that her association with British Intelligence was, 'the greatest possible devotion to the Mother Country, the pinnacle of what a woman who is also a soldier's fiancée can do.'

Gabrielle's unintentional involvement with espionage began in the earliest days. Her quick wits and her skill in helping young Belgian men, among them her fiancé Maurice, to cross the River Yser to join up with the Belgian Army, and her subsequent reporting on German troop and train movements through Belgium, caught the attention of the British authorities. After intelligence training in London, in July 1915, she returned to Brussels, where she created her own cell and network and, using a number of false identities, supplied the British with vital information on trains, troop movements and armaments. The British authorities saw her as one of their most reliable agents behind enemy lines.

With aerial reconnaissance in its infancy, human eyes were the most effective providers of information; a network of informers was necessary. Despite the complexity of the information required, Gabrielle's reports were invariably accurate and for a while she was adept at moving around undetected by the watchful Germans.

Frightened, but nevertheless refusing to be cowed by the dangers she faced, Gabrielle claimed that her death in service, would be 'like a soldier's'. However, the German occupiers became increasingly suspicious and despite successfully evading capture on one occasion, her luck gave out on 20 January 1916. Betrayed by a Dutchman working for the Germans, she admitted to her sister Hélène that she had let her guard down. Multiple interrogations followed her arrest, and she seized every opportunity to stress her violent hatred of the occupiers ('*tant est violente la haine que j'ai pour votre race!*'). Hélène's reported conversations with Gabrielle show a woman who was so outraged by the Germans' behaviour towards her compatriots that she would stop at nothing to hasten their defeat.

Unsurprisingly Gabrielle's words and attitude did little to endear her to her captors and sentence of 'Death by Firing Squad' was passed, which, according to Hélène, she accepted with 'impressive sangfroid', although she may have clung to the hope that it might be commuted to life imprisonment, as it had been for several other Belgian and French women found guilty of spying.

DEFIANT TO THE END

On 1 April 1916, dressed in white, with pink ribbons in her hair (stressing her purity and her femininity), and rejecting the steadying arm of a German soldier, Gabrielle approached the stake. Refusing the proffered blindfold, she told her assembled executioners, 'I do not need your help. You will see that a young Belgian woman knows how to die.' (*'Je n'ai pas besoin de votre aide. Vous allez voir comment une jeune fille belge sait mourir.'*) Seconds later, in a heap of 'white petticoats', she lay dead. Rumour has it two of the firing squad refused to shoot and were instantly executed themselves.

On 27 March 1919, her body was exhumed. Queen Elisabeth of the Belgians and Prime Minister Delacroix attended an elaborate funeral; Gabrielle Petit was posthumously awarded the *Croix de l'Ordre de Léopold*. Schoolchildren were subsequently issued with postcards quoting her last words (also inscribed on the statue) encouraging them to emulate her patriotism. The Belgian contributor to the post-war *Feminae Patriae Defensor* (1934) considered it somewhat surprising, although reassuring, that 'even those from the humblest and most uneducated classes' could experience such fervid love of their country. Gabrielle's statue at Place Saint-Jean in Brussels is not the representation of a martyred victim but of a defiant 'ordinary' woman who, cognisant of the risks she was taking, accepted that her own life, when weighed against Belgium's cause, counted for little.

Some women were sole agents. Others used extensive networks of family and trusted friends. They frequently acted as couriers and set up letter-boxes, assisted escaping servicemen, and reported on German activities, often connected with troop and ammunition transportation. One such family were the Grandprez from the East Belgian Ardennes. Although several family members were involved, newspapers focused on the execution of middle-aged Elise, whilst her brother and the family friend who died with her were seen as almost bit players. The story of their end is simply told. Betrayed in January 1917 by a Dutch-born naturalised Belgian, the Grandprez and their friend André Grégoire were arrested and tried. André, Elise and Constant Grandprez were condemned to death, the others to life imprisonment. Like Gabrielle Petit, Elise was determined to demonstrate that a Belgian woman remained visibly patriotic to the end. Nuns from a nearby convent visited her daily, bringing her black, red, and yellow hair ribbons on alternate days. On 8 May, with head held high she walked to the firing range. Withdrawing three tiny

Belgian flags from the neckline of her dress, she handed one each to the men sharing her fate. Bidding them to 'have courage', she held the third flag in her own hand. Apparently she died with the words, '*Vive la Belgique*' on her lips.

Before the war, Belgian Martha Cnockaert was a second-year medical student at the University of Ghent; an accomplished linguist, she spoke Flemish, French, German and English. Her world was torn asunder on 2 August 1914, when her comfortable home near Westroosebeke was razed to the ground by a 'Grey Wave' of German soldiery. Barely escaping with their lives, she and her well to-do parents found themselves in Roulers [*Roeslare*] near the German Front Line at Dixmuide; to survive, her family ran a café frequented by German troops, three of whom were billeted on them. Many affluent Belgians now found themselves working in lowly positions, often acting as servants and washerwomen for the German soldiers. Whilst women in free countries knitted socks for their soldiers, Belgian women were forced to wash those belonging to the enemy. Due to her medical training, Martha began nursing at the Roulers (German) Military Hospital. There were occasions, when, like Edith Cavell and Marie de Croy, she facilitated the escape of Allied soldiers who had been brought in as patients, generally paying people to help and funding this out of her own pocket. She was cynical about how humankind would undertake for money what they would not undertake out of patriotism.

Martha knew and accepted the risk that if caught she would face the death penalty. As a patriot, she loathed the humiliation Germany was inflicting upon her homeland; as a humanitarian she empathised with the sufferings of her German patients; as a human being she saw that not all soldiers were evil; her loyalties were dividing. Her documented feelings towards individual soldiers assist our understanding of the actions of those who post-war were branded as *collaboratrices*. Continuing to hate a person with whom one has daily interactions can be hard. These women's experiences were in contrast to those of the majority of British women who had no contact with German individuals and saw 'the Hun' as uniformly evil.

Martha's initial reaction to the family friend who recruited her as a spy was 'horror'. Like Gabrielle Petit, she 'knew that spies existed... had regarded them as things inhuman and far removed from my own sphere.' Martha's mother, who would live to regret her defiant words, was more enthusiastic, 'I give her willingly and proudly, just as I have given my sons.' Martha's acquiescence only occurred after considerable soul-searching, mental anguish and fear for her life, 'Everyone was suspected by the Germans of being a spy... Spy mania was soon fanned into a flame.' If even the innocent were suspect and were not infrequently 'shot out of hand', what fate would befall a woman who had assumed the role?

Seemingly rare in spy literature, Martha came to acknowledge that her activities had humanitarian consequences. After the Allied bombing of Roulers Station, 'It was I who was responsible for the hellish scene that was now being enacted... I threw myself on my bed... and wept as though my heart was breaking.' She describes in unflinching detail how her actions had killed friend and foe alike. 'I wandered along an endless street of smoking ruins where the way was strewn with mangled corpses whose glassy eyeballs watched me accusingly.' Perhaps, unlike soldiers who have the sense of a collective, ordered action to shield behind, she recognises her own culpability in the deaths of the unknown soldiers and also 'my little German officer friend of the Railway Transport', who had unwittingly divulged secret information and, because of her transmission to the British, left behind two young orphaned daughters in Hanover. However much she might tell herself, 'I was serving my country,' there are times when the mantra fails to exonerate her.

The German doctors having no reason to suspect her of complicity in the recent raid, her espionage and medical work continued in parallel, indeed 'His Royal Highness the King of Wurtemburg has graciously indicated that you have been awarded the Iron Cross for fine work with this hospital.' This stemmed primarily from her 'services in the field' following the latest fiendish development in warfare: the first gas attack on 22 April 1915. Working near Langemark, in a field hospital 'packed with French soldiers, beating and fighting the air for breath... their faces contorted out of all human shape,' she now knew what the strange-shaped cylindrical objects she had seen being stock-piled at Roulers (and had reported to the British) were for – and that the Germans had no antidote to the poison they had unleashed.

Martha's role as a nurse gave her greater freedom of movement than was accorded to most Belgians who were 'under the jurisdiction of the German Military Code'. Curfews were strictly enforced, but being able to go abroad at night allowed her to undertake clandestine, illegal activities. Her Iron Cross increased the Germans' trust in her and when a

Colonel invited her to Brussels 'to see the opera, eat decent food', she accepted, less for gastronomic purposes than because a trip to Brussels might provide her with certain information requested by her British spymasters. Aware that more would be required of her than pleasant company, and that she might not be able to hold the Herr Colonel at arm's length, she answers her own question, 'Why had I done it? For the sake of ravished Belgium.' She tried to convince herself that being 'ravished' would simply equate her fate with her Motherland's. However, when the Colonel made plain the payment expected for his hospitality, she successfully escaped. In Brussels, she saw how her countrywomen were 'caught in a holocaust [of degradation] over which they had no control.' She realised that many Belgian women faced a stark choice: become what is now euphemistically referred to as a 'comfort woman', or starve.

Back in Roulers, the net began closing round Martha. Her reluctance to become a German agent, as one of the officers billeted upon her family had proposed, may have aroused suspicion. Forgetting the warning given to her in her earliest days, 'If you are caught, it will probably be your own fault,' she fell into the trap set for her and was arrested and threatened with sexual assault by her interrogator, 'Are you going to tell me – or shall I have to resort to – other measures?' She 'refused to say a word' which might implicate others in her network. Resisting all forms of coercion (there is no hint that she was raped, unless this has been omitted from her 1932 autobiography), she was brought to trial, agreeing in her heart with the wardress who taunts her, 'There is but one fate for a spy!' Her refusal to speak anything but Flemish, her mother tongue, throughout the trial was a comforting act of defiance against her captors, who knew she spoke fluent German. The death sentence having been called for and passed, the Oberatz of Roulers Military Hospital, Dr Herbert Stolz, spoke in her defence, 'The accused may have been acting as a spy in the interests of her country... But knowing the accused as I do know her, I believe that she worked as a nurse purely in the interests of humanity.'

Stolz brought to the Court's attention the Iron Cross citation: Martha had 'risked her life in the field'. Her sentence was commuted to 'Life Imprisonment' in Ghent. 'So I began an unending regime without soul or mercy but buoyed up with the burning conviction that deliverance would come.' The Oberatz's occasional visits and his conviction that the war had to end soon, provided hope even as her health deteriorated. In

November 1918, two years after her arrest, weakened almost beyond recognition, 'out we streamed, half-crazed men and women' into the arms of the 'British advance guard.'

In due course, Martha's 'demobilisation papers and her prison pay arrived from the British Intelligence Commission', along with the news of being Mentioned in Sir Douglas Haig's 8 November 1918 Despatches. In 1919 the British Secretary of State for War, Winston Churchill, commended her 'gallant and distinguished service in the field'. However, the British authorities refused to meet her claim for reimbursement of expenses entailed in moving British soldiers back to their own lines. Yet, even in her pride at her decorations, including the French and the Belgian *Legions d'Honneur*, and her joy that once again Belgium was a free nation, ambiguity remained: 'I shall always remember some of those nobler emissaries, men of all ranks, who came with the Grey Wave.'

With a second war looming, German interest in Martha Cnockaert (now McKenna) was rekindled. Perhaps the 1933 film about her and her publication of spy novels had reminded them of her actions. Living in Manchester with her English husband during the Second World War, she was listed in 'The Black Book' of prominent subjects who were to be arrested following the anticipated successful Nazi invasion of Britain. When this second war ended, she returned to her native Westroosebeke, where she died in 1966, a largely forgotten, four times decorated, reluctant agent who 'took the only course open to me' – both as nurse and as spy.

'We could and did "do it"'

Social privilege enabled aristocratic women to find ways of getting to the Front, but others were equally keen to serve. Refusing to accept that in wartime, irrespective of her skills, training and expertise, a 'Dear lady [*should*] go home and sit still', professional women defiantly left their native shores and went where need outweighed the prejudice which deprived Britain's armed services of some of the finest medical care, professional skills and technology available. Frequently, the Allied medical services which welcomed these independent units, staffed and funded by women, were so woefully inadequate that often the best that could be offered to the wounded was a thin straw mattress shared between three men, where the dying often lay with the just-living.

Whilst women with social position or professional medical skills were aware of the part that they could play in wartime, those trapped behind enemy lines, irrespective of class or expertise, found themselves adopting hitherto unimaginable roles.

Precisely how many women were loosely involved in spying and undercover work is impossible to calculate. Some, such as Dr Alice Hutchison, simply kept their eyes and ears open and passed on information which they hoped might be useful. A number of officially recruited spies paid with their lives for their espionage activities; the lives of some were spared, their sentences commuted to life imprisonment. Not all survived the hardships of incarceration, starvation rations, and almost non-existent medical attention. Whilst the majority of agents appear to have slipped through undetected, for others, Germany's long memory endangered them next time round.

Rejected in the case of doctors and recruited in the case of spies largely because of their gender, the theatres of war in which they served and the nature of these women's war work has left the majority of them shrouded in mystery. Bravest of the brave, many rank amongst the most forgotten women of the Great European War for Civilisation.

CHAPTER 5

'We Too Wore Khaki':
Servicewomen on the Home
and War Fronts

'I was a first day volunteer,'
(Waac Ada Gummershall)

Images of young men from across the social spectrum of Great Britain and her Empire flocking to the recruiting stations on the day war was declared are seared into our collective consciousness. Women, despite the military's perception of their lack of usefulness to a nation at war, also found ways to wear a khaki uniform and contribute to the 'Great War for Civilisation'.

'Neither Fish, Flesh nor Fowl, but Thundering Good Red Herring': The First Aid Nursing Yeomanry
Lying wounded on the South African veldt during the Boer War, Sergeant Edward Baker visualised a female nurse galloping across the field on horseback and delivering him to a military dressing-station. Out of this vision, the First Aid Nursing Yeomanry, or FANY as it was soon dubbed, was born in 1907. Drilled by Edward Baker in cavalry techniques, horse-drawn ambulance driving, stretcher-bearing and first aid, the FANY soon began to attract press interest.

The February 1909 *Daily Graphic* referred to these 'aristocratic amazons-in-arms', who looked 'dashing in their scarlet' and included amongst their members 'Lady Ernestine Hunt, the eldest daughter of the Marquis of Aylesbury'. The doings of aristocrats sold newspapers and the FANY was definitely an upper/upper middle-class organisation, comprising about 100 members, each personally recommended by an existing member. They paid yearly membership fees of a guinea and were trained in first aid, horsemanship, veterinary work, signalling and camp cookery. They attended an annual camp, providing their own horses and uniforms, thereby deftly excluding less socially privileged recruits who had neither the mount nor the financial wherewithal to fund membership.

The initial rather glamorous uniform of dark blue riding skirts with a military-style scarlet tunic and cap was soon superseded by a daring button-through khaki skirt, which revealed elegant breeches for riding astride. One woman (whose service with the FANY was short-lived) ensured that her frilly white drawers were visible under her khaki skirt. A fur coat would eventually be added, as FANYs toiled through the biting winters of 1917 and 1918 driving ambulances whose windscreens had been removed to prevent possible injuries caused by flying glass.

By 1910, this first-ever officially recognised, uniformed women's service was well established and, although early members sometimes 'felt like freaks' when parading in uniform, they relished the occasional salute thrown by soldiers and military personnel. Free-spirited and with the confidence that their social status almost automatically bestowed on them, these women were generally endowed with a sense of humour and a desire to push the boundaries of Edwardian femininity. By 1912, Baker (who had elevated himself to the rank of Captain) fades from the scene; it is possible that his gender and his class lost him favour, as some FANYs considered him a social upstart.

Many FANYs were skilled drivers as well as horsewomen, and a number had won automobile races 'on' (the terminology used at the time) their fathers' or even their own vehicles. Their driving rather than their horsemanship skills would stand them in excellent stead in the years ahead. Little did these first volunteers know that under the highly individual leadership of their new Corps Commander Grace Ashley-Smith, later McDougall, this women's unit would, by the end of the War, have earned a total of 135 decorations, and medals from the British, French and Belgians and the first ever Military Medal awarded to a woman. Yet, as important to them as the decorations was their contribution to changing the British Establishment's perception of women's usefulness in war.

Although en route to South Africa when War was declared, Grace Ashley-Smith jumped ship in Gibraltar and arrived back in England in early September 1914. She was determined the FANY would play their part in the war effort overseas – the stated goal of all their peacetime training and activities. If the War Office's avowed belief was that a woman's place in wartime was strictly at home, Grace begged to differ.

With Belgium now in turmoil and both sides rapidly entrenching, there was already a desperate need for medical services to care for the huge numbers of hideously wounded casualties. To compound the misery, a typhus epidemic soon raged. Dressed in her FANY uniform, Grace arrived alone in Belgium, eager to blaze a trail which the rest of her Corps would follow. With little actual nursing experience, but an intuitive understanding of germ theory, she, like the members of the Scottish Women's Hospital Units in Serbia, set about disinfecting wards and implementing more sanitary procedures. Through hard work, ingenuity and outward calmness in face of the men's terrible injuries, she proved herself indispensable to the medical staff. Other FANYs soon joined her in a Belgian Hospital at Lamarck; all who came into contact with them were impressed.

Grace's ambition was for her Corps to serve not as nurses, but as ambulance drivers. Through a mixture of bluff, guile, and the self-confidence born of her social class, she succeeded in providing ambulance services to the Belgians, the British, and finally even to the most sceptical of all, the French – who had particular anxieties about independent women being allowed close to military personnel and institutions. The FANYs' driving skills won the heartfelt admiration of their patients, 'When the cars are full of wounded,' wrote one British officer, quoted in the 1916 FANY *Gazette*, 'no-one could be more patient, considerate and gentle than the FANY, but if the car be empty, they drive like bats out of hell.'

Although outwardly slightly glamorous, ambulance-driving brought even the most resilient FANYs close to breaking-point. Showing exemplary skill and courage, they drove their ambulances loaded with severely wounded and dying men over inhospitable terrain and in inclement weather. They frequently worked 20- or 30-hour shifts, seeing sights, smelling odours and hearing language that would have made their patrician parents faint. Having delivered their cargoes of wounded or dead soldiers to hospitals or morgues, they were also responsible for cleaning and maintaining their vehicles, ready for the next shift. One FANY wrote, 'Though the blanket hid the poor swollen figure, no blanket could hide the smell or the liquid that oozed from him. The journey to the mortuary took only a few minutes, but getting the interior of the car clean and sweet before the "lea" journey was no easy task. It all seemed such a tragic waste.'

FANYs themselves came into contact with war's most horrific weapons. One early morning in late April 1915, Betty Hutchinson and Ida Lewis were serving as cooks near Hellfire Corner on the Ypres-Menin Road. They woke to the sound of firing, and everyone 'began to cough and choke'. In a description pre-dating Wilfred Owen's poem 'Dulce et Decorum est' by two years, Betty wrote, 'Out of the queer green haze that hung over everything came an unending stream of soldiers, stumbling, staggering, gasping, all a livid green colour... It was the first gas attack.'

The FANYs offered what meagre assistance they could to the predominantly Canadian soldiers and returned to their post – to prepare breakfast. 'The men received it not a minute late, just as if no battle had been raging and we had been occupied with no unusual duties.' The British authorities, aware of the ineffectiveness of British-issued gas masks and of the superiority of the Belgian variety, asked the women to give 'details of the respirators issued by the Belgians and the chemicals they contained, whether we considered them effective at any distance from gas.' Presumably they did not divulge that they had fashioned relatively efficient gas masks for themselves – 'out of Mr Southall's hygienic towels for ladies.' Betty and Ida were decorated for their bravery in this incident, adding to the medal tally that the Corps had already begun to accumulate. This might have been the first gas attack involving FANYs, but it was neither the first nor the last time FANYs found themselves under fire.

Educated partly in French-speaking Switzerland, one FANY, Pat Beauchamp, arrived on the Western Front early in 1915 desperate to serve as an ambulance driver but aware that FANYs were deployed wherever and whenever required. Her extensive memoirs employ the rather upbeat tone that so many women, irrespective of their war work, adopted in their accounts published during and immediately after hostilities. One of Pat's first duties was to visit the Belgian trenches, bringing much-needed first aid and other donated supplies. The lorry journey and the writing begin light-heartedly, although underlying class tensions between the professional matron and Pat, the volunteer FANY, simmer. At one point, this less socially privileged professional, who had not had the opportunity to acquire fluency in a foreign language, instructed, 'You-with-your-

French go into that café and ask for the ladies' room.' A mischievous soldier directed Pat to a nearby brothel, where, 'about thirty or forty men were lined up being marshaled in one by one by a Sergeant-Major.' Gleefully, she pointed the other woman towards the required comfort stop.

Pat's laughter at her socially inferior, yet professionally superior colleague's discomfort was short-lived; turning a corner, seconds after a shell had landed, 'We climbed out hastily, taking dressings with us. The sight was one that I shall never forget. Four men had been blown to pieces on that road and it gave me an intense shock to realise that a few minutes earlier those remains had been living men walking along the road... everywhere there was blood and worse.' Having done all they could to help, their mutual antagonism now buried at least temporarily, the two women continued their journey to the Front. 'I shall never forget that trench... We squelched along a narrow strip of plank with the trenches on one side and a sort of cesspool on the other – sanitary arrangements seemed non-existent, – and I prayed that I would not slip.' Sanitary, or more precisely insanitary, arrangements would become one of the many miseries FANYs learnt to cope with.

Despite fulfilling many roles, Pat's real enthusiasm was, like most FANYs, for driving and maintaining ambulances. One fateful day she was driving a lorry in Calais. Crossing the railway lines, to her 'horror', she 'saw a train coming full speed out of the tunnel.' Unable to reverse, she was forced to drive forward in a desperate race against the speeding train. The train, caught the rear of the lorry and, 'I felt myself being hurled from the car into the air to fall and be swept along for some distance. ... Presently I was left lying in a crumpled heap on the ground... I tried to move but found it impossible.'

Her leg having been amputated, Pat was evacuated to a British hospital in Calais; she, like many other sick or wounded women, was considered an inconvenience. There was a feeling that wartime nursing should be of soldiers, not uniformed women who had infiltrated the war zone. Before a visit by King George V to the wounded soldiers who were to parade in the grounds, the hospital matron told her, 'it's quite unnecessary for you to appear, especially in that soft shoe.' She was instructed to watch from a window. The (male) Colonel of the hospital insisted that, despite the offending soft shoe, Pat parade in her uniform, 'two rows of foreign medals bedeck[ing] her khaki jacket.' Despite His Majesty expressing distress at her boasting no British medals for her actions under fire and her long and selfless service, none was ever forthcoming. Unable to return to service before the end of the war, she was one of many FANYs who returned to Active Service in World War Two.

When inspecting a group of FANYs in 1917, the Calais Surgeon-General Woodhouse had said that he did not know whether they were 'fish, flesh or fowl but you are thundering good red herring'. In reality, they were relatively young women, catapulted out of their comfortable drawing-rooms into a world turned on its head. In their dedication and their service they lived up to their motto, *Arduis Invictus*, informally translated as 'I cope' or, even in the words of one Tommy, 'First Anywhere'. Like other uniformed women's services, they proved to the War Office, and indeed the public at large, that women had a part to play in war beyond nursing, knitting and organising canteens.

The Embodiment of 'Our Ally England':
Flora Sandes, an Unconventional Soldier

Born in January 1876 into a traditional middle-class household of five boys and three girls, young Flora Sandes prayed every night that she would awaken the next day as a boy. On Sunday mornings, she would sit in her father's church in Marlesford in Suffolk, reading the memorial to Lemuel Shuldham, a Cornet in the Scots Grey killed at the Battle of Waterloo, 'Far in advance within sight of the enemy lines'. She too longed to become a soldier – if only she could.

Having completed her education at a finishing school in Geneva, where the young ladies were expected to appear every morning, 'freshly bathed and in clean linen, finger nails scrubbed and clipped short', the unladylike Flora set about acquiring skills that most of her contemporaries would have considered unfeminine. These included becoming an accurate shot, spending long hours in the saddle galloping unchaperoned across East Anglia, and consuming considerable amounts of alcohol as well as smoking heavily. Proficient in both French and German, she became a skilled shorthand typist and planned to 'type her way around the world'. After working in Cairo, she moved to the United States, where she allegedly shot a man in self-defence. Returning to England she became an accomplished driver; by 1914 she had clocked up over 70,000 miles behind the wheel and she was furious when, in 1914, the RAC banned women from Reliability Trials. She also joined an underground rifle range in London, where she was noted as being an excellent shot with a service revolver.

Unsurprisingly, the embryonic FANY appealed to Flora. On the surface her skills and personality perfectly matched the Unit's requirements. An early stretcher bearing/riding event ended in both triumph and disaster. Believing she had won the annual competition (which involved galloping across a field to rescue a 'wounded' man, dressing his wounds, placing him upon a wheeled stretcher harnessed to a horse, and then returning him to the Field Ambulance tent), to her dismay she was disqualified. In the judges' opinion, whilst she may have rescued her 'casualty', her excessive speed galloping to cross the finish line first would have turned him into a corpse before arriving at the field hospital. When the pair subsequently drowned their sorrows in a pint of light ale rather than the more genteel lemonade other women favoured, she transgressed both gender and class boundaries; the 'casualty' was a Private in the Territorials, and women of her class were not supposed to fraternise with other ranks. Her propensities to drink and to fraternise would stand her in good stead in the years ahead. Her involvement with the FANY proved short-lived: her spirit was too unconventional even for those independent women.

As well as acquiring driving, shooting and drinking skills, Flora, like countless other women in the first decade of the twentieth century, had enrolled on a Red Cross First Aid course, hoping that when the widely anticipated European War finally broke out she would at least be able to nurse soldiers, if not fight as one. In early August 1914, this wish seemed close to realisation until the Matron who interviewed her looked disdainfully at her Red Cross Nursing certificates and assured her that, as the War would only last until Christmas, 'There are plenty of trained professional nurses ready and able to handle all the wounded this war is likely to produce.' Perhaps the Matron had detected Flora's wayward spirit, and thought that she appeared unlikely to conform to the pattern of compliant Angel of Mercy that the nursing organisations sought in early volunteers.

Furious but not undeterred, Flora joined the Serb/American Red Cross Unit formed by Mabel Grouitch, the American wife of the Serbian Under-Secretary of State for Foreign Affairs. With 36 others, she left England on 12 August 1914. During their exceedingly uncomfortable journey to the Balkans, one woman lost her wallet and another (Flora's especial friend), her reputation, 'neither ever to be seen again'. Three weeks later, they alighted on Serbian soil. Flora's life was about to be transformed.

111

By December 1914, she was working in a typhus-ridden hospital in Valjevo, proving a competent nurse, anaesthetist and even surgeon as, one by one, the professional and volunteer personnel succumbed to disease. She, like the few surviving doctors and nurses, chose not to go to bed: the scant hours and days of life that remained were best not wasted asleep. Twenty-one doctors died in Valjevo in the spring of 1915 – as well as many British volunteer doctors and nurses. Despite succumbing to typhus, Flora survived and, perhaps presciently, set about improving the Serbian she had already started to learn.

Serbia's capital, Belgrade, fell in October 1915, and many volunteer units started to evacuate. However, Flora herself began edging closer to the Front, initially as a member of a Serbian Field Ambulance Unit, and finally enrolling (as a woman) in the 4th Company of the 2nd Regiment of the 1st Serbian Army. Although not the Serbian Army's only female soldier, she was the only British one. The General presiding over the enrolment ceremony warned her that if she remained with the Army she would face hard times, 'like nothing you have ever experienced'. Undeterred, and to General Vasić's delight, she confirmed her willingness to serve. Vasić told her, 'Your presence will encourage the soldiers. You represent the whole of England to them. I thank you and wish you luck.' This solitary representative of England was poised to take part not in a glorious frontline action, but in a tragic retreat over the Albanian Mountains, where survival required more than just the luck she had been wished.

Private, subsequently Corporal Sandes was not the only British woman swept up in this infamous exodus, forever remembered as the Retreat from Serbia. More than an army in retreat, this was the passing of the remnants of a whole nation into exile. Far worse even than Napoleon's infamous Retreat from Moscow, the columns comprised not only soldiers, but also thousands of old men, women, children and volunteer units. However, unlike her compatriots who were mostly neutral medical personnel, Flora retreated as a soldier, fighting rearguard actions against an enemy noted for its cruelty to prisoners, to the wounded, and to women. Close to starvation, filthy dirty and exhausted, on 31 December 1915 she and her few surviving Serb comrades staggered across the Albanian border to a hostile reception. Despite the near unimaginable hardships they had all endured ('You seem to be nothing but pain from the crown of your aching head to the soles of your blistered feet'), she had revelled in the approval of her comrades and officers, who accepted her as one of them; the easy relationship in the Serb Army between officers and men was far more in keeping with her unconventional spirit than the strict non-fraternisation rules of the British Army.

Promoted to Sergeant, Flora was constantly involved in fighting as the fortunes of war ebbed and flowed, occasionally in Serbia's favour, generally against it. In the autumn of 1916 she was involved in brutal warfare against the Bulgarians in the Serb mountains, 'Days and weeks went by during which one never took one's boots off; always on the alert, contesting one mountain top after another… daily increasing casualties among officers and men.'

Soon, Flora too became a casualty. Severely wounded in November 1916, by a fluke her revolver saved her life, protecting her from the full impact of a bomb which would otherwise have killed her. When her many shrapnel wounds were investigated without the benefit of anaesthetic, the surgeon stuck a cigarette in her mouth and told her to 'Shut up' and remember she 'was a soldier'. She was initially admitted to a small field hospital run by the SWH. When deemed fit enough to move, she was transferred to the 41st British Military Hospital for Serbian soldiers in Salonika. The British matron initially resisted Flora's request to be treated as the soldier she was, wondering instead if this strange NCO was a camp-follower who would quickly rise from her bed of suffering and, despite her 24 wounds, ply her trade. Flora became something of a *cause célèbre*; international correspondents came to take a look at her and English-speaking newspapers published articles about this unusual Serb soldier. The Serb Army found itself inundated with recruitment requests from other foreign women who wished to emulate Flora, whom one writer (with perhaps unintentional irony) referred to as 'The Lovely Sergeant.'

In hospital, Flora became the first woman to receive Serbia's highest award for gallantry in the field, the Kara George Star, bringing automatic promotion to Sergeant-Major. Ironically, although foreign awards bestowed on men by Allied nations are cited in the *London Gazette* (the official British journal which publishes names of recipients of awards), similar mention was not then made of women recipients. Thus Flora, along with the many FANYs and other British women who received *inter alia* French, Belgian and Serbian decorations, was never gazetted. Six months later, Flora was passed fit for active service. She spent many subsequent months in the field, as well as in bars – where she drank her fellow NCOs under the table. She was occasionally disconcerted when chatted up by prostitutes unaware of her gender. In 1919, having survived her third brush with death, (a severe attack of influenza which was successfully treated by a veterinary surgeon with doses of horse linctus), the much-decorated Sergeant-Major Sandes was commissioned into the Serbian Army; an Act of Parliament was passed to enable her to take up the rank of Captain – not because she was a woman, but because she was a foreigner.

After the war, with her service in the peacetime Serbian Army having ended, Flora and Yuri Yudenitch, the White Russian husband whom she married in 1927, lived in a number of European capitals including Belgrade, where she was reportedly the city's first taxi cab driver. In the author's copy of her autobiography, there are original annotations from a friend, including one commenting negatively on a hat that Flora was coerced into buying so as to become a 'lady' again, and a postcard from Flora to this friend dated 1927, shows how she longed for the excitement-packed days and vodka-drinking nights when she was a soldier in the Serbian Army.

War had not yet finished with Captain Sandes, however. On 5 April 1941, with the Nazis poised to invade Belgrade and the fate of Serbia (now Yugoslavia) hanging in the balance, Flora declared 'I am ready and willing to fight again for the people with whom I have lived for half a century.' She was as good as her word. Knowing that once commissioned a Serbian Officer stays on the reserve list forever, she re-enlisted in the Army. Now aged 65, with 500 cigarettes stuffed into her kitbag she once again set off to war – despite confessing to feeling a little less enthusiastic this time around. Her service was short-lived. Realising the impossibility of withstanding the onslaught of the Nazis, her Company was soon disbanded; officers and men making their way home as best they could. A few months later, the Gestapo arrested her as an Enemy Alien. Sharing a foetid cell with 13 other women, apparently 'communists, prostitutes and thieves', as well as an American journalist, she got on well with them all and even with the Prison Commandant, with whom she felt, in a different situation, she could have become friends. Eventually released, she was still forced to report on a weekly basis to the Gestapo until Yugoslavia's liberation in 1944. She made a point of always arriving in military uniform.

Widowed in 1941, in 1946 Flora returned to Suffolk (her family set her up in a small house, perhaps aptly named 'Folly's End'), where she successfully did battle with the new Yugoslav government; she was determined to receive the full Army pension to which she was entitled. However, like so many women who had served in the Great War (and indeed the Second World War), she never really found her way back to Civvy Street and she struggled to fulfil the gendered role society expected of her. Even in the 1950s she was haunted by memories of the wild days and nights spent as a soldier amongst soldiers:

> Sometimes now when playing family bridge... the memory of those wild nights comes over me and I wonder whether it was really myself or only something I dreamed. Suddenly, the scented drawing-room fades away into the stone walls of a tiny hut... Now I see myself in mudstained, bloodstained khaki breeches and tunic, and my vanity bag becomes a revolver. [*Then I remember*] I am a 'lady' now, not a 'soldier and a man'; also that Serbian soil is resting lightly on the graves of many of those happy comrades I have been seeing in my dreams.

Until late November 1956, long white hair blowing in the wind, Captain Flora Sandes, Gold Kara George Star (with Swords), twice Mentioned in Despatches, zoomed around the Suffolk lanes in a motorised wheelchair, terrorising horses, cattle and pedestrians alike. The woman who in 1908 had galloped so fast across the finishing line that she would have killed her casualty never lost, even as an octogenarian, her taste for speed and excitement.

Flora's close friend Doctor Katherine Macphail, who spent most of the War and many subsequent decades either in Serbia or helping the Serbs, once commented, 'I never met so many queer British people as I had in the Balkans,' adding as an afterthought, 'it was more an obsession that took hold of me.' Certainly, with its tragic history and gallant soldiers, Serbia was an obsession that took hold of Flora; an obsession which allowed her to live a life that, in her native England, would have been beyond her wildest dreams.

'Neither Spy, Whore nor Camp Follower': Dorothy Lawrence (aka Sapper Dennis Smith)

Despatches by professional war correspondents first appeared in the leading London papers during the Crimean War, giving readers eyewitness accounts of events unfolding at the Front. The public's thirst for news about distant, and less distant, wars became unquenchable, British and American war correspondents had swarmed over the American Civil War battlefields rushing to file reports of sometimes questionable accuracy. It goes without saying that communications from the Front dealing with military matters were expected to be written by men. War was the supreme masculine preserve; should a woman dare to wish to write about war, she should concentrate on the 'human' perspective – and write from the Home not the War Front. Although in the latter years of the Great War there were several (American) female correspondents reporting from the war zone, they generally wrote about hospitals, wounded children and women.

Although the British public's appetite for news was insatiable, newspapers' and journalists' relationship with His Majesty's War Office was frequently inharmonious; accredited male journalists found multiple obstacles obstructing them. Even in Britain's *fin-de-siècle* Imperial campaigns, Kitchener believed that any journalist who found his way to the Front Line should be arrested. When his ubiquitous finger told the (male) population, 'Your Country Needs You', this need did not include those who wished to report on the war. Between August 1914 and May 1915, Britain and France's War Offices erected so effective a barrier between the field forces and the outside world that war correspondents were treated as outlaws. In a desperate attempt to satisfy avid readers at home some decided to take matters into their own hands and roamed across the war zone. Eventually, in May 1915, the British High Command relented: five accredited male war correspondents would be permitted to report from the Western Front.

In August 1914, eager to 'do her bit', 19-year-old Dorothy Lawrence rushed back to England from Paris, her temporary home. Her 12 separate offers to undertake voluntary war-work fell on deaf ears, usually, she felt, because she had no money either to fund herself or donate to the volunteer units that were heading to the war zone. Deciding that if she could not serve the war effort then she would write about it, she elected to become a war correspondent. After all, she reminded herself, pre-war, she had had a few articles published by *The Times*.

Dorothy's earliest interaction with newspaper editors was hardly encouraging. One editor of what she simply describes as a 'very fine paper' asked, 'Do you suppose we're going to send a woman out there when even our own war-correspondents can't get out for love nor money?' However, a chance, almost throw-away, remark from another editor who was probably 'speaking heedlessly', provided all the encouragement she needed, 'Of course, if you could get to the Front.'

Investing £2 in a bicycle 'a bargain' and another £3 to get across the Channel, she set out for the Front as an unaccredited war correspondent. In the spring of 1915, describing herself as, 'the picture of unloveliness' – an unloveliness which increased when, with half a crown in her pocket, she pedalled from Paris to Creil, a French base camp outside the range but within earshot of the guns. She confided her ambitions of getting 'right into the firing-line' to some *poilus* (French private soldiers) who were fascinated by this *'petite Anglaise'*; one even suggested that she should disguise herself as one of them. However, they realised that whilst her French was good, her English accent would betray her; nevertheless, the seed of an idea was planted. It would eventually be put into action.

Leaving Creil, Dorothy reached Senlis, almost certainly one of many towns in the proscribed zone, where no foreigner or native not connected with military operations was allowed to enter. Dorothy's perceptive, descriptive remarks bring to life the pathos and brutality of the recent German invasion as well as the randomness of war; any newspaper broad-minded enough to employ her would not have been disappointed by her despatches. After a short while, the local gendarmes became suspicious of her presence: was she a spy, or perhaps a camp follower? They ordered her to leave. She 'had not the slightest intention of obeying'.

Hiding in the surrounding countryside, Dorothy decided to rethink her strategy, as she still had no means of getting to the fighting line. She turned back to Paris, where she befriended two English Tommies billeted in the city, telling them she planned to 'get out to the Front as a soldier'. Within a week, they had supplied her with an entire Sapper's uniform. To reduce her 'robust figure to masculine slimness', she 'enveloped [*her*]self in swathes of bandages, like a mummy' and, with her accomplices, she paraded round Paris in uniform, learning the rudiments of drill. With her hair cut short in true Tommy style, she set off for 'the firing-line'. She arrived in Albert, in the summer of 1915 a city of 'abject ruin'. With the Front Line then still slightly mobile, she was almost 'in front of the front'.

A chance encounter with a Lancashire miner, Sapper Tom Dunn, provided her with a Royal Engineer badge, name and number. Dunn (who subsequently vouched for the veracity of her story when she published her autobiography) agreed to assist her in her ruse and, hidden in a ruined dug-out, she prepared to spend her first night enduring the nightly 'Enemy Hate' directed at the Virgin of Albert. This once perpendicular, iconic statue atop Albert's famous cathedral had been dislodged by enemy fire in the early fighting. The Germans were determined to finish the job as she remained a symbol of Anglo-French defiance. In the interim, she provided a useful ranging-point. Under the alias Sapper Dennis Smith of the 179th Tunnelling Company, and with an improvised dog-tag to prove her credentials, Dorothy spent 10 days and nights in the direct line of fire as 'shots whizzed by at the Cathedral target, travelling shells passed overhead every few minutes.'

Her sojourn was short-lived. Weakened by hunger and rheumatism from the endless nights she had spent in the open and subject to fainting fits, Dorothy decided to give herself up. The disruption caused by her infiltration of the British Expeditionary Force appeared disproportionate. A full-scale investigation followed. She was shunted across the French countryside, Colonels and Major-Generals at a loss what to do with her. At one point, three full generals including General Sir Charles Monro, soon to receive the poisoned chalice of finding a way to conclude the disastrous Gallipoli campaign, and 20 staff officers interrogated her; other senior staff appeared merely to have a look. She was clearly not fulfilling any, to the male mind-set, obvious female wartime role: spy, whore (as by her own admission she had no idea what a 'camp follower' was), nor, unfortunately, did she even claim to be motivated by patriotism – she was no modern Joan of Arc. She simply wanted to share the troops' experiences, arguably to serve her own ends; she admitted to having reason to believe the *Daily Mail* would buy her story.

With Sapper Smith/Dorothy Lawrence under arrest, the military set about damage limitation. She was incarcerated for two weeks in a convent; the nuns called her admiringly the 'female desperado'. In the evenings, 'knots of black-robed figures used to gather round me… utterly enthralled at the adventures of a woman who had got out to the big world', the big male world of war. Having safely returned her to the correct feminine sphere, the authorities lost interest in her (perhaps they had more important matters pending, such as the September 1915 Battle of Loos and, for Monro, his imminent departure for Gallipoli).

Having been forced into signing the Defence Of the Realm Act (DORA) as the price of her release from custody, Dorothy was barred from publishing any account of her exploits. Although a photograph of her in Land Army uniform appears in her autobiography, any record of her WLA service has proved impossible to trace. Her 1919 autobiography attracted little attention. Her honesty about the financial intentions behind her 'service' may have done her few commercial favours. In 1925, Dorothy claimed that her adoptive father, a Church Guardian, had raped her. The disbelieving authorities confined her to Colney Hatch Lunatic Asylum. Still institutionalised, she died in 1964, her story and her escapades as a would-be war correspondent and soldier long forgotten.

'I've worn a khaki uniform... Significant indeed': The Women's Auxiliary Army Corps

By late December 1916, with casualties on the Western Front inexorably mounting and the pressing need for fit men to replace the dead and wounded, the War Office asked Lieutenant-General Sir Henry Lawson, General Officer-in-Chief (Northern Command) to prepare a report detailing the number of men carrying out non-combatant roles in France. This led, from April 1917, to a concerted press and poster recruitment campaign: this time it was women who were 'Urgently Wanted', both at home and abroad, to 'take the place of men'. Naturally, they were not wanted as combatants but as 'Cooks, Clerks, Waitresses and all kinds of Domestic Workers'. Posters also explicitly stated these women would 'work with the forces'. They would be enrolled in a new Women's Auxiliary Army Corps or WAAC, members becoming known as Waacs.

By 1917, uniformed women's corps abounded, but these consisted primarily of volunteers whose social class and status enabled them to be, if not totally self-funding, then able to supplement their minimal stipends through personal means. This new corps was aimed very directly at those from less privileged backgrounds for whom, irrespective of patriotism, 'Good Wages, Quarters, Rations, Uniform' were essential. As with munitions workers, patriotism among working-class women surprised many more gently-born citizens; some of the early Waacs were unfairly accused of being motivated by 'false patriotism'. It was felt that, unlike their social 'betters', they could not be familiar with ideals of honour and service simply for their country's sake. Waacs' writings and other archived material show how unjust such accusations were. Working-class Waac Betty Donaldson remembered, despite 'the rather hideous uniform, such was our patriotism... we were delighted with ourselves'. The wider

British public remained dubious about both the women's motivation and their intended role; the country must be scraping the bottom of the barrel if women had to be sent. Once again, women would prove the sceptics wrong.

Within weeks of the first advertising campaign, thousands of women had enrolled (initially they 'enlisted' but, due to angst about this term being used for men in the Services, the terminology changed) in the WAAC. As had happened in 1914 with would-be soldiers, the authorities were often horrified by the poor state of the women's physical and dental health, and many were rejected as unfit. Others were offered free dental or medical care for the first time in their lives. Those who were accepted marched and drilled enthusiastically, much to the public's bemusement. One aristocratic woman explained confidently to another wondering who these 'creatures' might be that they were 'something connected with the Salvation Army'.

As the promised uniform would be the visible sign of these women's patriotic service, the WAAC Commandants sought suitable apparel. Although femininity seemed desirable, sexuality needed to be contained: the 'khaki jacket chosen [*for Other Ranks*] had side pockets... but no breast pockets...These would emphasize the bustline.' Women were expected to provide their own more personal items. It came as something of a shock to the authorities to discover that some women did not possess undergarments, knickers being beyond their means. Reactions to the uniform varied, but Waacs soon realised that their ideas on dress were irrelevant and eventually they became reconciled to and proud of their uniform, seeing it as the outward symbol of their involvement in the war effort.

However proud they may have felt of their khaki-coloured coat-frock, clumsy-looking shoes and round, brown felt hats, Waacs had essentially been recruited for what could best be described as uniformed domestic and clerical service. In June 1918, of the just under 3,000 Waacs for whom figures are available, around 2,200 were in 'typical' women's jobs, with a mere 225 being employed in the more 'masculine' roles of carpenters, welders, smiths, mechanics and electricians, whilst a few were drivers.

Not all women were given the roles they aspired to. Worker 18375 Elizabeth ('Johnnie') Johnston, a trained telegraphist, had learned that the WAAC were recruiting drivers so, against her parents' wishes, she hastily learnt to drive. She was enrolled, and sent to Rouen as – a telephonist. Her lively letters, published in 1920, provide a vivid account of her

120

WAAC experiences, as well as her need for 'a huge lump of humour somewhere. This experience would kill lots of folk, myself included if I took it too seriously.' She soon realised that class tensions spilled over into WAAC life. Some Officials (the rank of officer was disallowed) were either unwilling or unable to mix, 'They are truly to be pitied, who look down their noses, and draw in their skirts, while they give thanks they are not as other women are.' Johnnie was one of the 9,625 Waacs who, 'to the envious cheers of those left behind [*most of whom never left Blighty*], set sail for France and the Great Adventure.'

Partly due to their being recruited to 'free up a man for the Front', Waacs were frequently loathed by those women whose men were now 'freed up', and by the men themselves, although many were simply deployed elsewhere on the Lines of Communication. Public perception of the Waacs was, at least initially, often negative, best summed up by one titled lady's cook, who referred to them as ''orrible Army women'.

It was not only those at home who were astringent towards Waacs. VAD Aileen Woodroffe, an affluent solicitor's daughter who served in hospitals in Calais, wrote to a friend, 'I travelled on a train today with some WAAC. They do not do well running about on the loose, not speaking the language, being rather conspicuous and exceedingly stupid and giggly.' There are many other similar comments. She admitted that for the soldiers, 'it is a recognised thing to have a WAAC friend', adding, 'there is nothing for these wretched men to do after hours.' Her sympathy for the 'wretched' man does not extend to Waacs – who had not had the benefits in life such as learning to speak a foreign language, which she seems to take for granted, and who also had 'nothing to do after hours'.

If some were angry about men being moved closer to the firing line due to the Waacs' arrival, others, including newspaper reporters, expressed concerns about the possible lax morals Woodroffe hints at. Were these women being recruited to staff army brothels? So intense did this outcry become that in March 1918 the Ministry of Labour sent a committee of five women over to France to investigate 'immorality'. Unsurprisingly, as the WAAC officials imposed strict segregation rules, nothing untoward was uncovered. The investigators admitted the rumours were unfounded and wrote what Helen Gwynne-Vaughan, WAAC Chief-Controller in France, termed 'an admirable report'. As she herself wryly admitted in *Service with the Army*, (1942) 'immorality is an excellent stick with which to beat a Corps of women.'

Some of the working-class women found the restricted relations between the genders – the norm amongst the more privileged – hard to understand. When drawing up rules, Gwynne-Vaughan believed her approach to potential relationships was pragmatic and open-minded: 'walking out' would be tolerated – within strict limits. Not all Waacs were impressed to find they were only allowed to walk with their Best Boy in designated areas, a rule that applied in both England and France. A former munitions worker, Waac Olive Taylor, was bemused, '"Out of bounds" was three miles away and one was not allowed to speak to a soldier within bounds… So if a girl became acquainted with a nice soldier she had to run three miles to say hello and run back again.' However, she realised not all soldiers were 'nice', asking wryly, 'What did it matter to them if a girl lost her good name and ended up in the workhouse with a baby?'

Not all were cautious and there were 'exceptional cases', as Gwynne-Vaughan termed them. In May 1918 the first Waac baby in France was born. One Waac who absented herself after 'elevenses' was subsequently 'discovered on her bed with a baby'. She was treated with sympathy. Like Woolwich Arsenal Superintendent Lillian Barker, Gwynne-Vaughan refused to take disciplinary action against pregnant Waacs, considering it unfair to 'take such action against one parent when it would not be taken against the other'.

Slowly, aided by sympathetic press coverage and the patronage of Queen Mary, the tide turned towards the Waacs (dubbed '*Les Tommettes*' by the French), particularly when an outraged British public discovered that women, even those in non-combatant roles, could become enemy targets. Air raids were not a new phenomenon and the women became used to them as the German advance, codenamed 'Operation Michael', brought their Abbeville Camp within striking distance. During these raids Controller Gwynne-Vaughan tried to keep morale high by reading uplifting texts to those sheltering in cellars, although she had trouble keeping at bay her realisation that, 'a direct hit would result in our being drowned in the drains of Abbeville, an unattractive prospect.'

On the night of 18 May 1918, Camp II in Abbeville on the Montreuil road took a direct hit by 'the largest bomb that had been used at that time'. This hinted at things to come. Although no lives were lost, 'huts were blown to pieces' and 'uniforms were scattered far and wide, some garments landing on the branches of the trees.' To Gwynne-Vaughan's pride, irrespective of the motley array of clothes they were dressed in, 'every woman was in her office or cookhouse at the normal time.' Echoing the FANY account of the first gas attack, women fulfilling their appointed duties, irrespective of enemy action, is a source of pride. This was far from the only occasion when QM/WAAC camps were subject to enemy bombing raids.

After demobilisation, Waacs suffered similar, arguably greater, difficulties compared to those experienced by serving men as they returned to an alien, even hostile, environment. Many previously unskilled women had hoped that the skills they had acquired in order to assist the Army would be valued in the post-war world, enabling them to continue to better themselves, improve their lives and increase their earning capacity. Their hopes proved ill-founded. Male survivors were given priority in the job market; when skilled women applied for less skilled work they were turned down as 'overqualified'. Although many had joined the Corps to escape a life 'Downstairs', now they found that despite a 'Servant Shortage' they were not even considered desirable servants. 'No Waacs Need Apply' was frequently appended to job advertisements. Unjustified concerns about Waacs' morals resurfaced in the harsh post-war world.

In 1921, veterans formed an Old Comrades Association and its vibrant newsletter kept ex-servicewomen in touch, with meetings and reunions becoming the highlight of many lives. The newsletter also carried 'Positions Wanted/Offered' advertisements, and those who had a position to offer were begged to consider a Waac. The Association bought a small holiday home, 'Shanghai' in St Leonard's-on-Sea. For many women, a short stay allowed them to rekindle the camaraderie and memories of their service days when, despite its tragedies, heartbreak and horror, the war was, as one Waac remembered, 'not all sorrow and all pain'. Like old soldiers, Waacs both wanted and needed to remember 'the dear dead days that never come again'. For many, perhaps even for the majority, those 'dear dead days', when they 'had done their little share/To win the War', were the most fulfilling of their lives.

'Perfect Ladies, or the Prigs and Prudes':
The Women's Royal Naval Service

On 26 November 1917, aware of the success of the WAAC, the First Lord of the Admiralty informed His Majesty that, 'it is recommended that a separate Women's Service should be instituted for the purpose of substituting women for men on certain work on shore directly connected with the Royal Navy.' The letter hoped that 'Your Majesty may be pleased to express your approval of these proposals.' Pleased or not, the letter was returned rubber-stamped, 'The King has signified his approval.' What the Sailor King (George V) really thought of the proposal is unknown, but recruitment via the press and posters for the required 10,000 women began. Dame Katharine Furse, former Head of the VAD (London) for the Red Cross, had already accepted the Directorship of the Women's Royal Naval Service, or Wrens as they became known (luckily the title 'Women's Auxiliary Naval Corps', with the acronym WANCS, had been rejected). As it was considered that uniforms and appearance were 'important' to females, designs were quickly submitted and approved.

The officers' uniform of tailored suits and tricorne hats proved popular with would-be officers. However, like the Waacs, some Ratings were underwhelmed by the 'rough serge coat-frock, very heavy greatcoat, heavy boots and shoes, woollen ribbed stockings and blue and white soufflé-type hat' and, for those who went to their duties by launch, 'an oilskin and sou'wester', which made them appear 'such frumps'. Others felt that their skirts, eight to twelve inches off the ground, were 'dashingly smart'.

Unlike the predominantly working-class Waacs, many Wrens had Navy backgrounds and, as the Navy forbade fraternising across ranks, socialising with their officer fathers/brothers became problematic. One Wren was surprised to find that she needed a permit even to go out with her father. She swiftly 'applied for as many [permits] as I could, putting down the names of all my relatives and friends so that I might always have a permit available if anyone came home unexpectedly.' Another was posted to Admiralty House, Queenstown, Ireland, where her brother was Assistant Paymaster. They shared a flat and one day they were spotted walking together, 'about fifty yards before going our different ways to work, ten shillings was deducted from my pay as a fine for walking in public with an officer.' Was, one wonders, the brother similarly fined?

No recruiting advertisements mentioned a life on the ocean waves and the WRNS soon acquired the unofficial motto, 'Never at Sea'. Superstition about women on board ship and angst about how they might climb ladders in skirts kept the majority on terra firma. Occasionally they worked aboard ships that were in harbour, but only very rarely were they at sea, although Gladys Wilburn 'captained' a large motor launch. Her Top Secret work consisted of towing a model about after dark, hidden by canvas screens. However, 'the war ended before it could be used'. Another's work was relatively unusual, 'The harbour was heavily mined, and my work was connected with guiding our ships in and out – sloops, Q-boats, destroyers and minesweepers.' She, like Gladys, was closer to the sea than most of her colleagues. Despite not working on board ships, some Wrens at least had the opportunity of serving overseas, on the Western Front and in Malta, Gibraltar, and Genoa. Eight ratings and officers stationed in the Scillies 'acted as a kind of hostess to the base, keeping an eye on its manners, morals and socks.'

Wrens, like Waacs, were predominantly required as cooks, waitresses, laundresses, book-keepers, telegraphists and motor drivers; those who did not already possess these skills would be trained either beforehand or, in the case of waitresses and laundresses, 'on the job'. One member of the galley staff at the Royal Naval College Greenwich probably did not need excessive training for her 'chief occupation, making mountains of toast – an eye-scorching operation'. Dorothy Gaitskell (politician Hugh Gaitskell's sister) was instructed to lay fires; she shamefacedly confessed to a senior Commandant that she had 'never done this sort of thing before'.

Katharine Furse was determined to weld her fledgling corps if not into a fighting unit, then into one of which the Senior Service could be proud. Recruits who were not up to the job for which they had originally been recruited were downgraded. The highest standards of behaviour were expected: each woman was given a confidential card for her pocket-book with guidance on the required conduct for women in 'the circumstances of Naval Service'. At Christmas 1917 and again in 1918, every member was sent a card bearing both a message from Furse and Nelson's *Eve of Trafalgar* prayer, suitably adapted, reminding Wrens that, 'The Empire expects that every woman will do her duty.'

Whilst almost every woman was undoubtedly determined to do her duty, some fell foul of the many rules and regulations. One hungry Wren, Rose Edmunds, was confined to quarters for ten days for being handed sandwiches by her mother when marching from barracks to her hostel. On another occasion the unfortunate Rose was spat at by a German prisoner, and she spat back. Another ten days confined to quarters followed. Wrens, she was informed, should conduct themselves in a suitable manner whatever the provocation. Furse's 'nice gels' had to be 'Perfect Ladies'.

Wrens' morals were supposed to be above reproach. Serious misdemeanours would not be tolerated, and hints of sexual misconduct stamped out. Furse appeared to believe the unfounded rumours of Waacs' immorality, 'It is desperately hard on the WRNS that we should be involved in the WAAC trouble.' Nevertheless, she, like Gwynne-Vaughan, treated the rare pregnant Wren with sympathy; we 'saw them safely through the process of child-bearing'. In her post-war autobiography *Hearts and Pomegranates*, Furse notes 'our Medical Directors and I agreed that we should do more to maintain a moral code by humane treatment than by punishment and the response certainly justified this belief.' As according to the Medical Director of the WRNS, Dr Dorothy Hare, there was only one identified case of STD, the need for 'humane treatment' was not tested to the full. Perhaps this explains why the Perfect Ladies were dubbed 'Prigs and Prudes'?

When peace was declared, the WRNS were still, in relation to the WAAC, a small corps. Their maximum strength only reached 5,054 ratings and 438 officers. Despite their small numbers, as auxiliaries of the Senior Service they were well represented at the Peace Parade of 19 July 1919. One Wren participant – signing herself simply 'W.R.N.S.', wrote a detailed letter describing how they had 'drilled incessantly' for this proud moment when, 12 abreast, 12 naval nurses, 108 Ratings, Petty Officers and senior staff were 'the first service women' in this first procession of the Services in which women had ever participated. Those who marched were, to their delight, given 'the most magnificent clap and cheer' by the senior admirals. The 'huge blister on each little toe' was, for 'W.R.N.S.', a small price to pay. On 23 July, the Second Sea Lord wrote, congratulating Furse on the Corps' 'marching and appearance', concluding, 'The WRNS had thoroughly earned the right to be represented on this historic occasion with the Royal Navy.'

Many WRNS officers and ratings hoped that post-war some would be kept on, if not as permanent members then at least as part of a Volunteer Reserve. Despite senior admirals' accolades, this never materialised. All that was left to the women of the Senior Service was their Association and their newsletter, *The Wren*. Penned across a file dated 15 August 1922 which discussed a revived WRNS scheme were the words, 'Dead. Scheme dropped by Board Order.'

Turbulence in the Air:
The Women's Royal Air Force

Although not acknowledged as national heroines, the QMAAC and

WRNS Commandants received multiple plaudits for successfully nurturing their respective women's services. By contrast, the Honourable Violet Douglas-Pennant, the WRAF's early Commandant, was ignominiously dismissed on 28 August 1918, five months after the Corps' inception. On appointment, she had all the required credentials – birth, connections and relevant experience leading organisations. Just a week before her actual dismissal, she was assured that she was the right person for the job. What happened next became something of a national scandal.

Post-war an investigation via a Select Committee of the House of Lords failed to clear the air. There was mention of 'information' coming to the attention of the inquiry which made her dismissal inevitable. Yet, she was unable to defend herself, because she was never told the nature of that information, which was nothing more than rumour. She was eventually sued for libel and financially broken. She died in 1945, the case never fully laid to rest. Her overtly liberal political views and her reputation as a social reformer may have done her no favours with the Establishment. *Under the Searchlight*, written in 1922 to try to clear her much-blackened name, indicates that she was making every attempt to create a female service of which the new Royal Air Force would be proud. Her text, whilst highlighting the multiple difficulties she faced, provides insight into the WRAF's earliest days and the women who, in her words, were taking 'the greatest pride in their particular jobs'.

The story begins on 1 April 1918, when the Royal Flying Corps and the Royal Naval Air Service amalgamated to form the Royal Air Force. Women already working as civilian subordinates with these services could apply to the embryonic Women's Royal Air Force to become (inevitably) 'Clerks, Waitresses, Cooks', and, more unusually, 'Motor Cyclists'. The aim was to recruit about 90,000 women in order to release men for other work. There were also opportunities for women to acquire a wide range of technical skills, including aircraft maintenance and even, for a very few, learning to fly.

Some transferred from the WRNS and the QMAAC, not always to their former colleagues' delight. There is something caustic about Waac Isabelle Grindlay's valedictory poem to I. Cruden, 'Go, dainty maid, your needle ply/Among those daring men who fly.' Almost certainly plying her needle as a sail-maker (the fabrics that covered an aircraft's wooden frame were called sails), Cruden would have been one of 24 skilled airwomen in a workshop whose work consisted of fitting, stretching and stitching the linen covers on to the frames. To the envy of their colleagues, sail-makers had 'no real dirty work' and 'nice clean overalls'. Completed sails were passed to 'Dopers', who painted layers of a liquid cellulose varnish, or dope, over the fabric-covered airframe. In order to combat the dope's poisonous fumes (recognised as deleterious to workers' health), an extra cup of tea and a slice of toast were authorised, at a cost of 2d to the public purse. Sail-makers in the adjoining workshop, getting, in Wraf Gertrude George's words, the 'partial benefit of the smell', were allowed the tea but not the toast.

Researching the WRAF's chequered early history, two parallel stories emerge: those of enthusiastic recruits such as Wrafs Gertrude George and I. Cruden, and the ever-increasing antagonism between Douglas-Pennant and the Air Ministry, to whom the WRAF soon became 'taboo'. Occasionally the stories collide, perhaps nowhere more strongly than on the subject of airwomen's well-being and uniforms. Douglas-Pennant notes how uniforms, so important in 'stimulating [*women's*] esprit de corps and self-respect', had been delivered promptly for the QM/WAAC and the WRNS, but not for the WRAF. One reason behind the delay was that the Air Ministry originally retained a firm experienced in delivering mackintoshes but not in producing women's coats and skirts. Further complications arose when a consignment of men's boots was delivered – at considerable wasted expense.

For those who had to provide their own work clothes and overalls, and, ultimately for Douglas-Pennant herself, uniforms became a source of understandable anger. In June 1918, two (still uniformless) women went on strike, threatening to bring approximately 1,600 co-workers at the Regent's Park Depot out with them. They told Douglas-Pennant that, 'they were striking against their treatment by the Air Ministry [*who when they joined up*] had promised them uniforms and a bonus as well as pay.' With neither the uniforms nor the bonus forthcoming, they 'were obliged to provide overalls at their own expense'. Despite spending most of a Sunday attempting to boil the grease out of the overalls, 'they were fined on Monday morning for their untidy appearance.'

Whilst Douglas-Pennant's previous experience with young working-class men and women helped her to understand their anger, it put her at odds with those who could not conceive of the importance of being provided with work garments which protected the owner's personal clothes. Significantly, once the women felt that they had received a sympathetic hearing, they returned to work and no strike followed. Decades later, one former Wraf remembered, that 'No uniform was provided', so many simply bought their own 'khaki breeches and skirt'. Many civilians considered these breeches scandalous, overlooking how frequently Wrafs worked outside in all weathers, maintaining the aircraft upon which pilots' lives depended.

When eventually the uniforms arrived (resembling those of the WAAC but in grey-blue as opposed to the original khaki), reactions were mixed. Almost inevitably some attempted to add personal touches, coordinating stockings with the grey-blue as these 'looked so nice'. Gertrude George notes how, 'Again and again the forbidden articles of apparel broke out in a fresh place when all the other legs were decorously black, [*just as*] the Quarter-mistress was congratulating herself the fight was o'er.' Some Wrafs tolerated unpleasant fatigues merely to retain some individuality. One involved scrubbing the hut floor when the 'rapidity with which the water in the pails became liquid mud was only equalled by the apparent hopelessness of ever reaching the original surface of the floor'. The scrubbers 'all agreed that the hut was much bigger than they had previously imagined it to be'. But they continued to defy the Quarter-mistress!

Anticipating some women taking greater liberties than wearing coloured stockings, provisions were made, from the outset, for those who contracted STDs or became pregnant. The WRAF Chief Medical Officer, Dr Letitia Fairfield, calculated that she needed 'four hospitals in different parts of the country'. As with the other services, the CMO had grossly overestimated. Memoirist Gertrude George was convinced that those taking advantage of the war's unexpected 'freedom and opportunities' were in the minority. She was right: amongst the 1,000 Wrafs serving with the Army of Occupation of the Rhine there was only one unmarried pregnancy.

If concerns over women's sexual mores proved unnecessary, those over the living accommodation originally proposed were well-founded. On one early occasion, Douglas-Pennant was asked to take over a house 'full of dry rot and almost pitch dark... unfit for human habitation'. She refused. She was not looking for luxurious quarters, nor even those up to peace-time standards, but the women could not live in hutments where, 'in wet weather the latrines washed down on the huts immediately below them.' If nothing else, she added, this was a certain way to ensure widespread illness. Oblivious to the fight that had led to hutments being of at least an adequate standard, Gertrude comments how these became a 'harbour of refuge' and the modicum of comfort that they offered was 'thoroughly appreciated'.

Following Douglas-Pennant's abrupt dismissal, Helen Gwynne-Vaughan was appointed Commandant. With a heavy heart, she told Waacs who paraded at Étaples to bid her farewell, as 'henceforward it would be my duty to try to make another service better and smarter than they and, please, they were not to let me.' Those drilling the early Wrafs were determined to turn them into as fine a body as the other women's services. Gertrude remembered, 'Invariably courteous our instructor was nevertheless a strict disciplinarian and inflexibly determined on getting the best out of us. The number of fours we formed would have made a sum long enough to appal the most precocious child... We endeavoured to drill even as our brothers did.' Another remembered being told to 'Get fell-in'; then, 'In a voice like the crack o'doom the Drill Sergeant put us through our paces as though we were candidates for the Brigade of Guards – but he was forbidden to swear at us.'

Apart from those who served with the Army of Occupation, most Wrafs' service lasted under a year. Like the Waacs and the Wrens they took great pride in their involvement despite, and this is the only time Gertrude alludes to it, 'much criticism [*having*] been levelled at the Women's Royal Air Force – criticism which is fundamentally unjust, because based only on fragmentary knowledge.' Their demob papers bearing the harsh words, 'Services no longer required', caused many Wrafs a 'keen pang of regret'. Gertrude noted, 'now the days of uniform were over.' The uniforms worn by women in official and volunteer corps were the 'outward and visible sign... of forming part of a great community.' As predicted in the early days, this had fostered an *esprit de corps*, and the sense that all, regardless of class or rank, were 'banded together in a common cause'.

For the officers and rank and file of the WRAF, all that was left to them as peace returned were their memories, pride in the part they had played in the war effort, and membership of their Old Comrades' Association which, as Gertrude noted, strove to keep alive their 'sense of comradeship towards each other and its principles of preparedness to help the country'. Despite its early problems, Air Vice-Marshal Sir Sefton Barker avowed that, by the end of 1918, the WRAF were 'the best turned out women's organisation in the country.'

When hostilities ceased, the QMAAC, the WRNS and the WRAF were rapidly de-mobilised, the FANYs returned home. But within 20 years war drums would beat again. This time the authorities acknowledged that women's service would be of vital importance to this subsequent war's outcome. The former QMAAC, (renamed the ATS and no longer graced by a Queen's name but by the presence of Princess Elizabeth), the WRNS, and the WRAF were re-formed.

A new generation of FANYs seized the opportunity to prove once again *'Arduis Invictus'*. Unlike Dorothy Lawrence, British war correspondent Claire Hollingworth was officially accredited; she was the first journalist of either gender to witness and report on final Nazi preparations for invading Poland – thereby scoring a notable scoop.

Flora Sandes' service spanned both wars. In autumn 1944, arriving for her compulsory weekly interview, she told Prison Commander Huber, 'I've come to say good-bye.' Furious, he asked her where she might be going, as she was not leaving Belgrade. She concurred; however, with the tide of war sweeping against the Nazis, she defiantly told him, 'You are'. She was determined to remind her captors that she was, as she had been throughout two World Wars, both a British woman and a Serb soldier.

CHAPTER 6

'Their Graves are Scattered and Their Names are Clean Forgotten': Women Who Died

'Seldom they enter into Song or Story,'
('For The Sisters Buried on Lemnos', Vera Brittain)

In June 1925 a restored stained glass window, known as the Five Sisters Window, was unveiled in York Minster. A plaque at its base stated that this was now, 'Sacred to the memory of the women of the Empire who gave their lives in the European War of 1914–1918.' Yorkshirewoman Helen Little, the driving force behind the restoration project, had initially proposed that, as the window was situated in York Minster, only Yorkshirewomen be invited to subscribe, but women from across the Empire were so eager to contribute that within nine weeks 32,000 women had donated well in excess of the required sum of £3,000. Contributors ranged from Princess Mary (£50) to the widow who, at considerable personal sacrifice, sent her whole week's pension.

In a nearby area of the Minster, somewhat tucked away in the Royal Air Force (or St Nicholas) Chapel, is an impressive set of ten wooden doors fashioned in the nature of a rood screen. Each door bears insignia of the various Corps in which women served. The names of all the women of the British Empire from that service who perished are inscribed. Not originally part of the memorial plan, the panels were commissioned using surplus money from the window restoration, and they form what Helen Little called a 'Roll of Honour of the Empire's female dead'. A few names, such as Edith Cavell, are familiar. Most are as anonymous as 15-year-old munitions worker Violet M. Brooks, who lost her life in November 1918, whilst she was, in her mother's words, 'working on Govnt. Purposes'.

Archbishop Lang officiated at the unveiling ceremony, the Duchess of York gave the address; the congregation included 800 individuals mourning, in Lang's words, '1,465 sisters of our race whose names remain forever here, written on the Minster's heart.' In purely statistical terms, the deaths of around 2,000 to 2,500 women seem but a drop in the ocean of blood spilt in the war. And, despite the Archbishop's words and the fundraisers' endeavours, the names, the physical sufferings, and the sacrifices of these women have largely faded from popular memory. Perhaps this is hardly surprising. In the early part of the twentieth century, war was seen as a male preserve and, with all combatant nations traumatised and seeking ways to honour their dead men, the women who died were largely overlooked. It is as though, as one American child was told when she tried to tell her classmates the story of her aunt's war service and death, women's war deaths 'don't count'. But their service did count and their deaths should too.

Initially, women's First World War contributions and deaths were not sidelined. On 10 April 1918, the British Red Cross held a memorial service at St Paul's Cathedral for 'all the nurses who have fallen during the war'. Unbeknownst to the organizers, at least another 194 nurses would subsequently 'fall'.

In his eulogy, the Archdeacon of London assured those nurses attending this service, 'You have had your chance and you have taken it – women who will be remembered with the soldiers in a never-to-be-forgotten page of history.' If the grieving mother of one QAIMNS(R) Staff Nurse was in the congregation, she may have raised a cynical eyebrow. She was locked in battle with the authorities about compensation for her 25-year-old daughter's death. Nursing training had cost money her family could ill afford but, with her promotion to Staff Nurse, Mrs Wallace felt that her daughter had started on a 'brilliant career'. Her letter, preserved in the IWM archive, states that she 'would therefore be obliged if you would do something for me or make enquiries how I should go about applying for compensation'. Mrs Wallace was not ashamed to admit to being in straitened circumstances, with a 'large young family to support alone'. Yet, despite her best endeavours she 'did not get a penny', even though, in language similar to that used by the Archdeacon, she reminded the authorities that her daughter's sacrifice was similar to that of soldiers who fell in combat and whose families received compensation.

Ten days later, another memorial service was held in St Paul's

Cathedral. The Bishop of London officiated. This was to memorialise the unknown numbers of killed and wounded war workers; chief amongst these were the munitions workers. Demand for tickets to this service was such that the organising chairman noted, 'the Cathedral could be filled five or six times over.' One can only imagine the heartbreak the paucity of available tickets must have caused to those whose loved ones had been killed or maimed.

Although there is relatively little documented testimony relating to munitions workers' deaths, some of the events surrounding fatalities can be pieced together. Irrespective of its cause, each worker's death left a family bereaved of a wife or mother, a sister, sweetheart or friend.

Munitions Workers: 'Destruction hovers o'er their bench'

When presenting her findings to the War Cabinet Committee on Women's Health in 1919, Dr Janet Campbell concluded that women's health 'had improved during the war years.' Be this as it may, one area in which women's health certainly did not improve was in the munitions factories. Working excessively long hours, even by the standards of the day, women handled dangerous, frequently lethal materials and a number paid with their lives. Fearful of damaging morale, the government endeavoured to hush calamities up through heavy-handed use of DORA.

Explosions occurred in factories from December 1914, seemingly at first with no loss of life. However, at 10.27pm on 5 December 1916, almost a year after what appears to have been a well-run, productive factory opened, tragedy struck in Room 42 of the National Filling Factory, Barnbow, Britain's premier shell factory where, recruited from across West Yorkshire, 16,000 of the 17,000 employees were female. A number of the 170 'Barnbow Lassies' at work that night were maimed or severely injured, while 35 were killed, including 27-year-old Martha Alderson from Tadcaster, whose husband Samuel was serving in France.

Decades later, his great-niece remembers Samuel talking of the tragedies that had destroyed his young family (two infant children had predeceased their mother). Despite remarrying, when his second wife was out of earshot he liked to remember, 'my Martha'; he died, childless, in 1961. In one respect, Samuel was luckier than some, as, relatively unusually, Martha's body was recovered and she had a burial service and grave. Some women were only identifiable by the identity disks that they, like soldiers, wore round their necks.

Linking these factory deaths to those in the field, Field Marshall Sir Douglas Haig issued a special Order of the Day from the British HQ in France, paying tribute to the devotion and sacrifice of the Barnbow munitions workers. His praise was justified, once 'the cocktail of blood and water' had been cleaned from the floor, and within hours of the explosion women volunteered to return to Room 42 and resume work. The *Manchester Guardian* only reported the disaster three days later, in morale-boosting terms: 'England is very proud of the pluck, endurance and determination of her munitions girls... [*who*] have come through the whole ordeal without panic or collapse.' Perhaps to maintain morale, no mention was made of the 35 who did not 'come through'.

One widely reported explosion occurred at Silvertown in London's teeming East End, destroying not only a large part of the TNT factory, but also a significant part of the surrounding area. Although the 1843 Metropolitan Building Act had sought to regulate the emplacement of factories handling noxious products, Silvertown lay beyond its reach and by 1914 it was a hellhole of factories where a cocktail of highly flammable substances, including rubber and rubber by-products, were manufactured. Tate and Lyle's sugar factory was then, as now, in the vicinity. In 1915, the government decreed that one of Silvertown's factories, Brunner Mond and Company, should produce the highly explosive TNT. Aware of the consequential hazards, the owners unsuccessfully resisted the edict.

The siting of the factory, with Woolwich Arsenal almost directly opposite on the other side of the Thames, compounded the dangers: an explosion in one factory could endanger the other. Not only was the Arsenal at risk from any explosion, so too were the inhabitants of the terraces of small, densely-packed houses in Silvertown's nearby streets. As the factory owners had feared, the worst happened at 6.52pm on 19 January 1917. A huge explosion, heard over 100 miles away in Southampton and Norwich, ripped a large area of Silvertown from the face of the Earth. Shock-waves were felt all over London and Essex; the ensuing fires were visible in Guildford and Maidstone.

In addition to the loss of life, some 60,000 to 70,000 properties were damaged at the, then enormous, cost of £2,500,000. Suffragette and pacifist Sylvia Pankhurst reported the tragedy in the following week's *The Woman's Dreadnought,* in language that could be describing devastation at the Front: 'There were just shells of houses, the windows broken, the doors gone, and the ceilings and floors fallen in.' In a ghoulish rush to the disaster scene, 'motor-cars filled with well-dressed sightseers slipped along.' On this occasion, perhaps due to the publicity surrounding the disaster, the Government 'without admitting any liability, [*agreed to*] pay reasonable claims for damage to property and personal injuries'. Whether what the government considered 'reasonable' correlated with how much the injured may have needed to sustain themselves is a moot point.

Fearful of lowering public morale even further, and desperate to maintain a supply of factory workers, by 1917 censorship of factory disasters was commonplace; when, as with Silvertown, this was impossible, only the minimum information was provided. Nevertheless, on 2 October 1917, the Minister of Munitions officially announced that a serious fire and explosion had occurred at a munitions factory. Although the disaster's location was effectively concealed, this was the White Lund Factory at Morecambe Bay. The *Blackpool Herald* reported that 'missiles firing over Lancaster and into Morecambe Bay, may have been visible down the coast.'

Eighteen-year-old factory worker Olive Taylor's memoirs of the disaster, preserved at the IWM, are vivid:

> huge explosions... shook everything. There was quite a lot of panic as the 12 foot high gates remained closed... The rush for the gates had the weaker people on the ground, yet others still climbed over them to try & climb the gates while the police tried to hold them back... I had no hope of escaping the holocaust but somehow I was not scared... Several people threw themselves into a river which ran at the back of the works. We never knew how many died... At the end of the week with that huge place still smouldering we were paid off and given a railway ticket home.

Like Olive, many workers simply never knew 'how many died'. She subsequently joined the WAAC.

One of the worst factory disasters occurred on 1 July 1918 (the second anniversary of the Battle of the Somme), at the National Shell Filling Factory in Chilwell, Nottinghamshire, just as the night shift began. To add to the bitter irony of the date, the factory founder and owner, Viscount Chetwynd, claimed, undoubtedly with justification, that the greatest number of shells fired during the Battle of the Somme had been manufactured in Chilwell.

Much of the factory was destroyed when eight tons of TNT exploded at 7.12pm, killing 134 people, including 35 women, and injuring at least 250 others. Despite the national press merely reporting '60 feared dead in Midlands factory explosion', the truth was horrific. Off-shift crane driver Lottie Barker remembered running pell-mell to the factory. In language that resembles descriptions of Hiroshima in 1945, she saw a 'mushroom spiral of smoke... rising into the sky'. She wrote of 'men, women and young people burnt, practically all their clothing burnt, torn and dishevelled... limbs torn off, eyes and hair literally gone... carts, lorries and ambulances making their way with their gruesome loads to the hospitals.' The sounds of the unfolding horrors were audible some 30 miles away, haunting Lottie for years. Eleven-year-old witness Kate Abdy remembered and graphically described the scenes of horror: 'I raced towards the works after hearing the huge bang and saw the awful sight of debris hanging in the golden sky, so clear that the bodies of those unfortunate people seemed to be suspended for some time, spread eagled, before slowly coming earthwards.'

Eight months later, the Duke of Portland unveiled a memorial to all who died on this terrible night. As well as remembering the victims of the 'V.C Factory' as it became known, the memorial provides statistical information about the factory's output, perhaps trying to justify the fatalities. Fifty years later, it was restored and rededicated, 'In recognition of the bravery and fortitude of the employees.'

Whilst a number of factory disasters led to multiple deaths, accidents and smaller explosions also led to fatalities. Although owners and supervisors did their best to surround these in secrecy, workers knew of them – and still carried on, often showing considerable bravery. The grief that they felt when a colleague was killed is demonstrated not only by the overwhelming demand for tickets to the St Paul's Memorial Service for War Workers, but also in smaller, local incidents. The funeral for a worker killed in an explosion at Swansea in July 1917 was postponed until the August Bank Holiday Monday to enable the maximum number of workers to attend. In an extant photograph, the grief on the mourners' faces is palpable, the long line of women workers, some wearing their munitions badges, stretches into the distance.

Accidents caused by human error occurred even in the best factories. R.A.

Lister's in Dursley, Gloucestershire, a large-scale pre-war employer, was rapidly converted to the production of petrol engines, lighting sets and munitions components and had a solid reputation for safety. Although no blame can be laid at the factory's doors, on 8 May 1918, one employee, Doris Wyatt, succumbed to a fatal accident. The *Dursley Gazette* related how she:

> was working at a lathe and by some means or other she became entangled with the machine. Her head was badly crushed and she died almost immediately. A sad feature of the fatality was that her father and fiancé were working close at hand and were among the first on the scene. No-one actually witnessed the accident so that the manner in which it occurred is a matter for surmise. The deceased was 23 years of age and had been engaged on munitions for some time past. She was a capable worker and very popular with her workmates and her untimely end is keenly lamented.

The subsequent inquest revealed that a few days earlier, Doris had dropped a shell on one of her fingers, injuring it quite badly. Whether anxious not to lose time (and pay) or out of a sense of patriotism, she reported for work on the fateful night, which was a hot one, further raising the temperature inside the factory. Suffering from the heat as well as her painful hand, she opened her overalls to cool down and fell forwards. Her blouse was caught in the rotating machinery and she was dragged in. No blame was attached to Lister's; indeed its care of women workers was lauded.

In a manner reminiscent of the Swansea workers' funeral, hundreds of factory women, wearing their caps and overalls with a black armband, joined the funeral cortège, headed by the factory owner, Sir Ashton Lister, as it wound its sorrowful way to the Dursley Tabernacle, where the memorial plaque funded by Doris' co-workers remains a visible mark of respect for their now long-dead colleague. In a manner similar to that of soldiers' regimental badges, a munitions worker badge is placed at the top of the memorial, and the inscription equates Doris' death with that of a fighting man: she too died 'whilst engaged on war work'. In his address at the dedications service, Sir Ashton wondered:

> Who could even have guessed that our women folk would have occupied the position they were doing in every walk of life where useful and self-sacrificing work was necessary?

138

They had risen to the occasion and saved the Country. In doing so they made for themselves a position in the world from which they had been kept too long.

Whilst explosions and accidents led to the deaths of countless women, others died as a result of handling noxious chemicals. Deaths from TNT poisoning peaked in 1916; in late 1916 DORA was further extended to prevent the press from reporting these cases. Nevertheless, the 12 December 1916 National Union of Women's Suffrage Societies *Bulletin* reported, in the '6 months to October 31st, 41 munitions workers died from T.N.T poisoning'.

In her letter to the IWM, a Mrs Hart recounted how, '14 pints of poisoned blood', caused by exposure to TNT, were taken from her daughter Dorothy Willis at the Military Hospital, Edmonton. (Dorothy's husband was then serving in Salonika.) Another worker who, like Dorothy, died of TNT poisoning, and also left a young husband, was Lottie Meade. Her poignant story is simply told. By 1915, she had four surviving children aged between seven and one. On 11 October 1916 she died in the Kensington Infirmary. Her death certificate gives the cause of death as: 'coma due to disease of the liver, heart and kidneys consequent upon poisoning by tri-nitro-toluene.' The post-mortem and inquest subsequently recorded a verdict of death by misadventure.

Lottie's husband Frederick did not get home from France in time to see his wife alive. He survived the war and, like others mourning a munitions worker, he donated a precious photograph to the IWM Women's Work Collection, writing, 'I am forwarding on 2 of her photos which are only old ones but I can['*t*] have a fresh one took of her so would you kindly let me know which one you would like of her please return her photos as I have not got any more to get a photo from like them thanking you very much for what you are doing. Yours faithfully, Mr F.G. Meade.' Perhaps he would be comforted to know that his beloved Lottie is one of the few women workers featuring in the IWM's online exhibition, 'People of the Great War: Shaping the Modern World Centenary'.

Nurses and Doctors: 'She lived among suffering, dying in the serving'
Most munitions workers' deaths occurred later in the war. Nurses and

medical personnel sustained casualties from the outset. In September 1914 the first wounded Army sisters returned to England; a suitably outraged *Daily Mail* reported, 'One of them was badly shot in the head while doing her duty in a field hospital.' Territorial Forces Nursing Service Staff Nurse Minnie Thompson, attached to No.2 London General Hospital, is the first nurse to have lost her life as a result of war service. The *BJN* provided extensive coverage of her funeral, 'conducted with full military honours'. The *Last Post* sounded as the coffin was lowered, 'announcing with its unforgettable wail that the work of Minnie Thompson was, as far as this life is concerned, over'. Unbeknownst to the editor, this was the first of many hundreds of medical women's war-related deaths which would be reported in the journal under the subheading 'The Passing Bell'.

Female personnel died in all theatres of war. One early fatality was 37-year-old Dr Elizabeth Ross. Amongst the first Scottish women to obtain a medical degree, she is reputed to have been the first female Ship's Surgeon. When war broke out, she offered to serve in the typhus-ridden Serbian town of Kragujevatz, which by early 1915 was suffering almost Biblical horrors. The Serbian medical services, primitive by Western European standards, were stretched beyond breaking point, and disease endangered the lives of military and nursing personnel alike. Elizabeth's niece remembers hearing that, 'When she arrived there were no nurses. They would put two single beds together and put three patients in them.'

Despite some of her compatriots wondering, 'how you can bear to work here', she just said "well, somebody's got to do it".' She survived less than three weeks, dying on Valentine's Day 1915. Her colleague Louisa Jordan volunteered to nurse her, dying herself three weeks later. All but forgotten in their native land, the Serbs continue to revere the memory of these and the many other British women who came from so far away, to a country they had previously never heard of, to care for the wounded and suffering, giving their lives in so doing. An annual ceremony of remembrance is held in their honour at Nish, Serbia, on 14 February.

One of the last nurses to lose her life was deeply admired and widely respected Matron Beatrice Jones. On 6 May 1916 she had led 250 nurses to Mesopotamia to organise the first hospital for British troops, who were 'dying like flies' in 'indescribable conditions'. She served there until her death on 14 January 1921. Dedicated almost beyond the grave, she 'had arranged every minute detail of her work, so that 'the running of the hospital was not disorganised even for an hour'. Obituaries in *BJN* portray a much-loved, dedicated professional who 'gave her life for the good of our sick and wounded under the most trying circumstances and climate, with never a thought for herself.' Laid to rest in in the Baghdad (North Gate) Cemetery, currently 'out of bounds' to visitors from her native land, she is the only woman amongst 4,555 casualties.

Soldiers suffering from and even dying as a result of shell-shock is common knowledge. Less well known is that this also affected nurses and, as with soldiers, for some, like 28-year-old Staff Nurse Phyllis Pearse, it proved fatal. Having to remain calm and professional when confronted with the horrors of technological warfare, and at times feeling guilty that they were complicit in patching up lives that might in truth have been better lost, added to the mental as well as professional burdens nurses shouldered, which a number hint at in their personal writings.

The first mention of Phyllis' condition occurs in Matron Maud McCarthy's April 1915 War Diary. Phyllis was transferred from '10 General to 8 General suffering from what appears to be nervous breakdown'. The transfer did little good; by 27 April McCarthy records that Phyllis and a Miss Stewart were leaving from Rouen for England, '2 sisters going down with them'. Perhaps McCarthy hoped that returning Phyllis to England would resolve the matter. However, on 29 April she learned by telephone that 'Miss Pearse who was on her way home... had thrown herself out of the window and was killed.'

As the war progressed, McCarthy became familiar with the need to evacuate shell-shocked nurses, and there are frequent mentions of the condition in her diary. Nurses' memoirs of both the Western and Eastern Fronts make reference to friends and colleagues stretched beyond breaking-point. Amongst the saddest is Red Cross Ambulance Convoy volunteer Nellie Taylor who, known to be suffering mentally, successfully evaded her attendants and, at 5am on 27 June 1918, flung herself over the cliffs near Le Tréport. Her body was recovered; in one nurse's words, it 'was quite smashed in every part'.

Many nurses and nursing personnel died violent deaths, some at the hands of the enemy as a result of air raids or bombardments. QAIMNS Sister Janet Lois Griffiths' elderly parents received a much-cherished letter, subsequently donated to the IWM, from Alfred Keogh, Director General of the Army Medical Service. Lois 'was gallantly killed [*in Alexandria*] while trying to save others'. She 'was one of a number of nurses travelling on an ambulance waggon, which was run into at a level-crossing by a train. She was sitting on the back of the waggon and, seeing the danger, jumped off to help the other nurses to alight and was killed while gallantly attempting to save them' (*BJN*). Her parents may have been comforted to know that the Alexandra DMS and indeed the GOC were amongst the mourners at her distant funeral service; in June 1916 she was posthumously Mentioned in Despatches.

Twenty-six-year-old Staff Nurse Nelly Spindler's death, during the August 1917 Battle of Passchendaele, caused particular outrage. Her path to war was not untypical of that of a young woman of the time with a vocation for nursing. The daughter of a Wakefield Chief Inspector of Police, by 1914 she was a Staff Nurse in the QAIMNS; in 1917 she was working at Casualty Clearing Station 44, a tented hospital at Brandhoek (Belgium). Specialising in abdominal wounds, which due to the excessive loss of blood needed to be treated as rapidly as possible, this CCS was situated unusually close to the Front Line. Proximity to a railway siding and also a munitions dump made it particularly vulnerable to enemy fire; staff simply accepted the risk.

Kate Luard, the QAIMNS sister-in-charge of nearby CCS 32, wrote extensively about Nellie's death in her post-war autobiography, vividly bringing readers close to the vulnerability of medical personnel and the ways in which they tried to dismiss potential attacks as being 'all in the day's work'.

> The business began about 10 a.m. Two came pretty close after each other and both just cleared us and No.44. The third crashed between Sister E's ward in our lines and the Sisters' Quarters of No.44. Bits came over everywhere, pitching at one's feet as we rushed to the scene of the action, and one just missed one of my Night Sisters getting into bed in our Compound. I knew by the crash where it must have gone and found Sister E. as white as paper but smiling happily and comforting the terrified patients. Bits tore through her Ward but hurt no one. Having to be thoroughly jovial to the patients on these occasions helps us considerably ourselves. Then I came on to the shell-hole and the wrecked tents in the Sisters' Quarters at 44. A group of stricken M.O.'s were standing about and in one tent the Sister was dying. The piece went through her from back to front near her heart. She

was only conscious a few minutes and only lived 20 minutes. She was in bed asleep. The Sister who shared her tent had been sent down the day before because she couldn't stand the noise and the day and night conditions. The Sister who should have been in the tent which was nearest was out for a walk or she would have been blown to bits; everything in her tent was; so it was in my empty Ward next to Sister E. [*Elizabeth Eckett*]. It all made one feel sick.

The *BJN* devoted considerable space to Nellie's death, providing a hint of her character: 'she was right in the danger zone, but while recognising it her letters were hopeful and cheery'. Her burial 'with full military honours' at Lijssenthoek Military Cemetery was attended by several very high-ranking officers and 'as many sisters as could be spared'. It appears that nurses' deaths still had the power to shock and outrage even the High Command and their funerals being attended by generals and senior staff was a common occurrence.

Nellie was one of a number of QAIMNS nurses to die from enemy action. Between March and June 1918, air raids on CCS and Base Hospitals killed 13 nursing sisters. The bombing of medical facilities, strictly against the rules of engagement, was seen as particularly dastardly and caused journalistic outrage. For *BJN*, raids on facilities 'bearing the sign of the Red Cross [*were*] acts of inconceivable barbarity'. Deaths of nurses as a direct result of attacks on hospitals in more distant theatres of war appear less widely publicised, although the *BJN* was quick to condemn these, reporting at some length how in March 1917, 'regardless of the Red Cross prominently displayed', an enemy air raid destroyed the hospital close to Monastir (Salonika) where Staff Nurses Marshall and Dewar were working. Marshall, previously Mentioned in Despatches and recipient of the French *Croix de Guerre avec Palme*, was killed outright; Dewar, mortally wounded while tending to a patient, died soon afterwards.

A quick glance at the official causes of nurses' deaths often reveals that some, like many soldiers', were caused by 'sickness', although on further investigation this 'sickness' is directly attributable to their war service. American nurse Helen Fairchild is a case in point. Very soon after the USA entered the War, she wrote her mother an excited letter, dated 22 May 1917 to say that she was 'on her way to Europe'. Once in France her letters home trace her metamorphosis into an experienced military nurse. At Abbeville Gas School, she and colleagues: 'spent the day learning about poison gas and how to protect ourselves. We were each given our own gas mask – a complicated ugly thing, but an item we must keep with us at all times... So you see I'll be well protected from effects of gas if I ever come into contact with it.' Working in CCS 4 near the Front Line (Ypres–Passchendaele area) she rapidly became all too familiar with gas and its after effects.

Like many nurses, Helen gave her gas mask to a soldier; her compassionate action has since been proved to have contributed to her death in January 1918. Her family were told that her death was caused by complications from chloroform used during surgery for a stomach ulcer, yet painstaking research by Helen's niece, Nelle Fairchild Rote, revealed a different story. So irrefutable was Nelle's evidence that Helen's death was caused by gas poisoning that in the final days of his Presidency, Bill Clinton honoured her memory with the Certificate awarded to American service personnel who lose their lives in 'the service of our country in the Armed Forces'.

The many letters sent to Helen's parents from her colleagues, friends, Matron McCarthy and even Sir Arthur Sloggett, DGMS GHQ, show that she was deeply loved and widely mourned. In Sloggett's words she had 'given her life for the British Army'. Thanks to Nelle's efforts, Helen's memory is still revered: in her native Watsontown, Pennyslvania, the Nurse Helen Fairchild Memorial Bridge was opened to traffic in November 2005 and in 2010 in Dozinghem, Belgium, a ceremony was held to mark her devoted service to the wounded of the Allied armies. One of 286 American Army and Navy nurses who died on active service, not to mention a number of volunteers working with the French Red Cross, Helen's name, unlike those of so many nurses who died as a result of their war service, truly does 'live for evermore'.

A similar case to Helen's may be that of Agnes Forneri of the Canadian Army Nursing Service, who served in France during the Battle of Passchendaele. Invalided back to England in January 1918 for convalescence from what was described as 'ptomaine poisoning and bronchitis', her medical report noted that her illness was due to the strain of 'active service conditions'. Back on duty at No.12 Canadian General Hospital in Bramshott in April 1918, she collapsed with a violent stomach haemorrhage, and despite transfusions and an operation she died a week later.

144

Whilst the cause of her death is given as 'multiple peptic ulcers', it is highly probable that the strain of her service (and exposure to gas) took its toll on her like so many medical personnel in war zones. The obituary writer for her local paper felt 'it is most fitting that our dear Canadian sisters should be buried like soldiers and in a soldier's grave, for they are indeed as brave and true as any soldier and "faithful unto death".' As nurses are supposed to succour the wounded and are not expected to die themselves, it was often hard for mourners to accept their deaths and, as happened with Agnes, these were often described in militaristic terms.

A sad footnote to Agnes' story is the reunion that she had hoped would take place with her younger brother David never occurred: he was killed just before she arrived on the Western Front.

Deaths at Sea: 'All these have no other grave than the sea'

Being on board ship in wartime was hazardous for all passengers. There is a long list of women whose bodies were lost at sea and are recorded on memorials to the drowned. One of the earliest disasters to claim nurses' lives occurred on 23 October 1915, when 10 New Zealand nurses perished and one was seriously injured. They were en route for Salonika when the *Marquette*, carrying the ammunition column of the 31st British Division, was torpedoed in the Aegean Sea. Staff Nurse Margaret Rogers, writing to her father in New Zealand shortly before her death, had said, 'There is no romance about war; it spells suffering, hunger, filth. How thankful I am every day that I came to do what I could to help and relieve our brave boys.'

Margaret was subsequently identified by the name engraved on her wristwatch when a Royal Navy minesweeper found her body in a lifeboat. Pictures of *Marquette*'s casualties figured prominently in New Zealand local newspapers, as did the lucky escape of one nurse, allegedly saved because her regulation veil was seen floating on the surface of the water. As well as a veil, New Zealand nurses' uniforms consisted of pantaloons, two petticoats, a starched grey dress with a long full skirt, long sleeves and a stiff collar and cuffs, a full-length starched white apron, a red cape and a white veil. Such clothes would have instantly become waterlogged, dragging many to their deaths. Anger about the sinking was fuelled when one contemporary account claimed:

Some lifeboats were not lowered efficiently and overturned as they were launched. One of the lifeboats on the port side fell on another already in the water, and the nurses from that boat spilled out in the confusion. Catherine Fox was flung into the sea. Eyewitnesses said her friend Mary Gorman, a strong swimmer, saw this happen and knowing that Catherine could not swim she jumped into the water to save her. They were not seen again. On the starboard side a boat filled with nurses was lowered at one end but not the other leaving it hanging vertically sending the occupants into the sea. This boat had to be abandoned as it had a huge hole on one side. Other lifeboats were not seaworthy, as they had been damaged by the mules on board. Many of the deaths and injuries to the nurses were due to inexperienced men [*soldiers helping out as some crew members had not turned up at their stations for various reasons*] lowering the lifeboats and the angle of the sinking ship. Acting-Matron Cameron was severely injured and never fully recovered from her injuries.

According to the *BJN* she had been 'seriously ill with broncho-pneumonia and paralysed on left side'.

Only one nurses' lifeboat got successfully away, and this 'was half filled with water'. The survivors floated for hours in intense cold, clinging to rafts and debris before being picked up, utterly exhausted, by rescue ships. Survivors were evacuated from Salonika to Alexandria, their recent departure point. One newspaper article confidently assured readers that, 'the dependants of those nurses who have lost their lives are provided for under the War Pensions Act. The Minister of Defence said any allotments of pay to dependants made by those nurses who lost their lives would be continued.'.

However, if the experience of the aforementioned Nurse Wallace's mother is anything to go by, these words may have been optimistic. A *BJN* article the following summer gives an insight into Matron Cameron's injuries (and perhaps her straitened financial position). She wished to resign her subscription to the *Journal* and Association as, 'having been disabled in the wreck of the *Marquette* she was unable to read'. Free membership of the Association was offered to her.

Outrage about the loss of these nurses' lives peaked when it became apparent that HMHS *Grantilly Castle*, following the same route as the *Marquette*, had been travelling empty in order to pick up patients; she could legitimately have transported the medical personnel. According to

146

the Geneva Convention, hospital ships, like medical facilities on land, were supposed to be immune from attack as long as no combat troops or material were being carried, thus the attack on *Marquette* was legitimate.

Disasters continued. On 16 November 1916, there were 1,066 people on board HMHS *Britannic* (sister ship to the *Titanic*) sailing to pick up wounded from Mudros (a small Greek port on the Mediterranean island of Lemnos, where countless casualties from Gallipoli were nursed). *Britannic*'s surgeon believed she was, 'the most wonderful hospital ship that ever sailed the seas.' Suddenly, as one survivor remembered, 'A BANG sent a shiver down the length of the ship'; within 45 minutes she had sunk.

Opinion is still divided as to whether the explosion was caused by a mine or a torpedo from an enemy submarine. Former *Titanic* stewardess and now VAD Violet Jessop was on board. Having survived one shipwreck, she knew what to expect. She put her toothbrush into the pocket of her uniform and, acting strictly against regulations, she fastened her life-belt over the 'new coat for which I had saved so long' and boarded her assigned life-boat. She regretted this action, as very soon her precious, now waterlogged coat threatened to 'drag me down deeper into the heaving seas'. Had *Britannic* had her full complement of 3,389, the scale of the disaster would have mirrored that of the *Titanic*. An RAMC officer summed up the nurses' behaviour in terms applicable to many accounts of disasters on hospital ships:

> I know that women can be brave, but I never dreamed they could rise to such heights of cool, unflinching courage as those nurses did when under [*Boer War*] veteran Matron Dowse, they lined up on deck like so many soldiers and unconcernedly and calmly waited their turn to enter the boats. We men are proud of them, and we can only hope England will hear of their courage. They were magnificent.

Along with many other 'Distressed British Seamen', Violet Jessop was repatriated on 1 June 1917. She worked in a bank until signing on again with the White Star Line in 1920. Her fractured skull went undetected for many years.

In January 1917, to the outrage of the International Committee of the Red Cross (ICRC) and the wider public, the 'German Government embarked on the policy of unrestricted submarine warfare... they determined to sink hospital ships systematically in their blocked zone' (*The War on Hospital Ships*). The ICRC's subsequent communiqué pointed out that, 'In torpedoing hospital ships, [*Germany*] is not attacking combatants but defenceless beings, wounded or mutilated in war and women who are devoting themselves to the work of relief and charity.'

Unrepentant, on the night of 20–21 March 1917,without warning, Germany torpedoed HMHS *Asturias* which, the Admiralty confirmed, had all the 'proper distinguishing Red Cross signs brilliantly illuminated'. Miraculously, QAIMNS Sister J. Phillips and Mercantile Marine Stewardess Bridget Trenerry were the only female fatalities. Sixty-five-year-old Bridget is amongst the oldest uniformed personnel (male or female) to have died as a direct result of serving with the Armed Forces.

Three weeks later, HMHS *Salta* struck a mine at the entrance of Le Havre naval base and sank rapidly. Nine nurses drowned; few bodies were recovered. *BJN* felt that: 'Heinous as the crimes of Germany have been in the last three years none are more dastardly than the war she has waged in defiance of all her obligations under the Geneva Convention, on sick and wounded men, and on doctors and nurses in attendance upon them.' Even prior to the declaration of open warfare on the fleet of approximately 100 hospital ships, naval nursing personnel undertook frequent lifeboat and other survival drills; in addition, they were taught to row the large lifeboats to ensure that they could do this competently during an evacuation.

Most QARNNS wore bathing costumes under their ward dresses and uniforms whilst aboard. In terms of practicality and ease of swimming, the costumes left much to be desired. Edwardian bathing dresses were generally made of wool and consisted of bloomers and a woollen sleeveless over-dress, stockings and laced footwear, although nurses almost certainly wore their own heavy boots. Whilst on board nursing and medical personnel were supposed to wear lifebelts, only taking them off when asleep. Several nurses' letters mention that they wear these all the time and tend to see them as uncomfortable encumbrances. Doubtless those who received the letters found the information somewhat reassuring.

Hospital ship personnel travelled thousands of miles in the course of their service. By 1918 South Africa war veteran QAIMNS Matron Katy Beaufroy had sailed some 60,000 miles and nursed some 30,000 patients. In 1916, she was appointed matron of HMHS *Dover Castle* and served for 15 months before sickness saved her from being on board when *Dover Castle* was torpedoed (twice) and sank at the end of May 1917. Despite this escape, Kate's luck ran out and she was among the nine nurses who drowned when HMHS *Glenart Castle* was torpedoed on 26 February 1918.

The *Birmingham Weekly Post* provided in-depth coverage of this 'Birmingham lady's' professional life and untimely death. Quick to condemn the loss of nurses' lives, *BJN* informed readers that two victims 'had just given up the greater part of a year to nursing German prisoners of war at Belmont, Surrey. We all know how hard this task is, and it seems an act of brutal ingratitude that their work for the enemy wounded should be requited with foul murder at the hands of the German Navy.' It is likely that survivors of the initial attack were subsequently shot by the submariners in an attempt to cover up the sinking of the *Glenart Castle*. After the war, the Admiralty endeavoured to charge with war crimes the captains of U-boats which had sunk hospital ships.

By 1918, service on board hospital ships was becoming increasingly hazardous. The late June sinking of Canadian HMHS *Llandovery Castle*, with the loss of 14 Canadian nurses, many of whom had been on active service in France and Flanders since the war's earliest days, caused understandable distress. Again survivors were fired upon. Sergeant A. Knight, one of the few survivors among the 97 hospital personnel on board, believed that nurses' 'sacrifices... will serve to inspire throughout the manhood and womanhood of the whole Empire a yet fuller sense of appreciation of the deep debt of gratitude this nation owes to the nursing service'. Although nowadays Knight's language appears flowery, his admiration for the nurses (12 of whom were in uniform and 2 in nightwear) is palpable:

> Unflinchingly and calmly, as steady and collected as if on parade, without a complaint or a single sign of emotion, our fourteen devoted nursing sisters faced the terrible ordeal of certain death – only a matter of minutes – as our lifeboat neared that mad whirlpool of waters where all human power was helpless.

Knight singled out Sister Margaret Marjorie ('Pearl') Fraser, who (like the nurses mentioned in *BJN*) was known to have nursed many German wounded. 'Many times had she been the first to give a drink of water to these parched enemy casualties. Many a time had she written down the dying statements of enemy officers, and men, transmitting them to their relatives through the Red Cross organisation.' He too felt it particularly inappropriate that Pearl should have fallen victim to this 'latest act of Hunnish barbarity'.

Civilian ships were also targeted. In a war that was so all-encompassing, that mail ships plied between countries seems surprising, daily life perforce continued against a backdrop of war. To protect vessels from attack, merchant ships sailing the Atlantic or more distant routes tended to be convoyed; those in waters nearer home were less likely to be so, increasing their vulnerability to submarine attack. On 5 October 1918, Germany asked President Wilson to facilitate peace negotiations. He stressed, however, that there could be no negotiations whilst merchant ships were still being sunk.

The following week, Reinhard Scheer, Admiral of the German High Seas, signalled all submarines to refrain from attacking merchant ships, but the embargo came too late for RMS (Royal Mail Ship) *Leinster*, which had left Holyhead on 10 October 1918 carrying 489 military and 180 civilian passengers. She was torpedoed by a German U-boat. Amongst the estimated 500 victims was WRNS 19-year-old shorthand typist Josephine Carr, the first Wren to be 'killed On Active Service'. Her colleague Maureen Water described the fatal moments when 'a second torpedo came on our side... I saw half the *Leinster* go up in the air... the ship was standing straight upright almost, propeller in the air, we were hardly three yards away. I prayed as I never did before.' Josephine's body, like those of many of the dead, disappeared.

However, London Hospital volunteer Clare McNally's body was found; perhaps this was some small consolation to her mother, who was already mourning the loss of Clare's father. A condolence letter assured her Clare had 'done good work voluntarily for more than two years'. Clare's coffin was carried to its grave between two files of Connaught Rangers, her dead father's regiment. The McNallys were one of the many families upon whom the war cast its long shadow across the generations.

When peace was declared over 1,000 families of nurses and medical personnel from across the British Empire and America were mourning a kinswoman. Many poignant letters and testimonials held in the IWM Women's Work Collection give particular insight into survivors' coping strategies. The (almost certainly) brother of 32-year-old QAIMNS Matron Mary MacGill donated to the museum photographs and newspaper cuttings relating to her 'funeral with military honours'. He proudly confirmed that, 'She went as a soldier goes.' Her obituary equated 'her quiet strength and her unbreakable endurance' with that of:

the bravest man who handles his rifle in the most desperate trench of Flanders; [*she was*] one of the bravest and finest of our women. She died in harness, few deaths are more noble than hers... There are few lives greater than her gentle and unselfish life, lived amid suffering, dying in the serving... Here was a heroine before whom all could bow in reverence.

Precisely six years after hostilities ended, acknowledging France's debt to the nurses and volunteer units without whose service the sufferings of the French *poilus* would have been even greater, a ceremony focusing solely on female medical personnel took place in Reims. An impressive monument commemorating the work and service of nurses of all Allied nations was unveiled on Esplanade Cères, a main thoroughfare of the city. The inscription reminds us how these women had fallen victim to bombs, torpedoes, enemy fire-power, disease and sheer exhaustion; their devotion to duty is equated to that of soldiers fighting in the field. Today, pilgrims who wish to peruse the *In Memoriam* book (*Livre d'Or*), lovingly preserved in the city's municipal archives, are still warmly welcomed. The book records the names of 979 nurses who had travelled from the four corners of the earth to alleviate the suffering of the French and died in a foreign field. Passers-by are requested to 'Remember Them'.

Service Women: 'This is woman's hour'
Although fewer in number than nurses or munitions workers, most of the Women's Corps suffered casualties, sometimes as a direct result of enemy action. Press reactions, parental grief and preserved condolence letters provide some insight into how these women were mourned.

Considerable fury was felt at home following the 30 May 1918 death of personnel at hospitals in Étaples, as well as nine members of the QMAAC, formerly the WAAC. A *BJN* contributor felt particularly outraged that this attack occurred on Corpus Christi night. As the British Government had acceded 'to the request of the Pope (who has, throughout

151

this war, shown himself an ally of Germany) that Cologne should not be bombed on Corpus Christi Day, these fiends were to be free for twenty-four hours to rush their murderers, ammunition and every death-dealing appliance over their network of lines, to the destruction of our defenders and allies.' These were the first deaths on active service of female members of the Armed, as opposed to the Nursing, Services.

Aerial attacks were not uncommon in May 1918 and Waacs took shelter in a system of nearby trenches. According to QMAAC Controller in France Helen Gwynne-Vaughan, who was in another camp on the fateful night, 'an aerial torpedo exploded in the trench, killing, wounding or burying all in that sector.' The dead women were buried at Abbeville Communal Cemetery Extension with full military honours. Although the press were eager to 'execrate the enemy for killing women', Gwynne-Vaughan reacted differently. Anxious to prevent Waacs being recalled home, she stressed that as 'we were replacing combatants, the enemy was entirely in order killing us if he could. The reporters saw the point... there was no [more] fuss in the Press.' The dead women had only very recently arrived in France; ironically, the established women 'felt it somehow inappropriate that this honour [of being killed] had fallen to new arrivals'.

Three women received the Military Medal for working beyond the call of duty to succour the wounded on that night. The camp's male Signal Officer requested that the Commander-in-Chief should Mention in Despatches various women's cool behaviour during subsequent raids. To Gwynne-Vaughan's delight he replied, 'We do not thank soldiers for devotion to duty; we do not propose to treat these women differently.' This rejection showed that the members of the QMAAC had been, in Gwynne-Vaughan's words, 'admitted to a great fellowship', including the fellowship of death. Some 182 Waacs died on active service.

Another of this night's fatalities was 21-year-old YMCA driver Betty Stevenson; she was one of several volunteers who drove parents of the wounded and dying to visit their loved ones in hospital. That the War Office gave next-of-kin the opportunity to visit their deceased (male and female) relatives is now little known. Women often served as relatives' escorts and provided considerable comfort. Betty's colleague, Lois Vidal, whilst perhaps slightly jealous of the younger woman's popularity and social status ('born with a silver spoon in her mouth'), referred to her as 'a fearless driver and excellent in emergencies' and 'a dear with the relatives... strong and tender'.

In her autobiography, *Magpie* (1934), Lois described the fateful air raid, a 'perfect hell in heaven went on above, lasting over an hour and a half. When the All Clear was sounded, [*we*] found that our garage and petrol store was ablaze.' Fearful that this would 'be sure to attract the Gothas on their return for a second doing', the drivers ran towards the woods. Six of them were caught by a returning Gotha. One other driver was injured, but Betty was dead on arrival at hospital. The General-Secretary of the Étaples Administrative District, Adam Scott, wrote to her parents with the information that, 'One bomb killed Betty instantaneously... nothing could be done... She was shot through the left temple... The funeral will take place... with full military honours as an officer of the British Army.' Taking some comfort from her daughter's award of the *Croix de Guerre avec Palme*, Mrs Stevenson, herself a former YMCA canteen worker, accepted that 'this is woman's hour; to a woman too it is given to lay down her life in a righteous cause.' From the many condolence letters Betty's parents received, the picture of a bubbly, delightful personality emerges, as does the shock that her death caused in the wider YMCA community.

Whilst the reasons for most serving women's deaths was straightforward, one is shrouded in uncertainty. On Christmas Day 1918, QMAAC Elizabeth 'Johnnie' Johnston, who had served overseas since 27 December 1917, fell to her death from the tower of St Ouen Church in Rouen. Was this caused by neurasthenia, or does the rather mysterious information that she had been seen at this church the previous week in the company of a young Canadian soldier called Donald Douglas Cameron, who attended her funeral, provide a clue? The secret lies with her in St Sever Cemetery, about which she had written nine months earlier, 'the cemetery is vast, and oh so beautifully kept', predominantly by the WAAC cemetery gardeners. The Town Clerk of the Jonhstons' native Anstruther subsequently wrote to her parents, expressing the sincere hope that: 'When the first pain of distress and sorrow passes may the pride in what that splendid girl of yours did for her country bring relief and comfort to you. Your grief is shared by the whole town.'

We two died: Multiple familial deaths

Stories of families losing several sons form part of the collective memory of the war; less widely known is that this same type of tragedy occurred with daughters. There are families where sets of sisters died whilst combatant brothers survived. The death of one sister, 'Canary' Dorothy Willis, is documented as her mother forwarded details to the IWM Women's Work Committee. Dorothy's younger sister, 19-year-old WRAF Sarah Hart, also died. Very unusually, possibly uniquely, they share a CWGC grave in their native Cambridgeshire village. This is highly unusual, as British munitions workers were not entitled to a CWGC headstone, although those who came from the Dominions were. Intriguingly, Dorothy is remembered on the village War Memorial, but Sarah's name is absent.

The deaths of Dorothea Cromwell and her identical twin Gladys (a respected poet) were well-documented in both the American and British press due both to their social status and circumstances surrounding their deaths. The twins (whose ancestors included Oliver Cromwell) had volunteered for service with the American Red Cross, initially at Chalons-sur-Marne, the scene of ferocious fighting, where they were under almost continuous bombardment. Transferred to Souilly, in the American sector at St Mihiel, they again experienced 'almost nightly bombardments [*and*] they saw men torn to pieces by shellfire, blinded by exploding bombs, horribly maimed by shrapnel.'

On 19 January 1919, following pressure from their influential brother (a three-time president of the New York Stock Exchange) to return home, the sisters boarded SS *La Lorraine* in Bordeaux. Newspapers relate that at 7pm on the first evening on board, as other passengers were dining, one woman leapt into the icy Garonne river, her twin following immediately afterwards, both rapidly disappearing into the swirling muddy water. Their bodies were never recovered but, according to press reports, suicide notes in their cabin indicated that 'their minds became unbalanced due to the terrible suffering they saw all around them for so many months. And that, combined with shell shock from the midnight bombardments caused them to "end it all" in the Garonne river.' Their brother, who initially refused to accept that his sisters were dead, let alone that they had formed a tragic suicide pact, never recovered from this tragedy.

Both women received a posthumous French *Croix de Guerre*. Their deaths sparked a public discussion of the effects of shell-shock on female war workers. In her March 1919 *Poetry* article, 'A Gold Star for Gladys Cromwell', editor Harriet Monroe feels that the 'self-drowning of... Gladys and Dorothea [*was due to*] the tragic result of over strain due to the months of contact with the dark realities of war'. It is a sign of the sensitivities of the time that Monroe refuses to call their deaths 'suicide', preferring the euphemism 'self-drowning'. A colleague commented on the twins' lengthy proximity to the firing-line, noting how serving men were given some leave after six weeks, but 'no-one seems to have ordered these girls to take a rest... At the end they were almost certainly suffering from abysmal depression, resulting from nerve-exhaustion.' Passengers' accounts of their 'nervous' behaviour on the ship fit the symptoms of what is now understood as Post-Traumatic Stress Disorder (PTSD).

Anne Duncanson had already lost two sons when, on 30 December 1917 HMHS *Aragon* was torpedoed off Alexandria with 25-year-old VAD Una Duncanson on board. Despite sinking within 15 minutes, all nursing personnel, if not their belongings, were rescued, as one survivor remembered: 'We had nothing in the wide world except what we stood in.' Not all survivors were as lucky second time around, as their rescue ship, HMS *Osmanieh*, struck a mine the following day. Una was one of eight nurses who died. The words on her CWGC headstone in Alexandria, which read, 'She hath done what she could', would apply equally to her mother, who lost three of her six children within the space of three years. Sadly, Mrs Duncanson was not alone in losing sons and daughters.

There are also cases of husbands and wives perishing. Sometimes, the couples' names are all that remains of their story, but occasionally, a little more information can be gleaned. In July 1916, 15 months after enlistment, 21-year-old law clerk Arthur Armer was serving in France. Initially a Lance Corporal, he was commissioned the following year. In 1917 he married Alice Crockley in Strood, Kent, the setting for many so-called 'khaki weddings'. According to Arthur's great-nephew, none of his family knew that he was married, but the wedding is duly noted in the registry of marriages. Although his service records do not reveal the precise date of his return to France, on 5 September 1917, within three months of his marriage, Arthur was killed.

Soon after, Alice enlisted in the WRAF. Despite seemingly living with her mother in Malmesbury, she may have wished for greater independence, as she enlisted as a 'Mobile', willing to serve at home or abroad. Employed as a storekeeper at a flying training station near Cirencester, Alice's service was short-lived. She developed influenza, then pneumonia and on 12 November 1918 she died. She is buried in Malmesbury, her husband in Belgium. In death as in life, war separated them.

The Gartside-Tippings married in 1890, he aged 47, she 18 years his junior. In September 1915 Lieutenant-Commander Henry Gartside-Tipping, the Royal Navy's oldest serving officer, was killed when HM Armed Yacht *Sanda* was sunk off Zeebrugge. His body was never recovered. Having worked voluntarily in a Munitions Workers' Canteen, Mary went overseas with the Women's Emergency Canteens for Soldiers (members were mainly society women and radical feminists), run under the auspices of the London Committee of the French Red Cross. Her service was short-lived. On 4 March 1917 she was shot and killed by a French soldier, who was apparently 'mentally ill'. Perhaps embarrassed by the tragedy, the French authorities instantly posthumously awarded the *Croix de Guerre*, which they had withheld from women since November 1916.

Mothers and sons also died. When war was declared, novelist, playwright, illustrator, vicar's wife and mother of two sons Mabel Dearmer was, by her own account, busy with her personal concerns. 'I knew nothing of European complications and cared less... I did not hate the enemy, I hated the spirit that made war possible.' Initially, she was more preoccupied by dealing with the abundance of plums in her garden than by the war. The enlistment of her sons, Geoffrey and Christopher, left her feeling deeply confused: 'I envied the proud mother who sends her sons, but could not share their feelings.' The letters she wrote to her friend Stephen Gwynne in 1915 provide a fascinating insight into her wartime life and inner turmoil.

Reading a request placed by the Stobart Unit in *The Times* for 'a clergyman to go out to Serbia to minister to the various British units, comprising some three hundred doctors and nurses who were at work there', Mabel's husband, Percy, volunteered. She accepted that he, too, 'was to follow my sons to danger and possible death'. But still she saw herself as a bystander of the tragedy unfolding around her. 'Then an idea struck me... I had no doubt and no hesitation.' She would accompany Percy. Despite looking at this middle-aged volunteer rather strangely, the Unit's leader, Mrs Stobart, agreed to take her as an 'orderly', warning her that she would need to learn many 'new things'. She would also have to leave behind her fashionable clothes, consisting that day of 'a green silk dress, a fur coat and long earrings'. Within a month, her 'costume' was very different.

A May 1915 letter written from Mabel's tent in Serbia in pouring rain describes her 'breeches and the heavy rubber boots... I wear my macintosh over this, which has been shortened to the knee and girt round the waist with a luggage-strap. It is quite true I am learning all sorts of new things'.

These included the 'best way of carrying off water round a tent'. Her letters reveal inward doubts; despite her outward enthusiasm she wondered whether she had the physical 'strength to stick this job'. Her documented introspections and her doubts shed insight on those that must have assailed other women of her age and younger. Eager to do what they could, many went to war fearful not of the dangers they might face, but of their own human frailties.

Once the Stobart Unit reached Kragujevatz, there was less time for self-scrutiny and, despite still hating the idea of war, Mabel welcomed being able to alleviate suffering. She saw medical service's unique irony, 'We are friends and enemies all together – half our wounded are Austrian – and the strangest of all, the head doctor of the Serbian Hospital is an Austrian prisoner. He is a wonderful man.' She reaches the conclusion, 'Everything is so curiously mixed up.'

Like many women's letters, Mabel's intermingle lively descriptions with the realities of war: bombs, wounds, suffering and its inevitable antidote – humour. On 12 June, she writes, 'Eleven people are down with this deadly fever [*enteric*]. I am not suffering from anything at present but fleas at night. Fleas!' Recounting a tea-party conversation with some '*very* respectable' people, 'there is never a tea-party in Serbia that doesn't begin with lice and end with latrines.'

Within two days of this witty letter, she too is 'knocked under with this fever – typhoid – but mild, owing to inoculations'. Her optimism was misplaced. After initially rallying, on 11 July 1915 Mabel Dearmer died. At her funeral in Kragujevatz Cathedral, the officiating Serb priest assured mourners Mabel had lived '"*sans peur et sans reproche*, [*fearlessly and blamelessly*] and died as bravely as any soldier'. In Stephen Gwynne's words, 'the anxious pain that was always at her heart can trouble her no more.'

Eleven weeks later, Mabel's younger son was also dead; both lie in foreign fields, she in Serbia, he in Turkey. Her elder son, Geoffrey, became Britain's oldest surviving war poet – he died in 1996 at the age of 103. One of his poems commemorates the death of his younger brother. His mother's war death is unrecorded; her grave is far from home and her sacrifice, like that of so many women, largely forgotten.

Edith Cavell: 'I meant to accomplish so much ...'
If most women's deaths are largely forgotten, one still looms large in the

157

popular imagination. The contemporary Belgian press deemed the execution of Edith Cavell, 'the bloodiest act of the war.' The bare facts are simple: when working with the Red Cross at the Berkendael Medical Institute in German-occupied Belgium, she helped Allied soldiers to escape, knowingly negating the neutral status bestowed on medical personnel. The Germans discovered her activities, and the legally conducted court-martial pronounced the death penalty.

Notwithstanding the legality of the case, social historian Mrs Peel considered Cavell's execution on 12 October 1915 to have been an act of 'Extraordinary Stupidity on Behalf of the German Government'. Exactly 90 years later, *The Guardian* reported, 'newly catalogued documents at the National Archives [*FO383/15*] reveal the desperate attempts by neutral American and Spanish diplomats to save [*Cavell's*] life. They also show the hand-wringing of British officials reluctant to get involved in her fate, clinging to a belief that Germany would not execute a woman who was regarded as a heroine.' Fortunately for Asquith's government, the press was unaware of this misplaced confidence.

Quick to win the propaganda battle, English newspapers depicted Cavell's execution and her last words in lurid terms. Enlistment figures rose to levels unseen since September 1914, as would-be soldiers sought to avenge her death. Photographs and posters depicting the dead 'heroine martyr' abounded. On 2 November 1915 *The Times* carried an advertisement for a 'Portrait Model of Nurse Edith Cavell' in Tussaud's 'Heroes of War Sea and Land' section. Sensing a possible commercial profit from the shockwaves engulfing the country, entry to the exhibition (open from 10am to 10pm) cost 1 shilling. Stone being more permanent than wax, long before the war ended £3,000 was raised from across the Empire for a memorial statue to be erected near Charing Cross, where it stands to this day.

On 15 May 1919, the body of Edith Cavell, the Empire's most famous war heroine, who said that she had 'meant to do so much but somehow I have failed to do it,' was repatriated. *The Times* documented the coffin's journey from Brussels to Dover, where it was reverentially placed in the South Eastern and Chatham Railway passenger luggage van No.132, its roof was painted white, so the crowds who lined the railway tracks could see where she lay, useful as the van was attached to a normal morning commuter train.

From Victoria, the coffin was transported to London's Westminster

Abbey ('admission by ticket only') to 'receive the nation's tribute to her memory', then onwards to her home town of Norwich. The funeral procession was covered in suitable detail by all sections of the popular and professional press; the effusive *Times* journalist assured readers that the 'crown of Cavell's patriotism was her womanliness and its sweetness of nature'. Restored in 2010 and now at Bodiam Station, luggage van No.132 serves as a memorial to the illustrious coffins (it also transported the remains of the Unknown Warrior) it ferried to London from overseas.

Contemporary interest in Cavell seemed insatiable; the *BJN* kept readers abreast of the progress of the monument and also published accounts by those who had undertaken pilgrimages to her place of execution in Brussels. Guides directed visitors to the exact spot where she fell. The *BJN* editor was convinced that Cavell 'lives in the hearts of her countrymen of England, in the bosom of Belgium, in the soul of France as none other has lived.'

Her life and in particular her death inspired the film *Dawn*. In rather chauvinistic fashion, the December 1927 *BJN* reported that, 'Miss Sybil Thorndike has been offered and accepted the part of Edith Cavell in "Dawn," Mr. Herbert Wilcox's forthcoming film.' Although an American had originally been cast, *BJN* felt it 'fitting that the part should be under-taken by an Englishwoman, and one of the talent and reputation of Miss Sybil Thorndike'.

Such was the adulation showered upon Edith Cavell in death that it is almost impossible to find the woman behind the martyr. However, Sister Catherine Black, who trained a few years after Cavell at the London Hospital, briefly lifts the veil on 'a quiet unobtrusive little woman whom no-one visualised in the light of a heroine.' A shy, retiring woman emerges from Black's pages, 'always reserved, even in her early youth [*she*] did not make friends easily.' When asked to go to Belgium in 1907 to pioneer the training of nurses and increase the sense of respectability of the nursing profession and of women working in general, she accepted this was her 'duty' and overcame her personal reluctance for the task. 'Duty', according to Catherine, was 'the one word to which [*she*] could never be deaf'.

Despite homesickness and loneliness, Edith Cavell 'was dedicated to a purpose and she achieved it, overcame obstacles and set-backs that would have daunted anyone else, fought discouragement like a tangible foe.' Although both nurses worked in Brussels, they lost touch, but when

Catherine Black heard of her death, she wrote a poignant vignette of this woman whose nursing background she shared: 'I could picture her hearing her sentence with steady resignation, putting on the green cloak of the London Hospital for the last time and walk[*ing*] out to face a German firing-party.' In these words we find Cavell the nurse as opposed to Cavell the icon.

Monuments to Edith Cavell proliferated across the Allied Nations: hospitals, statues, plaques, street names, even a metro stop in Brussels. Perhaps the most unusual is in Jasper National Park, Alberta, Canada: Mount Edith Cavell reaches into the sky at 3,363m; snow and ice falling off the mountains create the Cavell Glacier, which then carves into a lake, the Cavell Pond. There is something fitting in that a woman whose 'destiny' was, in Catherine Black's words, 'lonely from the very beginning,' but whose memory now towers above that of all Great War nurses, should be memorialised in soaring rock and ice.

Cavell's execution still arouses controversy. Whilst some excoriate the execution of a woman who was also a nurse, others recognise that by helping Allied prisoners to escape, she broke the neutrality imposed upon members of the Red Cross; criminal prosecution was the inevitable, indeed legitimate, reaction of the Germans. No one sums up the story of Edith Cavell more aptly than Major (Ret'd) Gordon Corrigan: 'Brave and patriotic she certainly was: murdered she was not. The Germans were fully entitled to shoot her, but it was a public relations disaster for them.'

'Dying in the service of her country and in the patriotic performance of her duty'

By and large women's deaths occurred later in the War; figures from the CWGC database of women casualties show that of the military graves in the Commission's perpetual care some 600 female deaths occurred between 1918 and 1919, as opposed to around 200 between 1914 and 1917. Social historian Caroline Playne believed that when deaths occurred later in the War, 'shocks concerning terrible happenings, losses, deaths, [*no longer*] struck us as beyond sane endurance. Later on... momentary faintness about such things passed into fixtures of endurance. The war had to be. Almost it was felt: "Woe to those who disturb our numbness, reawaken our sensitiveness by lessening our mechanical callousness".'

The *BJN*'s 'The Passing Bell' column and obituaries relating to nurses' war deaths substantiate Playne's argument. Significant editorial space was devoted to the September 1914 death of Nurse Minnie Thompson, but, as the war which was to be over by Christmas looked as though it might never end, many nurses' deaths went unrecorded in their professional journal. News of the deaths of nurses serving in far-flung theatres of war may never even have reached *BJN*. It appears as though, with the passage of time, the female deaths reported in either the professional or popular press were ones that, like Nelly Spindler's or the women who drowned in illegally-targeted hospital ships, had a propaganda value – they could be used to reinforce in the public's mind how dastardly the enemy was, how heinous his actions.

If many nurses' deaths were not reported due either to war-weariness or lack of knowledge, the deaths of munitions workers were actively suppressed. Under the terms of DORA, newspapers could be prosecuted for revealing details about deaths from TNT exposure or from explosions; news reports often rendered the factory unidentifiable and the names of the dead were never placed in the wider public domain. Only painstaking, and often frustrating, research reveals some identities behind the lists of munitions workers' names on the York Minster screen.

Some of the dead left widowed husbands to bring up children, others were hardly more than children themselves; war service cut short these women's lives, just as it did serving men's. In beautiful copperplate writing, Lottie Meade's husband wrote under the photograph he donated to the IWM that Lottie 'died of T.N.T poisoning contracted on duty'. A soldier himself, he equates her death with those of his comrades in the field. Her epitaph stands for hundreds of her co-workers.

Death in 'the patriotic performance of duty' became as integral to the female wartime experience as to the male. With the exception of Edith Cavell, who never sought martyrdom but somehow had it thrust upon her, nurses, munitions workers and all those who so willingly served their nation's cause found that, by and large, their nation soon forgot them. Without the efforts of the women who raised the money for the restoration of the Five Sisters Window, 'the memory of the women of the Empire who gave their lives in the European War of 1914–1918' would have been largely uncommemorated. Even the fact of the panels being tucked away in a side chapel of York Minster suggests that women's sacrifices are in some ways a sideline. Rather than being integral to the mainstream history of the Great War for Civilisation, women's deaths remain a largely forgotten footnote.

CHAPTER 7

'His Name Liveth For Evermore':
The One So Inexpressively Dear to Me

He has 'passed out of the sight of men by the path of duty and
self-sacrifice,'
(Inscription on the Dead Man's Penny)

During the war, few of the bereaved attended their loved ones' funerals, assuming that there had been a funeral and the dead soldier was not among the 254,176 'Missing', whose bodies had simply disappeared from the battlefields. Two years to the day, even to the hour, after hostilities ceased, an Unknown Warrior was buried in Westminster Abbey. One thousand invited women, including Army Nurses, were amongst the sorrowing congregation.

The Times correspondent confirmed, the 'humblest widow and mother had an equal part' in the obsequies, for each was a representative of the nation's sorrow. The ceremony's elaborate staging and ritual resembled nineteenth century state funerals, yet this was the burial of a man unknown and yet well-known, an ordinary soldier whose very anonymity represented modern warfare's facelessness. He represented, in *The Times'* words, 'our fathers, our husbands, our sons, our daughters'. This solemn act of committal was intended to comfort those mourning the approximately 800,000 British personnel who had perished in this Great War for Civilisation.

As the ceremonial funeral procession carrying the deeply symbolic corpse made its slow and dignified way from Victoria Station to Westminster Abbey, via the newly erected and assumed to be temporary Cenotaph, the eerie silence in the streets along which the cortège passed was broken only by the sounds of muffled sobs. This was the moment when the suppressed tide of grief, which had engulfed the nation for four long years of war, was given voice, reached its climax and was finally legitimised.

Few of those who had hailed the appearance of Their Majesties on the balcony at Buckingham Palace on 4 August 1914 could have imagined the hard and blood-soaked years that had lain ahead. Now, on that bleak November day in 1920 when George V laid the first of the many thousands of wreaths which swamped the Cenotaph he, like his watching subjects, had been irrevocably changed. Cheers had greeted him and his Queen that distant summer morning; now silence reigned. If the lights had gone out all over Europe, then the light had also metaphorically been snuffed out from the countless families the length and breadth of the land, whose homes would be forever bereft.

Although Britain's first casualty occurred on 21 August 1914, the *Daily Mail*'s 12 August letter column had featured Joan Seanton's letter suggesting that a 'national movement [*should*] be set afoot to discourage the wearing of mourning for soldiers and sailors… The almost universal mourning that must ensue will have an enervating effect when this will be disastrous'. The bereaved were actively encouraged to adopt a suitably stoic attitude towards death; this did not include wearing the traditional widows' weeds and garbs which had been the mainstay of female Victorian mourning. Hornchurch housewife Mrs Purbrook confided to her diary that those 'who wore no outward sign… were wise'.

Prior to the war, mourning wear and mourning rituals lasting for many months had been firmly prescribed. In addition to wearing the outward trappings of grief, death had its own mores and customs. Predominant amongst these was the idea of a 'good death', in which the beloved was eased out of this life into the next, surrounded by his or her loving and outwardly grieving family. The good death would be followed by the most elaborate funeral that could be afforded. Anything less suggested a lack of respect for the memory of the dear departed. Deprived of the cultural mourning practices of the late nineteenth and early twentieth centuries, the bereaved had to find alternative ways of negotiating the loss of their loved ones.

Daughters bereaved of fathers

Approximately 350,000 children lost a father to the Great War. Their last glimpses remained vivid. Ten-year-old Lucy Neale's mother was unable to face walking with her 31-year-old Sergeant husband and their daughter when his leave was over and so, 'He said good-bye to my mother who was crying, and we went off down the road.' Lucy walked up a hill with her father and then turned for home, 'He was still waving when I went and that was the last time I ever saw him.' Learning he had died (in Tanzania) in October 1917, a 'stunned' Lucy 'couldn't believe it'. For years she missed her father's nightly, 'Good night, Lulu'.

Although Lucy bid her father farewell on a road, many final partings occurred at railway stations (latterly only wives and children were allowed on to the platforms). The 'amount of tears on the station amongst the families who were there' made a lasting impression on one five-year-old, who always remembered the tears 'tumbling down' both her Lance Corporal father, John Jones (killed in action 22 November 1917), and her brother's faces when they bade each other farewell. Poet Edward Thomas' younger daughter remembered a similar experience. When Edward went overseas, the children accompanied him to the station for what would be the last time. Like Lucy Neale's mother, their mother Helen stayed behind, watching and watching 'until the mist and the hill hid him'.

Once in France, Edward, like most service personnel, wrote to his children, who naturally replied. Sixty-five years after his death, two precious pencil-written letters remained Myfanwy's most cherished possessions, as well as a painful memory. She had been, 'awkwardly filling in the pricked dots on a postcard with coloured wool, embroidering a wild duck to send to France [when] I saw the telegraph boy lean his bicycle against the fence. Mother stood reading the message with a face of stone. "No Answer" came like a croak, and the boy rode away.'

Decades later, Myfanwy remembered walking with her 'graven-faced' mother to the local post office, where 'wires were sent off to Mother's sisters, to Granny, and to [poet] Eleanor [Farjeon]'. For many children the stark moment their mothers heard of husbands' deaths remained vivid. Four-year-old Mary Morton remembered all her long life the arrival of what she called the 'tegrum' boy on a 1916 May morning. The message was blunt, 'Sergeant George Morton has been reported missing, believed killed in Arras.' The word 'believe' would have devastating consequences for Mary, her two sisters and her mother, who was 'shaking so much that she could scarcely hold the inevitable cup' of tea a kindly neighbour made.

Some women resigned themselves to the fact that their husbands were indeed dead; they remarried or formed new partnerships, only for their husbands to turn up after the Armistice. Seen as the ultimate treachery, such actions tore families apart. Sergeant George Morton returned home from a German POW camp in early January 1919. He found his place taken by another man and his wife heavily pregnant. George would have nothing further to do with her. Temporarily placing his children in an orphanage run by nuns for the children of ex-servicemen, he sought full custody through the courts. The subsequent divorce was reported in the local press in lurid if inaccurate terms, which included, 'Wounded Prisoner of War returns home to find his home empty, his children abandoned.'

Truth, and at least as far as the children were concerned this was far from it, was less important than sensationalism. As the presiding judge sadly commented when granting George full custody and their mother no access, 'There are almost as many tragedies at home as there are on the battlefields.' By rising as though from the dead, and with his mind clearly unbalanced, George condemned his daughters to a childhood of abuse by their stepmother. For these daughters, he would have been better off dead. There was nothing Mrs Morton could do to retain any rights over her children.

Like Myfanwy and Mary, Gertrude Farr clearly remembered the day the news of her father's death was confirmed. Puzzled as to why her 7 shilling 6 pence widow's pension and 5 shilling allowance for three-year-old Gertrude were no longer being paid, the young widow (also Gertrude) began making enquiries. She eventually discovered the reason at the local Post Office. Gertrude remembered her mother stuffing a letter into her breast, as though to 'close a hole in her heart'. This letter revealed that her husband Harry (unbeknownst to her one of the 306 British Empire soldiers found guilty through the process of capital courts martial) had been 'Shot At Dawn'.

Feeling his death to be a terrible stigma, Gertrude hid the truth from their daughter, who believed that her 25-year-old father had died in battle. Only in the 1950s did she learn that her probably shell-shocked parent had been executed for cowardice; her shock was considerable, yet it finally explained to her why, at the time, his family disowned his memory and ostracised his wife and daughter.

'Old Mother Farr', Harry's mother, who sent five sons to the Front, always said that no German bullet would get any of her sons. She was correct. The remaining Farr brothers returned unscathed. Perhaps due, in part, to the way his contemporary family had treated his memory, Farr's descendants were vocal campaigners for a pardon to be offered to those Shot At Dawn – a pardon finally, if controversially, offered by the UK Government in 2006 to all who shared Harry's fate.

Sisters bereaved of brothers: 'All the happy comradeship we knew'

In early twentieth century England, upper/middle-class brothers and sisters' lives differed considerably. Boys went off to boarding schools, sisters eagerly awaited their return for the school holidays. Brothers frequently provided a window into the wider world of their sisters' closely chaperoned lives. When a brother was killed or even went to war, his sister lost the person with whom she could most closely identify.

Mary and David Boyle appear to have been very close. Their early childhood spent together in the nursery cemented a bond that remained strong even though their genders meant their lives diverged as they grew to adulthood. In August 1914, David, a Regular Officer in the Lancashire Fusiliers, was rushed over to France with the vanguard of the BEF, whilst Mary remained at home, waiting and praying for him. Twenty-four-year-old David perished at Le Cateau on 26 August 1914, making Mary one of the first sisters to suffer bereavement.

In *Aftermath*, a series of 30 sonnets which she composed and dedicated to his memory, Mary works through the devastating sense of loss that his death has brought her. She compares the girl she was before he was killed to the woman she suddenly became; grief has aged her and she stares into a bleak future, wondering what life can hold for her now that one of the keepers of their personal story has been brutally taken from her. Not only has his death robbed her of a brother, she also mourns a lost future: David's anticipated children, her nieces and nephews, remain unconceived. Just as it would with mothers, this lost future weighs heavily upon sisters. Yet, grief can be selfish and although David left behind a widowed, grieving mother, Mary makes no mention of her; Mrs Boyle may have lost her son but Mary has lost her brother, and this is the focus of her grief.

Mary was not alone in so deeply mourning a sibling's passing. For New Zealand writer Katherine Mansfield, her younger brother's death in October 1915 was 'the greatest grief' of her life. In her diary, letters and a sonnet to 2nd Lieutenant Leslie Heron Beauchamp, nicknamed 'Chummie', she charts her loss and despair, hungrily seeking and sharing information with family about 'our dear one'. Three weeks after his death, caused by the accidental explosion of a hand grenade, she writes, 'not only am I not afraid of death – I welcome the idea... I will come as quickly as I can'. In words that could be penned to a lover, she adds, 'To you only do I belong, just as *you* belong to me.' She had been told that his last words were addressed to her, 'lift me, Katie, I can't breathe, lift me'.

Guilt, a common reaction to sudden death, may have complicated her mourning. She, the older sister, had not been there to help her younger brother when he pleaded for her. The following month she acknowledges, 'I am just as much dead as he is'. Her only comfort appears to have been reminiscing about events that happened when he was alive. She confesses to him in her *Journal* that she has almost lost the will to write anything other than to and about him, although she knows that she must do so for financial reasons. Eventually, she seems to resolve her dilemma by imagining that she is writing for 'my brother, my little boy brother' and her 15 February 1916 diary entry vows, 'I will not fail'. According to her husband, 'no single one of Katherine Mansfield's friends who went to the war returned alive from it', but the death of Chummie, six years her junior, was the hardest loss for her to resolve.

These middle-class, educated women found methods and time in which to record their grief for lost siblings. For sentiments of sisters from less privileged backgrounds, reported words are helpful. Padre (originally Private) R.F. Wearmouth, Chaplain to the Forces 1915–20, ministered to the wounded and dying from his base at 21 CCS at Corbie on the Somme. He painstakingly transcribed in his diary extracts from letters he received from families of men to whom he had ministered in their dying hours. 'The loss of my brother is a terrible one for us,' writes one sister. 'One thing consoles us and that is he died as he would have wished – giving the best he had willingly.' Another writes, 'I will try and bear up for Father and Mother's sake… Oh, he was a son, a brother in a thousand.'

The sister of 25-year-old Private A.A. Connell, who died on 29 September 1916, was so grief-stricken that a friend wrote on her behalf, 'She is so thankful to know that her brother had every care and attention… she is anxious to know if he mentioned her name or left any kind of message… They were so devoted to each other.' This sister was now alone in the world, her parents having previously died. It must have seemed to her, as it did to countless other bereaved sisters, that both her past and her future lay buried with him.

Not all siblings were close. Some sisters, particularly those occupied with their own war work, were not overwhelmed by grief. The daughter of a Liberal MP, Elsie Corbett was a volunteer nurse. Her published diary includes only a brief entry for Christmas Day 1916: 'Late that night I got a garbled cable that told me my younger brother had been killed.' Arthur had been killed on 4 December. Perhaps his death made relatively little impact upon her; she was pursuing her own war service in distant Serbia and he is only mentioned six times in her 182-page book, *The Red Cross in Serbia*. Or, as her memoirs were published almost 50 years later, he may simply have faded from her memory.

Another bereaved sister involved in her own work was Canadian Army Nurse, Lieutenant Clare Gass, whose war diaries detail her Western Front service. On 20 April 1917, she learned her brother, Blanchard, 'was killed on the 9th I think'; when confirmation of his and a cousin's deaths are received, there are few introspective comments, although on 4 May she notes having received letters from Major Ralston telling me of the last day of B. V., nicknamed 'our Happy Warrior'. His death is not, however, accorded greater space than the deaths of a number of patients in her care. Neither Elsie nor Clare appear to have grieved deeply; however, their characters may have precluded sorrowful written words or their nursing work may have hardened them, like soldiers, to war deaths.

Other war-workers were less immune. QAIMNS Kate Luard was deeply affected by her brother's death, and she took comfort when casualties who served at Gallipoli with her brother shared memories with her, writing in her autobiography, 'Major S. told me all about F[*rank*] on the 13th.' Perhaps the information was too personal for public publication: she simply promised, 'I am writing separately'.

Bereaved sweethearts: 'My heart, for loss of you, was broken' (Vera Brittain)

Belgium's Adinkerke Military Cemetery is the final resting place of 168 British and Commonwealth dead. One grave commemorates 19-year-old Lieutenant Frederick Philip Pemble of the recently formed Royal Air Force. Phil's 19-year-old shop assistant fiancée, Phyllis Iliff left a detailed account of her mourning which shows her attempts to cope with his loss. The first record of her grief is a poem written on 29 July 1918, dedicated to 'My darling Phil who died in France 29 June 1918.' The poem ends with words inscribed on many headstones: 'Till the Day Breaks and Shadows Flee Away.'

In a sonnet written a fortnight later, she confesses that in the depths of the night she imagines Phil returning to her to reassure her that, as he 'gave his life for England', she should accept the rightness of his sacrifice – a sentiment that recurs in many contemporary writings, almost certainly as a way of making the loss of a young life bearable and meaningful. Phyllis struggles unsuccessfully to obey this injunction, although there are hints that this idea had formed part of a last conversation before the young airman went overseas. Inconsolable because she was not with him when he died and could not even attend his funeral, she confesses to him that all she can hope for now is that her life too will soon end.

By 2 February 1919, the traditional style of her early poetry has turned to more modern prose. Now she starts to confront the yawning gap that his death has left in her life and although God may have held out a 'welcoming hand' to Phil, lying in the darkness, she realises what it means to be totally bereft. The letter is addressed to Phil and it hints at his fate, 'Your body which should have belonged to me, must have made a big hole in the ground. And I who could have made living beautiful for you even though you had been crippled, or disfigured or blinded may not touch or hear or see you anymore.'

Phyllis was far from alone in believing that a life caring for a crippled husband was preferable to a life as a spinster or widow – some women even offered in newspaper, personal advertisements, and 'Lonely Heart' columns to marry a wounded officer. One of the countless letters addressed to Padre Wearmouth begged him to assure a wounded sweetheart that his Meg 'wants him to live and if he is crippled [*she still*] want[*s*] him if he is in pieces'. She asked him to reassure her wounded beloved that 'his sweetheart will try to cheer up his mother all she can, as he asked me to when he went away if anything happened.' As the worst did happen, perhaps the bereaved mother and sweetheart were able to find some mutual comfort in sharing memories of the one who was, as Meg wrote, 'so inexpressively dear to me'. Meg and countless other women's assertions that they want their loved one to return irrespective of wounds or disability, makes the much-quoted lines from Siegfried Sassoon's poem 'The Glory of Women', 'You love us when we're home on leave/Or wounded in a mentionable place', seem the more misguided.

Perhaps unsurprisingly in view of his profession, Wearmouth received countless letters from correspondents affirming that God's ways are best and speaking of the comfort derived from attending church services. Not so young Phyllis: in her letter to Phil she mocks the church service she attended the previous Sunday. There are strong hints that not only is religion failing to sustain her, she does not even have a supportive network of women friends. She describes an incident at work where colleagues were far from sympathetic: 'I felt so awful I got up and went out of the room and into the dark stockroom and there among the darkness and dust, I cried and cried for about ten minutes.'

With no obvious living confidante, she turns to her dead one. Perhaps her misery is compounded by the knowledge that her friend Gladys' fiancé has (so far) survived the war and they are to be married the following week; women's covert jealousy of those whose loved ones survived is not uncommon, although often well-concealed in their writings. Phyllis' letter ends with the assertion, 'If ever I get married I shall burn this book, your dear letters and your still dearer photo's [*sic*] and go forth on my new life with only your glorious memory to help. All my love, dear one. Phyl.'

By the first anniversary of Phil's death, Phyllis considers her grief to be greater than that of any other woman's, 'Did anyone ever suffer as I have suffered?' Like Mary Boyle's for her brother David, her mourning appears entirely focused upon herself and all that she is suffering. By June 1919, again like Mary and so many other war-bereaved, she is finding some comfort in sleep. She dreamt, 'This morning at 1 a.m. you came to me as you have so often before and for a while I was in Paradise then comes the awaken [*sic*] as ever – alone, always alone.'

Nine months later, her grief still as raw, she wonders whether she is being punished for having worshipped Phil so much; this possibility has led her to atheism. 'An atheist I am and such shall remain. In other words, I deny the god of my Fathers.' This comment was far more shocking in 1918 than today. Belief that the war and, of course, war deaths were part of some divine plan sustained countless combatants and civilians throughout the years of conflict.

If denying religion in the early twentieth century was taboo, so too were sex and sexuality. Despite official fears that the illegitimate birth rate would spiral – not only among servicewomen – countless young sweethearts exercised self-restraint, seemingly not always initiated by the woman. QAIMNS Dorothy Turle longed at least to be kissed by her fiancé, Captain Ainslie. Posted to Gallipoli, he regrets *his* refusal to comply with *her* longing 'to be kissed. What a fool I was. You would not have to wait long now'. They waited forever; he died three weeks later.

Dorothy eventually married Ainslie's best friend, making, on her own admission, a companionable rather than a passionate marriage.

Like countless war-bereaved fiancés, Phyllis and Phil never consummated their love. She bitterly regrets the loss of his unconceived children. By November 1920 she has invented two 'dream children' about whom she writes to him on a regular basis – as though he were away on business and needs to be kept abreast of their progress. The modern reader may feel uncomfortable with this imaginary or 'dream husband', but for those who saw only empty years and a barren future, it was a coping mechanism. Perhaps assisted by the presence of these 'dream tiddlies', acceptance if not resolution may have occurred, for in October 1921, her final entry states, 'I sleep with the flowers in my room and tomorrow I will lay them on the cross that is all that I have to worship you from, as I have done for the past three years; three years can it possibly be less than three hundred?' As she laid the flowers lovingly brought from home on his grave, did 21-year-old Phyllis still feel, as she had in July 1919, 'that the war was over and my life with it. Though [*Peace*] may bring joy to thousands yet, to those breaking hearts it means the end of all things. Oh I wish I was dead'?

Despite her earlier assertion that she would burn the book, along with Phil's letters and photos, in 1922 Phyllis married Ralph Castle, who was over 40 years her senior. This was almost certainly a compromise, as many others including Dorothy Turle freely admitted their marriages to have been merely preferable to spending the rest of life alone. The words of Phyllis' young womanhood and her grief speak across the century; they give an insight into the complex mourning of those who, being neither the dead soldier's wife, mother, nor sister, were forced to find their own ways to confront the bleak and endless years that lay ahead.

Bereaved wives: 'I am engulfed in this despair' (Helen Thomas)

Charles (nick-named Dick) Doughty-Wylie was on the staff of Sir Ian Hamilton, the Commander in Chief of the Mediterranean Expeditionary Force, tasked with the invasion of Turkey. Following the hotly-contested landing on V-Beach at Gallipoli on 25 April 1915, Doughty-Wylie was instrumental in successfully driving forward a stalled attack on Turkish fortifications. At the height of his success (rare for that ill-fated campaign) in taking one of the first day objectives, Hill 141, Doughty-Wylie was shot through the head and lies where he fell in the only isolated grave on the Peninsula. His fearless leadership earned him a posthumous Victoria Cross.

Whilst Doughty-Wylie was fighting in Turkey, his wife Lilian was working in an English hospital in France. She heard, via her father-in-law, of Dick's fate five days after his death. Her meticulously archived notebooks record her disbelief, despair, and the intimate details of her mourning. Yet, whilst her personal life crumbled around her, she, like so many war-bereaved women, carried on with her professional duties, 'The shock was terrible. I don't quite know what I did for the first 60 seconds, I was nearly mad. Then I pulled myself together and went back to my dressings.' In disbelief, she sought further news, 'I never passed a day in such agony of misery it was physical as well as mental pain. I did my work in the theatre where there was an operation but I could have screamed aloud. Oh the suspense!' Despite the dreaded confirmation arriving on 2 May, she refused to believe it; surely as his wife, she would have sensed that he had died. Although her mother immediately offered to come to France to be with her, this was rejected, 'I particularly do not want any of my family to come out here. I find it easier to behave with the dignity of my position as the head of an English hospital by *myself*. Anybody close would only upset me.' Like a number of other serving women, war work took priority over personal grief.

Inevitably, as the wife of so prominent an officer, Lilian received many condolence messages. In stark contrast to many bereaved who, like Katherine Mansfield, cherished letters eulogising their loved one, copying these out by hand and circulating them amongst family members whilst the cherished original was preserved, Lilian described them as 'maudlin things'. For many, if not for Lilian, speaking or writing the loved one's name helped keep him or her alive a little longer.

One correspondent who seems to have brought Lilian some comfort was Gertrude Bell. Although there is a belief that Gertrude was Doughty-Wylie's mistress, there is no conclusive evidence, and indeed it is far more likely that theirs was a deep friendship rather than a sexual relationship. Lilian writes of the women's shared grief, 'June 12, I had a strange letter from Gerty on the 10th. She tells me that she saw Dick 2 days ago after [*she*] had heard of his death. It was 4 am quite light and she was wide awake. She suddenly saw him sitting on her bed, he was leaning slightly forward and his eyes were wet.'

Lilian also dreamed of her dead husband: 'I dreamed last night that Dick was wounded in the lower regions, that I had the severed part in my hand. It was a strange muddly dream.' On their wedding anniversary, 1 June, she records in great detail another dream in which Dick:

> said that the last words of his last letter to me saying 'all my love and kisses till we meet again' were meant to cancel that part of the marriage service that says 'till death us do part' and he asked me if I also would renew my marriage vow to him on the same terms. If so I could no longer consider myself his widow as widowhood meant the conclusion of the contract and I was renewing mine.

Lilian seems to take this injunction as reassurance that her wish of soon dying will be fulfilled, a wish not granted for decades, as she survived until 24 April 1961, having also served in World War Two.

Lilian was one of the approximately 190,000 women who were widowed as a result of the war. Helen Thomas, wife of poet Edward Thomas, writes movingly in *World Without End* of Edward's last days with his family. The passion and pain of their final hours together is palpable. Seven years later, she confessed to still grieving for 'my lover to whom I gave my whole being and in giving myself possessed myself as I can never do again'. She too was comforted by another woman who was close to her husband, the poet Eleanor Farjeon.

When Eleanor received the telegram telling her the dreaded news, she rushed to Helen's side. Helen greeted her with the words, 'I asked you to come because I thought I could comfort you – oh Eleanor, you'll have to comfort me.' This the grieving women attempted to do. Eleanor remembered how 'We held each other's hands… I put my arms around her and held her while she wept.' She movingly recreates these moments of intense grief when the two women who both loved Edward Thomas mourned together. Temporarily delaying her own grief, Eleanor ran the Thomas home, even sharing Helen's bed as she sought to sustain the grieving widow. Eleanor would, in time, work through her own grief by writing a biography exploring her own deeply complex relationship with Edward and his *Last Four Years*, acknowledging that he knew how much she loved him, although doubting whether his feelings for her extended beyond friendship.

Bereaved mothers, the hardest grief to bear: 'No mother's care to tend and watch' (Alexandra Grantham)

During the 99 years separating the battles of Waterloo and Mons, war deaths had touched relatively few British families. Simultaneously, the likelihood of children predeceasing parents due to natural causes had receded. Thanks to falling infant mortality rates, most parents could realistically expect their children to outlive them, leaving them with few emotional strategies for coping with a child's premature death and the overwhelming grief that this engenders. In mothers' writings for their lost sons, whether by the educated or the barely literate, we see mothers attempting to develop necessary coping strategies. Whilst many demonstrate how overwhelming parental grief can be when a beloved child is killed, others show that pride in the child's imagined heroism can temper grief and give a meaning to an otherwise meaningless death; these conflicting emotions frequently share the same space.

If, before the Derby Act and the 1916 introduction of Universal Male Conscription mothers had been conscripted, even bullied, into encouraging sons to enlist, they were also seen, and saw themselves, as epitomising the greatest of all human griefs: that of a mother for her child. Images of the *Mater Dolorosa* abounded in wartime Anglican England. Both genders used this as a way of linking contemporary mothers' sorrow to that of Mary, thereby helping some mothers to deal with what grief therapists consider the hardest bereavement of all to cope with, the death of an adult child.

Like countless other women, Alexandra Grantham experienced the Great War for Civilisation as both a mother and a wife. Whilst outwardly a stereotypical socially privileged British family, certain aspects of the Grantham's family life are less typical, for Alexandra was German by birth. Despite naturalisation through her marriage, in 1914 many would have considered her 'an enemy' and feelings ran high against those who were seen as 'aliens'. Having a husband and son in His Majesty's Army was not considered proof positive of loyalty to the British cause. Her loyalty would be put to the test.

By 22 September 1914, Captain Frederick Grantham was serving in France with the Royal Munster Fusiliers; his and Alexandra's eldest son, 19-year-old 2nd Lieutenant Hugo, was posted to Gallipoli. Still at home was three-year-old Godfrey, as well as 16-year-old Alexander, who would be safe – just as long as it was all over, if not by Christmas 1914 then at least by the following one.

In *Mater Dolorosa*, a series of elegiac poems written for Hugo, Alexandra gives an insight into overwhelming maternal grief, as she seeks to hold on to her memories and recalls the agonising moment of their physical separation. Like so many thousand such separations, it occurred at a station, where her valiant smile was specifically donned to mask her aching heart. She is intensely aware of women's need to be publicly cheerful, not only for their own, but also for their menfolk's sake.

Many of the women who were so roundly condemned for cheering the boys as they left for the Front were hiding breaking hearts with hollow smiles. Men may march to war to protect women, but in that moment of farewell, a gender reversal occurs: the woman must protect the man for, if she lets her guard down, he may be unable to cope. The gendering of warfare could hardly be more marked; soldiers stand by the train, waiting for the whistle to blow, wives and mothers 'wave with trembling hands' until the train is lost from sight. If men rush to follow their country's colours, women can only stare as the station master waves his green flag, then wander home with heavy hearts. Fears and tears must await the privacy of the echoing house with its discarded cricket bats and silent gramophones, and, come nightfall, the empty bed.

Alexandra followed as best she could the heavily censored accounts of the Gallipoli campaign. Maternal fears and pride coexist as first anxiety, then pride overwhelm her. Although Hugo barely mentioned this in a letter home, she was elated when, on 4 June 1915, Hugo was Mentioned in Despatches. She momentarily accepts the promise of military glory that at other times she vehemently criticises, and she voices personal pride in her child's manly achievements.

Although she learns that Frederick is 'Missing believed wounded', Hugo himself does not seem particularly worried about his father. In his 21 June 1915 letter (which must have reached her after his death) he simply wrote, 'in a fierce action the time goes like wildfire' and it is unsurprising that no one quite knows what has happened. In the rest of this undoubtedly last letter home, he provides uncomfortable details about the types of shells that land close to his trench, as well as the fact that he has, as all soldiers had to do, written his will. His mother was his beneficiary.

175

Fighting soon intensified for Hugo. At sunset on Monday, 28 June 1915, having been held in reserve all day, and supported by too few guns, Lieutenant Hugo Grantham and men of the Essex Regiment attacked an enemy trench. News soon reached Alexandra that never again 'on this wide earth' would her mother arms enfold her child. There will be no homecoming for Hugo, nor will she even be able to cradle his beloved body one last time. 'Too far, too dead [*his*] body lies'.

On 14 August 1915, a memorial service was held for the young lieutenant at All Saints Church, Maldon, Essex. In France, men of the Royal Munster Fusiliers were bringing in their dead who had lain in No Man's Land since 9 May. A dog-tag, bearing the name Captain Frederick Grantham, was found. His body had disappeared. However, by the time she received this confirmation, Alexandra's grief for Hugo was so overwhelming that she had no emotional energy left, indeed anger (a recognised reaction to bereavement) informs the few lines directed towards him; he has failed her at the very moment she most needed his support. Accusingly she writes, 'Can you not hear me weep?' She addresses him no more and directs her undivided grief, never anger, towards their dead son.

A tragic footnote to Alexandra's story is that on 21 June 1942, her youngest son, 30-year-old Pilot Officer Godfrey, was killed in a flying accident. A name on a panel at Le Touret Memorial to the Missing, France, a low headstone at Twelve Tree Copse Cemetery, in Turkey, and Grave 407 in St Wystan's Churchyard, Repton, England, were all that remained of three of her four beloved men.

In 1920, Alexandra Grantham fulminated against laws that deprived 'women of all rights of possession [*including*] of their children'. One mother who was deprived not only of her son, but also of what many people would have seen as a share of what was rightfully hers was the mother of the much-lauded sailor 'Boy VC', 16-year-old Jack Cornwell. Mortally wounded at the Battle of Jutland, he died on 2 June 1916. Posthumously gazetted VC, his widowed mother received Jack's medal from the King at Buckingham Palace with appropriate pomp and ceremony. Unsurprisingly, the stories of young Cornwell's gallantry appeared in newspapers across the British Empire. Over seven million children donated pennies to the benevolent Jack Cornwell Fund set up to honour the memory of this ordinary boy from East Ham, who had 'done his bit' in spectacular fashion, thereby giving youngsters from the most socially-deprived sections of society their very own war hero.

Sadly the country which had done and would continue to do so much to preserve and glorify the son's memory, did nothing for his impoverished widowed mother, Alice, who, to provide for her younger children, was forced to take a scrubbing job in a Stepney hostel, consisting of a gruelling, 12-hour day. Restrained and dignified, she refused publicly to criticise the way she had been treated, whilst admitting to an *East Ham Echo* journalist in April 1919 that 'It seems odd after all the fuss they made over my poor son that I should have to do this... I am not grumbling.'

Alice had much to grumble about, nevertheless. Her widow's pension was too meagre to support her remaining family and, despite her request to the Jack Cornwell Memorial Fund trustees, such meagre financial aid was forthcoming that when she died in October 1919, her family were so poor that the undertaker refused to proceed with the funeral without some guarantee that the expenses would be paid. Jack's siblings emigrated to Canada in 1923, leaving behind the country that had lionised their brother's memory and marginalised their destitute mother.

Alice Cornwell's son became a national icon with hundreds of columns of newspaper space dedicated to his actions; Alexandra Grantham memorialised her son in poetry. German sculptress Kathe Kollwitz expressed her grief for her 19-year-old son Peter in stone. Initially, like so many mothers she was happy, even proud, to accept his decision to volunteer. When he was killed, in October 1914, she records being overwhelmed by her 'sense of guilt, of remorse over the responsibility the older generation had for the slaughter of the young.' She wrote of her anguish at the youth of Europe massacring each other.

As Alexandra Grantham had done, she saw the commonality of maternal suffering: all mothers' sons had been 'betrayed'. Kathe admitted to a friend, 'There is in our lives a wound which will never heal. Nor should it.' In a manner not dissimilar to Phyllis Iliff's letters to Phil Pemble and Alexandra's poems to Hugo, she speaks directly to Peter: she will undertake a memorial to him, vowing, 'I shall do this work for you and for the others.' Twelve years later, after numerous false starts, she was finally satisfied, and she assures her son, 'In the autumn – Peter I will bring it to you.' Adjacent to Peter's grave in Roggevelde German Military Cemetery, Belgium, surrounded by bleak tablets naming a myriad of slaughtered young men, the statues of a kneeling father and mother huddle in prayer and supplication, expressing the totality of parental agony, guilt and grief.

Pilgrims to distant graves: 'Visits to serried ranks of headstones'

Following significant furore surrounding his initial burial in a humble grave, John Cornwell was reinterred in a more elaborate resting-place in East London's Manor Park Cemetery. For the brief time she outlived him, Alice could visit his grave. In her grief and guilt, Kathe Kollwitz visited her son's burial place, and Phyllis Iliff eventually placed flowers on Phil's grave. It was rumoured, although never confirmed, that Lilian Doughty-Wylie visited Charles' Gallipoli grave before the January 1916 evacuation of the Peninsula.

Alexandra Grantham was less fortunate: she, like thousands of others, recognised she would never place flowers on her child's grave. For many of those whose loved one had a known grave, a visit to that 'corner of a foreign field that is forever England' was almost impossible. For most, the sheer cost of such a journey was utterly prohibitive.

However, in the mid-1920s, the St Barnabas Society, founded by a former New Zealand Army Chaplain, organised a series of battlefield pilgrimages to *Ypres and The Somme* (1923), *Gallipoli and Salonika* (1926), *Ypres and the Menin Gate* (1927). Funded by public donations, some of the bereaved were taken to visit loved ones' final fighting and resting-places. Local and national newspapers praised this 'gallant organisation', which hoped that undertaking a pilgrimage might ease sorrow. Some female pilgrims found words in which to express and preserve for posterity the enormity of their own emotions and of those who travelled with them.

One Tasmanian nurse, who had served at 3rd Australian General Hospital on the island of Lemnos, returned on 1 September 1926 to lay a wreath in memory of 20 17-year-old Tasmanian cadets whom she had nursed and who had perished so far from home. Visiting an ANZAC cemetery on the Peninsula itself, one sibling commented that finally she 'could see traces of where the boys had been'. United in sorrow, an Australian mother stood with a 'sad-eyed girl holding two wreaths, one for her father and one for her

178

fiancé'. One New Zealand mother climbed four arduous miles to reach the top of Chunuk Bair to lay a wreath where her son died. She was overwhelmed to feel that, 'I have actually walked the way he went.'

Others scrambled all over the unforgiving terrain to 'know the manner of the country in which their boys fought and endured and fell'. The official St Barnabas record-keeper commented on 'the fortitude and determination shown by the women in the party' who found 'strength for their special missions'. QAIMNS sister Kate Luard, who had hungered for details of her brother's death, was amongst the Gallipoli pilgrims. Many of the bereaved derived some comfort from seeing where loved ones fought, died, and would forever remain.

Some St Barnabas pilgrims travelled more than 3,000 miles to stand for a few moments by a grave or a memorial and place 'a wreath beside it... a token, almost a heart's blood'; others 'took back home with them some blades of grass or a handful of soil from the loved one's cemetery. They were momentarily reunited with him. Not one of them but came away comforted.' Preserved letters suggest that those first pilgrims – among them – the elderly, the weak, and sometimes near illiterate – made on their return home a financial donation, often at considerable personal sacrifice, to allow another woman to find the solace that she herself had found. 'I am forwarding my boy's pension for your good work,' wrote one Leicester mother and another sent 'what I can spare... to help another mother get the satisfaction I have got'. One mother's words encapsulate the sentiments of all who undertook the sad journey, 'I have now seen the last resting-place of my loved one and that is a lot to a mother.' Like today's visitors to the, initially Imperial, now Commonwealth War Graves Commission cemeteries and memorials, they stood in awe as they gazed around, frequently overcome by the spirit of quiet and repose which permeated the cemeteries, feeling that, 'even in such bitter lands they abide in beauty and peace.'

Every night at 7.55pm, the traffic heading into and out of the Belgian city of Ypres (Ieper) through the Menin Gate comes to a halt. Between two and eight members of the Fire Brigade march solemnly to the exterior arch of the Gate and at precisely 8pm they raise their bugles and the plaintive notes of the Last Post rise into the night sky. Sometimes watched by a mere handful of the curious, at other times by many hundreds of pilgrims, this ritual has taken place in Ypres since 1929 (during the Second World War Nazi Occupation the brief ceremony was temporarily transferred to Brookwood in Surrey). Many of the watchers feel shivers go down their spines as the sad lament fills the air and, wherever their eyes rest, they see panels with the inscribed names of the 54,406 British, Australian, Canadian, Indian and South African forces who lost their lives in the Ypres Salient before 16 August 1917 and who have no known grave. (New Zealanders are primarily commemorated at Tyne Cot a few miles away, along with the names of servicemen from the British Empire and her Dominions who died after the 1917 date.)

Designed by Sir Reginald Blomfield, this Gate, arguably the most iconic of all the Memorials to the Missing of the Great War, was unveiled in an elaborate ceremony on 24 July 1927. 'Wipers', as it was dubbed during the war, bristled with official and Royal dignitaries. Largely funded by the St Barnabas Society, another group of honoured spectators also attended. These were the 700 mainly working-class mothers and wives, whose sons' and husbands' names were inscribed on the acres of panels, accompanied by some young girls who had lost brothers or a betrothed in the area.

The *Daily Mail* praised this female army: 'Mothers of heroes, women whose losses were bravely borne and whose duty has been nobly done.' In its sensitivity to the grief of the bereaved poor, the St Barnabas Society ensured that, 'every genuine applicant who applied in time received a ticket. For the aged poor and crippled who could not travel we have started a fund to provide them with an illustrated album of the visit and ceremony. At least 300 will receive this consolation.'

Accommodation in the town being at a premium, pilgrims were 'housed' in the trains that had brought them from England and the Association hired a cinema where they could eat, rest and share their emotions before and after the Unveiling. For some the experience was overwhelming:

> holding little bunches of flowers from English gardens, when they saw the long lines of names on the stone tears came into their eyes. Tom was there somewhere, a little name on the Menin Gate... The Menin Gate was left to the mothers of England. They came to it so bravely and calmly, holding their little posies of English flowers. 'That's him' they said, and cried a little. Then they hung their appealing flowers on the Menin Gate [*forming a*] little cluster... all from England.

One of the hundreds of wreaths placed that day spoke for so many, 'With proud thanksgiving from the Mothers of the Missing.'

Even today, nearly 90 years after it was unveiled, it is impossible to visit the Menin Gate and not find a British Legion poppy reverently placed against the name of a long dead but never forgotten family member. His name and a message engraved on the simple wooden tribute, bear witness that his body may have disappeared but his 'Name Liveth For Evermore'.

Elaborate ceremonies, intimate cemeteries, and pilgrimages to distant lands offered some comfort and closure, yet the heart-breaking truth remained: never again would the arms of the bereaved enfold the one who had been 'so in-expressively dear'. In vain had women prayed, 'dear God, bring him back.'

Conclusion

'I Was Very Proud of My Service'

When, at the eleventh hour of the eleventh day of the eleventh month, the guns fell silent, thousands of women had experienced a life unimaginable four years earlier. Whilst men had enlisted or been conscripted into His Majesty's Armed Forces, women had voluntarily offered their services. From the drawing room, the schoolroom, the hospital ward, the factory and the servants' hall, they had stepped into the breach created by men's absence, proving, in Dr Elsie Inglis' words, that women 'could do it' – whatever 'it' happened to be.

Initially informed that it was women's duty to become unofficial recruiting sergeants, some had complied. Many had proudly waved a beloved husband, brother, son or sweetheart off to war, accepting that she must not prevent him from doing his duty; her encouragement may even have helped him to recognise that his country needed him. Eager to send love, luck and comfort, women and children picked up their wool until the country resounded to the clicking of knitting needles; not only did the finished articles provide physical warmth, but the letters they included created a web of love between the home and the front.

In August 1914, an infinitesimal number of women had a designated role. The Army Medical Services soon realised that there were insufficient military/naval nurses to care for potential casualties. Professional nurses from civilian hospitals eagerly responded to the call for more nurses. Nurses travelled thousands of miles, from across the English-speaking world, often at considerable personal expense, to assist the Allied cause. In hospitals at home and overseas, in Casualty Clearing Stations, on ambulance trains, barges and ships, nurses did all in their power to alleviate suffering; the safety and the comfort, even the lives, of the wounded always came before their own. Their dedicated care hastened the recovery of thousands of troops. A woman's presence often comforted the fatally wounded or those who were beyond medical help. When asked to 'Kiss me for my mother', nurses and volunteers complied.

182

CONCLUSION

Unlike nurses, other women desperate to serve their country found their paths barred. Aristocrats, eager volunteers and trained doctors refused to be restrained by the barriers an at best chauvinistic and at worst misogynistic medical hierarchy had erected. They simply bypassed red tape and transported themselves and the units they had founded, and often funded, to the Front, earning the perpetual gratitude of many Allies whose medical services were stretched beyond breaking point. These Units took advances, retreats and imprisonment in their stride, the women coming to represent 'Our Ally, England'. As one Serbian journalist remarked, 'no wonder Britain is so great if her women are like that'!

By September 1915, an ammunition crisis loomed and women flocked into the factories. Often working 12-hour shifts, six days a week, they became 'the girl behind the man behind the gun'. Explosions and accidents were all in the day's work. If their fighting menfolk could 'stick it', so too would they. Civilians as well as an Army need feeding as well as supplying with munitions. With Britain's access to imported food seriously restricted and thousands of tons of foodstuff being lost to enemy action, it became women's duty to feed the nation. The Women's Land Army kept the spectre of famine that had stalked the land at bay. By speeding the plough, these women helped prevent German U-boats from starving the nation into submission.

In 1917, the High Command accepted that although women could not fulfil a combat role, they could replace men in the rear. Women responded to this call for another form of National Service. Whether the predominantly working-class women and erstwhile servants of the WAACS, the 'perfect ladies' whose family connections with the Navy led them to join the WRNS, or the 'nice gels' eager to acquire mechanical and even flying skills of the WRAF, they rose to the challenges of Service life. Initially considered ''orrible Army women' of loose morals, cynics revised their opinions. These militarised women were enthusiastically cheered when, in the Peace Day Celebrations, for the first time ever they marched alongside their brothers-in-arms.

Although before 1914 nurses had died on active service, female war casualties were still the exception. But as the panels in York Minster, the CWGC headstones, and the names on war memorials across the land bear witness, between 1914 and 1918, women too made the ultimate sacrifice. Killed in explosions, by poisoning, through accidents, as a direct result of enemy fire-power or even by execution, they and even their grieving relatives accepted that women's lives counted little when weighed against their nation's cause. Women too, in Gabrielle Petit's words, 'knew how to die'.

The majority of the 908,000 British and Colonial war dead would have been mourned by a woman. In their grief, some women sought another woman's comfort; some grieved alone, their imaginations creating a dream-world inhabited by ghostly brothers, sons, husbands, unborn children; others awaited an end to their now apparently meaningless lives. Children grew up fatherless; mothers and sisters acknowledged that there would be no future generation – their bloodline extinguished. Some women gained solace from the burial of the Unknown Warrior; maybe, just maybe, he was their own lost soldier. Visiting a loved one's final resting-place or treading the ground where he had last been seen brought closure to some. At the unveiling of the Menin Gate and through pilgrimages to distant battlefields, some women bade their soldier a final farewell, acknowledging that even though the world had stopped spinning, he was dead – forever.

For four years, women had been let out of the cages that had defined, confined and restricted their lives. As nurses, they pioneered treatments and cared for the psychologically as well as the physically wounded; some were wounded and psychologically damaged themselves. As physicians and surgeons they proved to male members of a traditionalist profession that women could perform surgery on and treat men, not just women and children. In the factories and in the fields, women demonstrated skills equal to those of the men they replaced. As servicewomen they experienced camaraderie and a sense of their own self-worth hitherto undreamed of, and accepted that they were legitimate enemy targets.

Thousands of women who had been engaged on war work hoped, perhaps naively, that the post-war world would be fit for heroines as well as heroes. Yet, this future did not materialise. As one volunteer put it, the war years were simply, 'Four years out of life.' The plaudits, military decorations and civilian honours women had received, the new freedoms they had enjoyed, and the independence they had experienced were strictly 'For the Duration'. Many felt that if their country no longer recognised their achievements, they would use their own abilities and resources to keep their memories alive. Their associations, reunions, magazines, newsletters and personal correspondence stretched over decades. Many ultimately bequeathed precious and intimate personal records and memorabilia to the Imperial War Museum Women's War Work Collection and to archives being formed across the Empire. Perhaps future generations would then understand women's integral contribution to the Great War for Civilisation.

However, for decades women's war work did not form part of the War's mainstream historiography, with women's contributions largely overlooked. Nevertheless, these hundreds of thousands of forgotten women war workers would doubtless have echoed Great Britain's last surviving veteran, WRAF Florence Green who, at the age of 110, more than 90 years after her enlistment in 1918, simply told a reporter, 'I was very proud of my service.'

Select Bibliography

Parliamentary Papers

Ministry of Munitions, Health of Munitions Workers' Committee, *Health of the Munition Worker*, (HMSO, 1917)

Morgan, Ben (comp.) Reconstruction Committee Sub-Committee on Women's Employment, *Memorandum and Tabular Report on The Employment of Women in Industries Together with a Detailed List of Processes on which they are so engaged*, (HMSO, June 1917)

Report of the War Cabinet Committee on Women in Industry, (HMSO, 1919)

English Census: 1871-1911

Archives

Australian War Memorial, Treloar Crescent, Campbell ACT 2612, Australia. Telephone: +0061 (02) 6243 4211 *www.awm.gov.au* Extensive information about Australian nurses

The British Library, 96 Euston Road, London NW1 2DB, Telephone: +0044 (0)843 208 1144 *www.bl.uk*

Imperial War Museum Department of Documents, Recorded Sound, Printed Books, and Women's Work Collection. Largest repository of material relating to women in the UK. Some associations' journals also held. IWM London, Lambeth Road, London SE1 6HZ UK Telephone: +0044 (0) 20 7416 5000 *www.iwm.org.uk*

National Archives Kew, Richmond, Surrey TW9 4DU Telephone: +0044 (0) 20 8876 3444 *www.nationalarchives.gov.uk* Search for nurses' and WAAC records. None held for WRAF or WRNS (fee payable to download)

National Army Museum, Royal Hospital Road, Chelsea, London SW3 4HT Telephone: +0044 (0) 20 7881 6606 *www.nam.ac.uk* Material relating to WAACS

Peter Liddle Collection, Leeds University Library, University of Leeds, Leeds LS2 9JT UK Telephone: +0044 (0) 113 343 5663 *www.library.leeds.ac.uk* Significant material donated by members of the SWH, WAAC, WLA, Nursing Services and private individuals, (Phyllis Iliff filed under DO 69).

Websites

www.ancestry.co.uk censuses 1881-1911 and Births, Marriages Deaths

www.cwgc.org lists graves of serving personnel in the Commission's perpetual care

www.newspapers.com The Times and many US newspapers can be viewed on line (subscription required)

www.scarletfinders.co.uk Maud McCarthy's Diaries available, transcribed by Sue Light from WO95/3988, 3989, 3990 and 3991

Newspapers, Periodicals, (1914-1920), and Association Magazines

Blackwoods Magazine
British Journal of Nursing
Cardonald Souvenir Magazine
Daily Graphic
Daily Mail
Daily Sketch
Dornock *Souvenir Magazine 1916-1919*
The Times
FANY *Gazette*

Books

Anderson, Agnes, *"Johnnie" of the QMAAC*, (Heath Cranton, 1920)

Beauchamp, Pat, *Fanny Goes to War*, (John Murray, 1919)

Beauchamp, Pat, *Fanny Went To War*, (George Routledge & Sons, 1940)

Black, Catherine, *King's Nurse, Beggar's Nurse* (Hurst and Blackett, 1939)

Bradford, May, *A Hospital Letter Writer* in France, (Methuen, 1920)

Brittain, Vera (ed. Alan Bishop with Terry Smart), *Chronicle of Youth – War Diary*, (Victor Gollancz, 1981)

Cosens, Monica, *Lloyd George's Munition Girls*, (Hutchison & Co., 1916)

Courtney, Kate, *Extracts From A Diary During The War*, (The Victor Press, 1928)

Dearmer, Mabel, *Letters From A Field Hospital*, (Macmillan & Co., 1916)

Grantham, Alexandra E., *Mater Dolorosa*, (Heinemann, 1915)

Greig, G., *Women's Work on the Land 1916*, (Jarrold and Sons, [1916])

Gwynne-Vaughan, Dame Helen, *Service with the Army*, (Hutchinson, [n.d.])

Hay, Ian, *One Hundred Years of Army Nursing*, (Cassell & Co., Ltd., 1953)

Hockin, Olive, *Two Girls on the Land, War-time on a Dartmoor Farm*, (Arnold, 1918)

Lawrence, Dorothy, *Sapper Dorothy Lawrence: The Only English Woman Soldier*, (John Lane, 1919)

Leighton, Clare, *Tempestuous Petticoat: the Story of an Invincible Edwardian*, (Rinehart & Company, New York 1947)

Luard, Kathleen, *Diary of a Nursing Sister on the Western Front*, (Blackwood, 1915)

Luard, Kathleen, *Unknown Warriors. Letters of K E Luard*, (Chatto & Windus, 1930)

Macaulay, Rose, *Three Days*, (Constable, 1919)

McDougall, Grace, *Nursing Adventures: A F.A.N.Y. in France*, (William Heinemann, 1917)

McKenna, Marthe, *I Was a Spy,* (Queensway Press, 1934)

Millicent, Duchess of Sutherland, *Six Weeks at the War*, (The Times, 1914)

Moreton, Mary, *A Cinder Glows,* (Eric Dobbey, 1993)

Mrs Alec-Tweedie, *Women and Soldiers*, (John Lane, 1918)

Narratives of Eye-Witnesses, *The War on Hospital Ships*, (T. Fisher Unwin, 1917)

Peel, Mrs C.S., *How We Lived Then 1914–1918*, (John Lane, The Bodley Head, 1929)

Nicholson, Juliet, *The Great Silence: Living in the Shadow of the Great War,* (John Murray 2009)

Playne, Caroline E., *Britain Holds On 1917–1918*, (George Allen and Unwin, 1933)

Playne, Caroline E., *Society at War 1914–1916*, (George Allen & Unwin, 1931)

Proctor, Tammy, *Female Intelligence Women and Espionage in the First World War,* (New York University Press 2006)

S., C.G.R., S., A.G, *Betty Stevenson, YMCA Sept. 3,.1896 – May 30, 1918*, (Longmans Green & Co., 1920)

Sandes, Flora, *An English Woman Sergeant in the Serbian Army*, (Hodder & Stoughton, 1916)

Sandes, Flora, *The Autobiography of a Woman Soldier*, (H F & G Witherby, 1927)

Sebastian, Hilda, *Lace Collars and Cocoa Cups* (Sarsen Publishing 1989)

SELECT BIBLIOGRAPHY

St Barnabas Society, *Gallipoli and Salonika*, (St. Barnabas Society, c.1926)

St Barnabas Society, *The Menin Gate Pilgrimage*, (St. Barnabas Society, c. 1927)

St Barnabas Society, *Ypres/The Somme*, (St. Barnabas Society, c.1923)

Tennent, R. J. MM, *Red Herrings of 1918,* (Creed [n.d])

Thomas, Helen, *World Without End*, (William Heinemann, 1931)

Thomas, Myfannwy, *One of those Fine Days*, (Carcanet New Press, Manchester 1982)

Van Emden, Richard & Humphries, Stephen, *Veterans: The Last Survivors of the Great War*, (Leo Cooper, Barnsley 1998)

Van Emden, Richard, *The Quick and the Dead,* (Bloomsbury, 2012)

Vidal, Lois, *Magpie*, (Faber and Faber, 1934)

Viscountess Wolseley, *Women and the Land,* (Chatto and Windus 1916)

Warner, Agnes, *My Beloved Poilus,* (Kessinger Publishing, 2009)

Wearmouth, R F., *Pages From a Padre's Diary*, (Wearmouth, North Shields [n.d.])

Wheelwright, Julie, *The Fatal Lover: Mata Hari and the Myth of Women in Espionage*, (Collins and Brown, 1992)

Woollacott, Angela, *On Her Their Lives Depend*, (University of California Press, 1994)

(For further bibliographic information see the author's website *www.firstworldwarwomen.co. uk*)

Index